Frank Pope is the Ocean Correspondent of *The Times* and a presenter for the BBC. Previously he worked on underwater expeditions all over the world under the auspices of Oxford MARE (Maritime Archaeological Research and Excavation Unit), including the excavation of Admiral Lord Nelson's flagship HMS *Agamemnon*. He divides his time between London and Nairobi.

72
HOURS

FRANK POPE

An Orion paperback

First published in Great Britain in 2012
by Orion
This paperback edition published in 2013
by Orion Books Ltd,
Orion House, 5 Upper St Martin's Lane,
London WC2H 9EA

An Hachette UK company

1 3 5 7 9 10 8 6 4 2

A CIP catalogue record for this book is available
from the British Library.

ISBN 978-1-4091-2697-3

Typeset by Input Data Services Ltd, Bridgwater, Somerset

Printed in Great Britain by CPI Group (UK) Ltd,
Croydon, CR0 4YY

The Orion Publishing Group's policy is to use papers that
are natural, renewable and recyclable products and
made from wood grown in sustainable forests. The logging
and manufacturing processes are expected to conform to
the environmental regulations of the country of origin.

www.orionbooks.co.uk

For Saba

AS-28
Priz-class submersible

Lazurit Design Bureau
Depth rating: 900m
Length: 13m

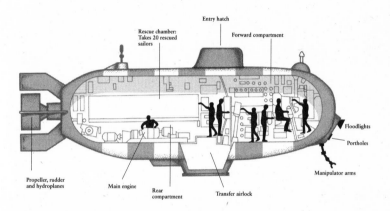

Entry hatch

Rescue chamber:
Takes 20 rescued
sailors

Forward compartment

Floodlights

Portholes

Manipulator arms

Propeller, rudder
and hydroplanes

Main engine

Rear
compartment

Transfer airlock

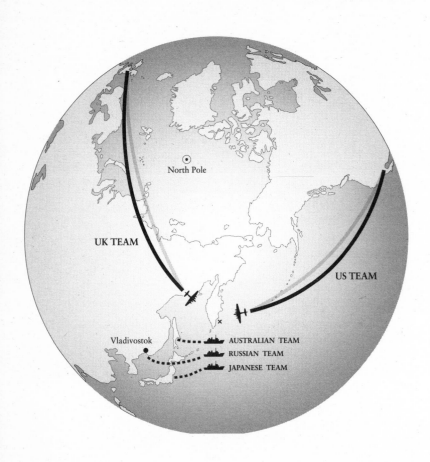

North Pole

UK TEAM

US TEAM

Vladivostok

AUSTRALIAN TEAM
RUSSIAN TEAM
JAPANESE TEAM

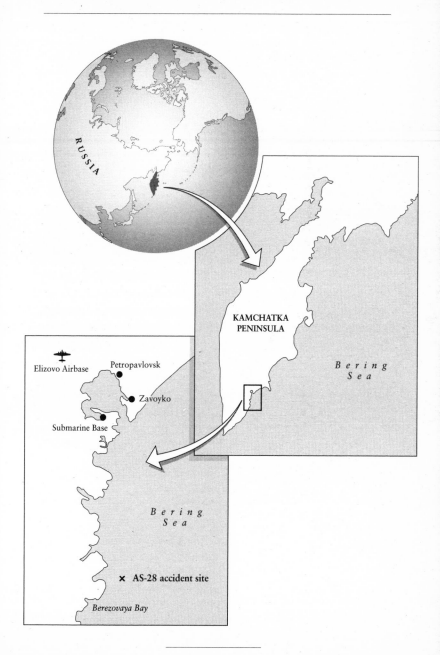

RUSSIA

KAMCHATKA
PENINSULA

B e r i n g
S e a

Elizovo Airbase

Petropavlovsk

Zavoyko

Submarine Base

B e r i n g
S e a

✕ AS-28 accident site

Berezovaya Bay

A Note on Sources

In the years that have passed since the events described in the following pages, Russians – both civilian and military – have become cautious of openly criticising the state. Beatings, harassment and arrest await those who speak out.

Extensive interviews were taped in the immediate aftermath of the incident, raw material to which I was generously given access by journalists and broadcasters. This gave me the perspective of some who later felt unable to talk. Other key players who did not agree to communicate with me had felt it necessary to change important aspects of their stories.

I have therefore not identified who was interviewed by whom and when. I have tried to use versions of events that were told with the greatest candour, that were remembered closest to the time and that I judged most likely to reflect the reality of what happened. Where the memories of those involved did not agree with one another, I consulted experts familiar with Russia and her Navy to reconstruct what happened that August as accurately as possible. Any errors are of course my own.

FP

PROLOGUE

Royal Naval Trafalgar-class Attack Submarine,
Submarine exercise area, North Atlantic

It should have been the one of the best moments of his career. Instead four men died a violent death beneath the waves.

Lieutenant Commander Ian Riches was at the final stage of one of the most punishing selection processes in the force: the submarine command – or 'Perisher' – course. Four weeks of exercises at sea were the culmination; a trial by fire designed to push candidates past their breaking point. At stake was the ultimate honour: the right to command a submarine.

Riches was about to take control of the 85-metre-long Trafalgar-class submarine for his next test. Two of the six candidates had already been failed and removed from the boat, but he was confident. Success was so close he could smell it.

The nuclear submarine was already running silent, pursued by a Naval frigate somewhere above her. Her corridors were filled with intense, hushed activity as the vessel slipped through the deep. Riches threaded through the passageways, the sound of his footfalls ringing loud in his ears as it echoed among dense pipework that lined both walls and ceiling. This was one of the most advanced weapons in the world, the front line of defence for Her Majesty's Government, and Riches knew every valve, gauge and dial.

He ducked through the forward hatch and into the Weapons Stowage Compartment that doubled as accommodation for the candidates. Four Tigerfish torpedoes were against one bulkhead, his bunk against the other. Grabbing his charts from beside the mattress he headed for the Control Room and checked his watch: 2 a.m.

The darkened control deck was calm when he stepped off the top rung of the ladder and informed the Duty Captain, one of his fellow candidates, that he'd been told to take over early. The departing officer looked relieved. His run of exercises had gone well, but laying mines while evading a warship in confined conditions was like playing an intense, high-stakes game of chess while blindfolded. He was ready for a break.

As the helmsman brought the submarine around in a long, sweeping turn to starboard to get into position for the next exercise, the Duty Captain began briefing Riches on the vessel's status. The report ran in a structured sequence. Mechanical condition came first. Then their position, surrounding seabed terrain, threats and current operations would all be described, after which Riches would be in the hot seat.

In a darkened room just a few metres away, the sonar controller sat listening to the eerie noises of the deep. In other circumstances he could rely on active 'pings', a sonic flashlight that would illuminate everything around the submarine. But the frigate still lurked somewhere above; an opponent that would detect them if someone dropped a spanner, let alone if the submarine sent out a sound pulse. Instead the sonar controller had to rely solely on the other sounds that were echoing around the undersea trench through which they were moving to tell him what lay close.

The pulsing green display in front of him gave a visual indication of which bearing the sounds were coming from, but distances remained hard to gauge.

The controller counted the engine sounds of various fishing vessels above. One, two, three targets. Then, to the north, a fourth sound, which he logged as Contact 05. It was a loud signature, slightly ragged. He'd keep an eye on it.

By 02.10 the submarine had straightened her course and was now heading to the northwest.

The sonar controller was watching Contact 05 ever more closely. It didn't look right. Suddenly the contact split into two and part of it began moving across his screen.

'Contact zero-five bearing 306 degrees, moving slowly right . . .' he said, his voice broadcasting across the Net, the open system of speakers that connects the Control Room with the darkened and acoustically shielded Sound Room.

The Duty Captain immediately broke off from the handover sequence and turned away to listen to his officers. 'Port fifteen,' he said, ordering an immediate course alteration.

'Contact zero-five bearing 330 degrees, moving fast right,' came the voice on the Net, more insistent now. The sonar target that had been on a constant bearing was suddenly passing fast. They were far too close.

'Port thirty,' he said.

A tense silence followed, broken by the Operations Officer reporting that the contact had been avoided, at a minimum distance of 200 metres away.

'Ease to ten, steer 260,' the Duty Captain said with evident relief, and turned back to Riches. 'Right, where were we?'

The two officers restarted the handover, but 30 seconds later a loud impact slammed through the submarine. Everybody braced, heads whipping forward to starboard where the noise had come from. The scene seemed to freeze for a long second. Then the crew's training kicked in, with each man running through checks and demanding status reports.

'Log speed increasing,' shouted the Ship Control Officer. 'Fifteen knots. Twenty knots. Thirty knots.' His voice was almost defensive. He had not ordered an increase in speed from the engine room, and engine RPM was constant, yet the speed indicated on his display was shooting up.

'Stop main engine!' ordered both the Duty Captain and the Ship Control Officer simultaneously.

But it was too late. An awful screeching noise began to reverberate through the submarine. Disaster had struck.

Thursday, 4 August 2005
15.30 Kamchatka
Berezovya Bay, 70 kilometres south of Petropavlovsk,
Kamchatka Peninsula, Russia's western Pacific coast

Thirteen years later, aboard the Russian Federation Navy's mini-submersible *AS-28*, 200 metres down off Russia's northeastern coast, 23-year-old Captain Lieutenant Vyacheslav Milachevsky took his hands from the controls and flexed his fingers. He'd been holding on too tight. This was only his seventh dive in the craft and his eyes were narrowed with concentration as they flicked between the three portholes.

The forward compartment was dark, save for the pulsing green light of the sonar that swept over damp metal equipment and the faces of the men squeezed in around it. The submersible was built for four, but today there were seven men on board.

They'd been down for five hours, close to the limit of the craft's six-hour endurance. There was no insulation, and the curved titanium hull was only a few degrees above freezing. There was no heating, other than the warmth radiating from the electric motors.

Milachevsky steeled himself with the thought that they would soon be able to step out into the warm sunlight, to stretch, smoke a cigarette and relieve themselves. There was no way he could know of the danger that lurked in the darkness ahead.

The dark waters off Russia's Pacific border had been the stage for many a silent, deadly, Cold War drama. Beyond the fuming volcanoes of the Kamchatka Peninsula, only thousands of miles of open ocean lay between Russia and its foes of old, the United States. As a result, the continental shelf was studded with top-secret military installations.

The Priz-class mini-submersible *AS-28* was currently operating near one of the enormous hydrophone arrays that had been deployed off a remote stretch of the peninsula to listen for the whisper of enemy submarines. Enormous steel cylinders filled with air supported a series of underwater microphones that captured the sounds of the deep and transmitted them to listening stations ashore. Anchored to the seabed and floating in mid-water, these chambers needed regular maintenance to keep them in position, while the hydrophones themselves needed to be cleaned and the cables connecting them to shore inspected.

This was all routine work, but that wasn't what the 44-foot *AS-28* was designed for. She was a rescue submersible. The flexible skirt that fitted to her bulky, downward-facing hatch to enable her to dock with stricken submarines had been removed, but her bulbous rear pressure chamber was still there, able to hold 20 rescued sailors at pressure, but doing no favours for her speed and manoeuvrability.

Manipulators extended from her bow like the forearms of a praying mantis. Designed to be able to clear debris from an escape hatch, they also allowed her to moonlight as a maintenance vehicle. It was working with these manipulators that Captain Lieutenant Milachevsky excelled: he prided himself on his precision with their claws. When he'd first practised – with *AS-28* on deck and the ship still in port – he'd smashed many of the bottles he'd been trying to pick up. But now he felt like he could thread a needle with the big titanium claws if Mother Russia required it of him.

Milachevsky's eyes passed between the porthole in front of him and those to either side. Down here the water was clear, allowing the submersible's lights to shine almost ten metres into the darkness to his left. Ordinarily he'd be flying using the sonar, the submariner's sixth sense that let him see far into the blackness. But right now he was navigating by sight alone. Through the starboard porthole he could see a vast wall of steel gliding past. The cylinder had acquired a dense camouflage of barnacles since its installation, but nothing could disguise its vast bulk on the sonar readout that pulsed by his left knee. It was as though half of the screen was malfunctioning – it had turned solid green.

He shook off the creeping fatigue and pushed his shoulders back.

His father had once sat in the same seat as he did now, also as the pilot of this submersible. Small, manoeuvrable and with the distinctive red-and-white striped hull of the Navy's rescue fleet, the *AS-28* had a place deep in the young pilot's heart. As a boy he'd watched his father step on board, and as a teenager had carved models of her during his long absences. Now he was at the helm.

What's more, crouched beside him was Gennady Vasiliyevich Bolonin. Bolonin was not a military man, but Milachevsky was proud to be piloting with him on board: he was the deputy chief designer at the esteemed Lazurit Design Bureau, and had been one of the principal members of the design team behind *AS-28*.

The fact that there were seven men on board made no difference to Milachevsky – it just meant an audience to appreciate his skills. The weight gain was negligible in the water, and the fact that their 120-hour emergency endurance would be almost halved made no difference – they were progressing well, and their mission should be over within the hour.

Standing on the bridge of the 427-foot-long, 7,960-tonne salvage submersible support ship *Georgy Kozmin,* 2nd Rank Captain Viktor Novikov scowled and lowered his binoculars. Despite the clear August air he couldn't make out the fishing boat's name through the rust that spread over the transom like lichen on old rock. He swore and stormed inside to hail the unknown boat on the VHF radio, but got no response. He might have guessed. There was no way of knowing if they were ignoring their radio or if it was broken. He could have sent one of the ship's boats to find out what they were doing, but it was a risk. If she broke down and needed rescuing, he'd have nothing left with which to recover the submersible. He shook his head, as if to rid himself of the irritation. There was nothing he could do even if he had been able to identify the boat. There was no way to tell if she had been trawling in this area or not. He'd caught others before, had them hauled before the Ministry and reprimanded. They knew it was illegal to fish in this top-secret area but still they came. The giant metal structures hidden beneath the surface created a haven for marine life and, for the fishermen, the quantity and size of the fish they caught there was evidently just too tempting.

Novikov turned and squinted into the sun, his practised eye scanning over the rusting deck. It had taken him twenty years of serving the Great Russian Navy to be given this command, but now he'd made it he almost wished he hadn't. Here he was in August, when all other self-respecting Russians were at their holiday homes, their *dachas*, and he had been pushed into servicing the array. The *Kozmin* was originally a timber-carrier refitted as a submarine rescue ship. Neither she nor the equipment she had on board were suitable for work as an underwater repair and maintenance vessel. Her mini-submersibles were built to save sailors from stricken nuclear boats, not for running maintenance duty on enormous underwater hydrophones. But it was the same old story everywhere in the Navy, throughout the Russian military: the infrastructure behind the nation's threatening and impressive profile was disintegrating.

He knew he should count himself lucky. Most of the surface fleet had not seen any money since 1991 thanks to the Navy's focus on nuclear-powered, ballistic-missile-carrying submarines, a policy that meant at least a trickle came through to the rescue fleet. That did nothing to ease his tension. The feeling was down to the *Kozmin*'s barren stern deck. *AS-28*'s sister submersible was 70 kilometres away, sitting on a dockside on wooden stocks, waiting for repairs. Launching one without the other ready to rescue her contravened all the training he'd undertaken at the Naval academy. Even *AS-28* should not have been launched, strictly speaking, given the maintenance that was due on her. And she shouldn't have been sent to do the kind of work he'd been asked to undertake. To cap it all, it was August and everyone was on holiday, including some of his best men. They got paid so little, the least he could do was let them take their precious August holiday.

Thursday, 4 August
16.00 Kamchatka
Petropavlosk-Kamchatsky

Queuing at the bakery on the ground floor of a featureless concrete apartment block in the south of Petropavlovsk, Tatiana Lepety-ukha finally reached the counter to find the woman in front of her had bought the last loaf. It would be two hours before a new batch would be ready. Tatiana pursed her lips and sniffed sharply. Nothing had been going right so far today.

It was never going to be a pleasant day. Her husband, Valery Lepetyukha, had been sent down in a Priz submersible for the first time in years despite his ill-health. She'd hoped these days – and the nervous feelings that always accompanied them – were over. As the wife of a Captain 1st Rank in the Russian Navy, she should be spared indignities like queuing for bread that ran out when she got to the counter, or having a car that refused to start. But there was something else, too, nagging her, that she couldn't put her finger on. The sun had been bright as she made her way to church to say her morning prayers, and there hadn't been a breath of wind on the streets. Maybe that was it. Maybe it was just too calm, too much of a contrast with the normal north-eastern weather.

As a sailor's wife she'd come to trust omens and portents. The sea was in her family's blood, going back as far as anyone could remember. The past three generations of men had been in the Navy, and she'd learnt to listen to what her heart was telling her. And right now something deep down in her body was worrying her. It wasn't that she didn't have faith in her husband: she had complete confidence in him. She also trusted in the Navy that her family had served for so long, or so she told herself. But though she believed wholeheartedly in the Russian Navy's intentions, she could not entirely ignore the breakdowns and Valery's private complaints. He and the crews were working hard, but there was no money to repair any of the things that needed repairing. Given the risks they ran while working, it didn't seem right. Strong though her patriotism was, her love for her husband was greater.

She was used to the long absences, and normally thought nothing of a two-month period apart. After all, when he had been a lieutenant, he was away for between nine and 12 months at a stretch. She'd learnt to lock away her emotions. But for some reason this time – although Valery had only been away for a week – thoughts of him kept bubbling up to the surface.

Fifty kilometres to the west of Petropavlovsk town, on the wide plains reaching out beneath the Yakki volcanoes, Yelena Milachevskaya's[1] thoughts were also probing beneath the Pacific, thinking of her man. While she was always brimful of pride for Slava, the pilot of *AS-28*, today she was worried. She was watching her twin girls play in the short, stubby grass, but the sun was making her tired eyes hurt as it glinted off the gold frames of her oval glasses. She'd woken in the early hours of the morning with a start. Staring into the darkness she'd tried to banish the swirling image that had bled from her dream, but every time she blinked it was there. She recognised the hand that seemed to float in front of her as her own, but its colours were unnaturally bright, and on her finger was a strange, ugly wedding ring. She'd woken herself up screaming, 'Take it away! That's not my ring!'

The afternoon sun was warm on Yelena's pale skin, but her soul felt cold. Everybody knew that the women in her family could predict the death of their husbands, and there could be no clearer portent than seeing another ring on her finger. She had felt panic rising inside her.

The Naval operator had calmed her down when he eventually answered the phone that morning. He'd become like a friend, thanks to Yelena's frequent calls. She liked to be kept updated, for even at the best of times she was very nervous of losing her Slava. Good men were very hard to find, she often said, especially

[1] In Russian, the female version of a surname has a different ending. The last name of Slava Milachevsky's wife is Milachevskaya.

in Petropavlovsk. While Yelena held the line the operator tried the *Georgy Kozmin*. He came back two minutes later to say that there was no reply. That was no reason for worry though, he said. The ship must simply be out of range. After all, the sea was flat calm, and no trouble had been reported.

But what about the strange wedding ring on her finger? Just because it was calm on the surface didn't mean that everything was fine. Yelena knew that better than most. Despite the bright day, the beautiful view and the laughter of the girls, her insides were starting to churn. She started thinking of all the times Slava had come home complaining about things going wrong with his submersible, the time that the electrics caught fire inside, burning up their precious oxygen. Or when a porthole burst and the freezing sea flooded in. The machine was in urgent need of an overhaul, having not been repaired for so many years. Slava was supposed to be accompanying it to Nizhny Novgorod at the end of August to help with the repairs. But that would be too late, she knew. Something terrible was going to happen. Her Slava was going to die. How was she going to break the news to the girls, his beloved twins?

Thursday, 4 August
16.15 Kamchatka
***AS-28*, 210 metres beneath Berezovya Bay**

With their work on the first face of the 100-metre-long hydrophone completed, Slava Milachevsky began to turn *AS-28* starboard into the current. The enormous structure disappeared into the black water, but he could feel its awesome size behind him, as though his mind had become sonar-enabled. He didn't even need to glance at the compass or the green sonar display to know that he'd judged the submersible's slip through the current well. When the wall of steel appeared in the porthole to his right he saw that the array was indeed lined up perfectly to the starboard once more, ready for their inspection of the other side. He didn't smile, but nodded to himself solemnly. Man and machine were working as one.

Around him the crew were all at their stations, monitoring the submersible's systems. Through the hatch behind him, the three Warrant Officers were in the second compartment keeping an eye on the engine and the electrical systems. All seemed well: *AS-28*'s motors were whirring, pushing the craft along at a steady two knots.

Captain 1st rank Valery Lepetyukha was sitting directly behind Milachevsky, his eyes ringed by dark circles. He surveyed the men, his thick, grey-flecked moustache twitching. He was experienced on the Priz class of submersible, but it had been a while since he'd been on board. Strictly speaking, he shouldn't be there: he'd lost one of his kidneys and a third of a lung to the surgeon's knife, and was supposed to be restricted to pushing papers at headquarters. The usual captain was away on leave – it was August, after all.

Gennady Bolonin was in the seat in front of him, watching the array glide past in the external floodlights. The civilian engineer was there to help with the work they were doing on the hydrophone array, as well as making some checks ahead of the bathyscaphe's upcoming refit.

Aware of Bolonin's importance and his expertise with the machine, Milachevsky was making an extra effort to pilot it smoothly. He responded instantly as the steering started pulling to starboard. He started feeding in left rudder, but still the submersible veered towards the array.

Captain Lepetyukha felt himself start to pitch forward softly, as though he was on a train that had started to slow.

'All stop! Full reverse engines!' he ordered, his voice shattering the quiet, echoing hum of the submersible's motors.

Milachevsky immediately pushed the thrust levers into the reverse position, but his whole body began to tense. Why had he not stopped as soon as he'd felt the restriction? Why did he just try to keep going straight? He cursed under his breath, eyes darting over the portholes, sonar display, warning panel and the periscope. That's when he saw it.

Slicing down through the black water ahead were several lines, draped over the side of the array and cutting across their path like a tripwire. His chest tightened. Whatever they were – ropes, cables or nets – they were bad news. He was only halfway through the thought when there was a terrible, grinding crash. *AS-28* had been dragged into the huge steel float, her starboard side scraping to a halt across its barnacle-encrusted surface.

Adrenaline had quickened Milachevsky's breathing, and he had to swallow before turning to make a report to the Captain. Lepetyukha listened, then stared at him calmly through rheumy eyes as if assessing the strength of his character.

It was Captain Lepetyukha's turn to peer through the periscope's binocular-shaped cowling. He had worked in submersibles for 30 years, and nothing came as too much of a surprise to him any more. The solution to all problems was a calculated approach and an absence of panic. In most underwater emergencies, the best option was to head straight back to the surface, and a less experienced captain might have decided to do so, hoping that the rope would slide over the hull and fall away beneath them. But Lepetyukha knew that just a small snag on a hatch fitting could trap them and there would be no telling where they were caught. The cable he could see in the glass was evidently not the one holding them in place. It was also so covered in weeds and other marine growth that it was not even possible to tell if it was made of wire or rope.

Lepetyukha rotated the scope around to the port, peering into the dark water, looking for other obstructions. If they'd snagged a fishing net, there was no telling how much more of it could be around.

It wouldn't be the first time the Pacific Fleet had suffered trouble with fishing gear. In the late 1990s, a new experimental submarine detection system called Dnestr-B had been installed in the area. The system had been producing good results when suddenly, in 1997, it went blind. When the Navy went to go and have a look what had happened, they could not find the 120-metre-long, 15-metre-high float from the array. It had disappeared. Nothing more was heard of it for three years until, in 2000, the world's news agencies began reporting that a huge, unidentified object had been spotted near Japanese shores. Somehow it had broken loose, very possibly having been snagged by a fishing net and dragged off its mooring.

If a fisherman tangled and lost a net on the hydrophone array there was no way he was going to report it as he was required to do. He would just cut the lines and let the evidence sink to the seabed. Captain Lepetyukha had become snagged before, but with patience and cunning – traits integral to the Russian Navy – it had always been possible to work free.

The drifting snow of particles in the water faded as the periscope panned sternwards and away from the bow floodlight, before becoming utterly black behind them. Lepetyukha's moustache twitched. He could see nothing: the stern light was not working. It was on the long list of repairs awaiting *AS-28* next month.

Milachevsky had not reported passing any other obstructions, and continuing ahead was a known risk. All eyes turned to the Captain. The Captain's eyes turned to Gennady Bolonin. It was a telling moment. As the senior officer all orders must come through Captain Lepetyukha, but of the two men it was the civilian who knew the craft better, and had spent more time underwater within it.

In this case, however, there was not much doubt as to what the next move should be.

'We must reverse around the cable,' the Captain ordered.

Milachevsky slowly engaged the motors in reverse. With no light astern, he kept the periscope forward, watching the rope slide off the bow. A few more feet and it would be clear. Then their creeping retreat began to slow. The pitch of the motors deepened. Both he and the captain involuntarily spun round to look towards the hatch to the second compartment, only to hear the solid clunk of a large electrical relay tripping, and the sound of the main motor whirring to a halt.

In the second compartment, Warrant Officers Sergei Belozerov and Anatoly Popov sat in stunned silence. At the first impact with the array, Popov's heart had missed a beat, but he'd soon calmed. He'd been trapped before, and after an hour or so they'd been able to work themselves free, and complete their task as normal. But this time the motor's automatic cut-out had activated. That could only mean that something had caught around the propeller, wrapping itself so tight that the main motor was on the edge of burning itself out, and so had shut down. This was new. With no way of manoeuvring it was now impossible for them to remove the net.

Thursday, 4 August 2005
04.20 UK – 16.20 **Kamchatka**
Royal Navy lodgings, Bristol

It was still dark outside, but the streetlights stabbed across the bare bedroom through chinks in the ill-cut curtains. Commander Riches had woken up for no good reason, but his legs were tangled in the duvet as though he'd been fighting it. If he'd been dreaming, he couldn't remember what about.

He lay awake for a while, trying to get back to sleep. It felt as though the dull, subsonic throb of the motorway in the distance was taunting him, each low swoosh of a truck mocking what his life had become. Perhaps in his dream he'd been back in a submarine, the sonar sweeping across an undersea landscape, probing for contacts.

He closed his eyes and tried to distance himself from the reality: a Services house tucked into the armpit of the M4/M5 motorway junction with no more excitement than a desk and a computer screen to look forward to when his nine-to-five day began.

That disastrous night back in 1990, on his Perisher command course, his submarine had also snared a net – but it was not him or his crew who had suffered. Three fishing vessels had been trawling in the area near them at the time. Although the fishermen knew there could be submarines below, it was up to the Navy crews to steer clear. That night the Hunter-Killer submarine was running silent, relying on passive sonar and able to gauge accurately only the direction from which a sound was coming, not the distance. At a crucial moment the noise of two fishing vessels had melded into one. Only when the submarine was far too close did the signals diverge. Seconds later, they were crashing through a trawl-net. Chains and cables wrapped themselves around the forward sonar dome, shearing off one of the two hull-mounted speed-sensors and causing its readings to go haywire (perhaps the cause of the loud bang heard through the vessel), but the 4,500 tonne submarine was barely slowed by the obstruction. On the surface it was a different story.

A 16-metre wooden fishing boat was mid-turn when suddenly the lines to her trawl-net wrenched the craft sideways with brutal force. Within seconds she was flipped upside down and dragged along the surface, her propeller thrashing the air faster and faster as her engine raced. No-one knows exactly how long the terrible, churning chaos lasted, but it was probably only a matter of seconds. The force rapidly overcame the vessel, and she was sucked beneath the surface. Three of her crew were still on board. The body of the fourth – the watchman – was only found when it appeared in a fisherman's trawl nearly five months later.

Following the immediate response to the tragedy, the fallout began. A breakdown in the structure and standard of watchkeeping on the submarine was blamed, and the careers of both the student Duty Captain and the Course Commander suddenly hung in the balance. Riches had been minutes from taking over as Duty

Captain, at which point the blame would have landed on his shoulders as well.

It was a lucky escape. Riches went on to pass the course, and spent the next three years as First Lieutenant (second-in-command) of HMS *Resolution*'s Starboard Crew (ballistic missile submarines have two crews to man the vessel around the clock), awaiting his first submarine command. But fate struck first. He was out on a training run when his left arm started tingling. He ignored it, and the feeling went away soon after he'd got his breath back. But on his next run the tingling was back, and a week later he reluctantly turned himself in to the doctor.

The doctor strapped him into a heart monitor, but as soon as Riches saw his face he knew he was in trouble. He should have known: his father had been living with angina, and his grandfather had died of a heart attack. Now they were going to have to operate on him. Somehow he'd blocked out the possibility that he too would be affected, thinking that by keeping fit he'd escape his genetic destiny.

There was a glimmer of hope, however. The cardiac specialist who treated him said airline pilots were able to get back in the cockpit if they proved themselves fit enough. But when he was transferred back to base, the Naval doctor there refused to consider it. Although a thoracic consultant not a cardiac specialist, he declared that Riches would never serve at sea again.

The newly qualified officer fought it, and won the chance to prove himself fit a year down the line. He trained hard, ran the London marathon, and by the time his medical exam came around he was declared fully fit. But the mud stuck. The Navy's promotion boards are an ancient ritual that are guided by a report from the candidate's Commanding Officer, and his had mentioned a serious illness. The implication was clear: there was no way that he should be left in command of a nuclear submarine. Although he'd jumped every hurdle and qualified for command, he finally resigned himself to the fact that his dream was over.

The next few years saw him working in a number of different

shore jobs, trying to work out which way he should go next. He had become a 'shiny-arsed inboard bastard', as they put it in the Navy. He wouldn't get to command a submarine, and he was certain he'd never make the rank of Commander. Then, out of the blue, a promotion signal came through with his name on it. He'd be Commander – in rank at least – after all. When he was summoned to see his 'Appointer' two months later, he was presented the list of jobs for which he was being considered. It wasn't long. There was one position: Submarine Escape and Rescue Equipment Manager at Abbey Wood on the outskirts of Bristol, starting in December 2003.

It was some consolation, but he knew he was now destined to roam the back-alleys of the Ministry of Defence for the rest of his Naval career. He knew he'd always be a submariner and would still wear the dolphins with pride, but he'd never be back at sea in a submarine in an operational role, doing what he did best.

Thursday, 4 August
16.30 Kamchatka
***AS-28*, 210 metres beneath Berezovya Bay**

Captain Lepetyukha's first thought was to keep everyone calm. There were some young, inexperienced sailors on board, and there was no sense in panicking them. They may have just reversed into a piece of free-floating net, or the process of entanglement may have torn it free, after all. But there was a good chance that whatever had tangled the propeller was connected to the array. Unfortunately, without a stern light there was no way they could check. He decided not to make a report to the *Georgy Kozmin* just yet. In the Russian Navy, all else being equal, it was better to do what you could by yourself first before passing on bad news.

He ordered Milachevsky to make a thorough scan around the

submersible while he had a muttered conversation with Bolonin over how best to proceed. When the lieutenant finished his inspection he reported the first rope was still there on the bow, and there now seemed to be another snagged beside one of the dome bolts. Though the young pilot was doing his best to disguise it, there was a hint of fear in his voice.

'We will use our positioning thrusters to move laterally,' Lepetyukha barked. If the cables were not snagged too tightly on the array, moving in a different direction might set them free.

The higher-pitched whine of the smaller positioning thrusters, mounted on both the stern and the bow, slowly filled the spherical steel chambers of *AS-28*. The craft began to ease away from the array, the cables scraping their barnacles against the hull. They'd managed to get a couple of metres' clearance when their momentum started to slow.

'Maximum power!' ordered Lepetyukha, but to no avail. The motors began to strain, and *AS-28* was no longer moving. 'All stop,' he snapped. As the sound of the motors died away, the swirling starfield of floodlit particles in the porthole began to shift to the left, then the hull jolted with a hollow metallic boom. *AS-28* had been drawn back against the array in the net's lethal embrace.

Only one direction was left open to him, the same direction that each crew member's mind was starting to reach towards. The surface. Blowing the ballast tanks would make the submersible lighter, launching it upwards. The time had now come to inform the *Georgy Kozmin* on the surface. The captain picked up the underwater telephone and gave a short, factual report outlining their position and measures attempted so far. Trying to send voice as high-frequency sound through the water made for frequent distortion, but with the *Kozmin* only 200 metres above them the apparatus was working fairly well. After giving his status report, Captain Lepetyukha stated that he was about to blow the ballast tanks in an effort to float free of the entanglement, and would make a new report once he'd carried out the manoeuvre.

Bolonin coughed, and all eyes turned to him. The clock had begun to tick, but the engineer had been in many a tight situation underwater, and knew that what would kill them most easily would be rushed decisions. He was all too aware of the lack of backup available. He felt like an ambitious mountaineer who'd been too focused on the summit ahead, and not paid enough attention to how they'd get down if something went wrong. Now they were in trouble and there was no one nearby with equipment that could help them.

Blowing the tanks came with risks beyond simply tightening the bonds that held them to the seabed. If one of the lines – perhaps the one wrapped around the propeller – held fast, they could quickly find themselves tilting off balance. Beyond a certain angle the acid would start leaking from the bank of batteries, creating acrid and poisonous chlorine gas that would rapidly choke them. Floating up was still the best option open to them, but it must be done with extreme caution. After explaining his concern, Bolonin nodded to the Captain, who gave the order.

Compressed air started exploding into the two ballast tanks that flanked the *AS-28*'s hull, pushing the seawater out of a valve at the bottom at a pressure of between 3,500 and 4,500 pounds per square inch. The surrounding seawater transmitted the sound perfectly, while the curved shape of the hull amplified it until it sounded like an express train passing a platform at full speed. Despite its deafening volume, the sound was a comforting one. Submariners have an intimate relationship with their buoyancy, for their craft are perpetually on the edge of sinking. The roar was not just the noise of returning to the surface, but also the sound of everyday routine. Even at the dockside, submarines blow out each of their tanks once a day to make sure they are correctly trimmed.

The cables lying over the submersible's nose began to tighten as she rose. Like the rest of the crew, Milachevsky gripped secure handholds. With no frame of reference except the tiny portholes in the bow, all but Bolonin darted their eyes about the cylindrical walls of the inside hull as though looking for clues as to what was about to happen. Then a sudden lurch sent loose items crashing to the deck as the stern slipped upwards a few feet but stopped again just as suddenly. Something was holding them – another cable had become wrapped behind the main fin. The tilt indicators showed they were already 13 degrees off level. Any more and they risked flipping the craft into a vertical position or on its side, and releasing the battery acid. Like a fly's attempts to escape a spider's web, the manoeuvring had served only to entrap the submersible more tightly. There was now no way they would be able to escape by themselves.

Thursday, 4 August
SS + 30 mins
17.00 Kamchatka
Russian Federation Navy Vessel *Georgy Kozmin*, Berezovya Bay

On the surface, Captain Novikov was struggling to find workable options for a rescue. Seven of the sailors under his command were trapped on the seabed, and every minute now was precious. Procedures would have him launch the second Priz submersible, *AS-29*, but it was sitting on the dockside in Petropavlovsk. It had been plundered for spares, and there was no way it could be rendered operational any time in the next week, even if all the parts were immediately available and the engineers weren't on holiday.

There was another Priz class rescue submersible in Vladivostok to the south, but despite being part of the same Pacific fleet, there was almost no functional connection between Primorye and Kamchatka when it came to the Navy. The distances were too large. It was part of the same problem that had plagued the Russian Navy since its inception – fleets defending the Black Sea, the Baltic, the north, and the Pacific were forced to operate in isolation from one another. The nearest operational Russian rescue submersible was four and a half days' sailing away.

In another kind of submarine, such a delay might be fine. But the Priz class, being rescue vehicles, were designed for quick runs to the seabed and back. Dives lasting six hours were already pushing the envelope. With extra oxygen and carbon-dioxide-removing chemicals the endurance might be stretched, but other factors would rapidly crowd in. The batteries, for one, were notoriously weak and would soon start to fade. Then there was the temperature: the hull was not insulated against the cold – on a dive of only a few hours, a thick sweater would do. But over a long immersion the cold would become a problem. And then there was the lack of food and water.

And what if they couldn't untangle the submersible? All of the Russian Navy's other submarines had standard hatches with flat, level flanges with which the Priz could mate. But the Priz class did not have them themselves. Nor did they carry equipment that would allow their crews to make an emergency buoyant ascent like other submarines in the fleet. If they had done, the crew of *AS-28* could have put on inflatable suits that would shoot them to the surface. But its crew were there to perform rescues, not save themselves. It was ironic, thought Novikov bitterly. They'd joked about it before, but now it was deadly serious. You couldn't get stuck in a worse vehicle than a Priz rescue submersible.

Thursday 4 August
SS + 1 h 30 mins
18.00 Kamchatka
AS-28, **210 metres beneath Berezovya Bay**

Standing close to the open hatch between the first and second compartments, Captain Lepetyukha began a terse announcement to the crew.

'The submersible has become temporarily disabled due to illegal fishing activity on the array that left a net draped around the antenna,' he announced. 'This is a completely ordinary situation. It has happened many times before. Assistance is being deployed from the surface as I speak.'

The last thing he wanted to do was alarm the less experienced crew. Panic in such a situation was worse than useless – it used up valuable oxygen. The more they allowed their pulses to quicken and their minds to race, the less time they would live.

Lepetyukha's first priority was to establish that the submersible's atmosphere was stable. The effect of oxygen and carbon dioxide on the human body changes dramatically with pressure. Although there was no reason to believe that the pressure hull had been damaged by the impact with the array's buoyancy chamber, it was imperative that all three must be monitored even more carefully than usual. If water was leaking in anywhere, the pressure inside the hull would start to creep up, changing how oxygen, nitrogen and carbon dioxide reacted with their bodies.

All the vehicle's non-essential systems would soon be shut down and crew activity reduced to a minimum in order to maximise their endurance. It did not mean they were about to run out of air, he reminded them. It was just that they now knew they could not surface alone, and needed to give their rescuers as long as possible to come to their aid.

He ordered the men to make an inventory of all emergency supplies on board – anything that could be used to keep them alive.

Then he asked Milachevsky to organise a duty watch to man the underwater telephone and monitor the oxygen and carbon dioxide levels. Each watch would last the standard four hours.

The inventory was ready after only ten minutes; there was only so much space to store such equipment. Running his eye down the list, Lepetyukha's heart sank. They had only three and a half litres of water and two packets of crackers between the seven of them. There were immersion suits on board, designed to extend survival in the water by a few hours by keeping the body core dry. These would help against the cold which all could already feel creeping into their bones, but there were only six. For the unlucky seventh man, a cobbled-together collection of woollen jumpers and coats would have to suffice.

For ordinary operations the volume of air inside *AS-28*'s hull was easily enough to last the six-hour deployment that the battery life allowed. In case of emergency they had a store of V-64 canisters filled with chemicals that would both absorb carbon dioxide and generate oxygen. On Lepetyukha's list he saw they had seven tins of V-64, each of which should last for eight hours at a push, making for 56 hours with four crew. They were seven, which gave them 32 hours. They'd better hope they didn't get anywhere close to that limit, he thought.

Next, Lepetyukha ordered the electrical systems to be shut down. Used lightly, the batteries would start to cool and lose power, but at least they would last longer. The Warrant Officers methodically powered down the sonar systems and disengaged the motor circuits, then flicked off the lights one by one. With a metallic clunk the outside floodlight was extinguished. The starboard porthole, previously filled with the multicoloured patchwork of barnacles that covered the array, went black. Inside, the dim cabin light was replaced by a single red, low-power interior emergency light, and the men were plunged into blood-red darkness.

Captain Lepetyukha took the first watch, along with Gennady Bolonin, the civilian engineer. Lepetyukha ordered the crew to stay silent, for talking used up energy, and energy consumed oxygen and produced carbon dioxide. What's more, he didn't want a verbal route by which despair might spread.

Most of the men moved into the stern compartment. Although it was almost identical in size to the forward section, there was less equipment inside. All seven of them would have been able to crush inside at once, hugging the fading warmth of the electric motors, but the communication panel was in the forward compartment, meaning at least one man had to remain up front.

Captain Lepetyukha looked his old friend Bolonin in the eye. The deep crow's feet of lines and laughter that creased the engineer's face were now set into a grim mask. The dim red light only made the contrast starker. The two men went back a long way, and it was not hard for them to know what the other was thinking. It was August. Next week they were supposed to be attending the five-year memorial for the 118 sailors who died when the Oscar II-class nuclear submarine *Kursk* sank in the Barents Sea, at the opposite end of Russia.

On 12 August 2000, the might of the Northern Fleet was north of the Kola Peninsula, two days into a large military exercise. *Kursk* was preparing to fire a test torpedo at a ship on the surface. At twice the length of a Boeing 747, by far the largest attack submarine in the world, it was the pride of the Russian Navy. But just prior to launch something went badly wrong. The torpedo's powerful propulsion system began to ignite before the order to launch had been given. The torpedo doors were still closed when the hydrogen peroxide propellant exploded with a force of more than a hundred kilograms of TNT. Exactly 135 seconds later the *Kursk* hit the seabed, triggering her remaining store of weapons, many of which were equipped with warheads. The front end of the submarine was torn apart, the explosion almost rupturing the final bulkhead that protected the vessel's two nuclear reactors.

Ninety-five men were killed in those first few minutes, but in the ninth compartment 23 officers and sailors had survived the detonations. Tapping noises were reported by surface vessels listening out for signs of life, but, despite the seabed being at a depth of only 200 metres, for a week the Russian Navy was unable to reach the submarine. A horrified world had looked on as foreign rescue teams were kept away from the site until a full seven days later, by which time all they found was a huge, silent steel tomb.

The catalogue of errors that had caused the *Kursk* tragedy had given fuel to elements of the Russian press as they stoked the population's fury against their apparently uncaring new president, Vladimir Putin. But despite government attempts to pin the accident on an attack or a collision with an American or British submarine, it was widely known that bad maintenance and poor infrastructure were to blame for the *Kursk* disaster. Those who survived the initial explosion and its aftershocks might have had a chance had it not been for more equipment troubles, combined with the Russian Navy's inertia and unwillingness to take the initiative.

Unfortunately – as both Bolonin and Lepetyukha knew – with no money to invest and no impetus for change, nothing had been done since to purge these problems from the Navy.

The scandal had altered one thing, however. Politicians had pushed for what was seen as mostly a cosmetic fix, a sticking-plaster for the diseased Navy and something to placate the mourners. The Navy had been allowed to acquire some new rescue equipment. It was nowhere near enough to refurbish the rescue capabilities of such a geographically dispersed navy, but it was something. Among these were eight 'atmospheric diving suits' from the Ocean Works International Corporation. Nicknamed 'Newtsuits', they functioned as human-shaped exoskeletons that could carry a man to 365 metres and still leave him able to move arms and legs. One had come to the Pacific fleet, Lepetyukha knew.

The Navy had also bought several of the latest undersea robots, or 'Remotely Operated Vehicles', from two British companies. Guided from a surface vessel via a long umbilical cable, they were able to operate in depths of thousands of metres and could do most of the work that a submersible could. They did so without having to house human operators. They were so much easier and cheaper to use that manned vehicles were becoming rare in the commercial world, and increasingly in the military too.

On the deck of the *Georgy Kozmin* were two of these brand-new robots, Bolonin and Lepetyukha both knew. One was a small, inspection ROV which carried only video cameras, but the other came equipped with cutters. Bolonin had used it himself, and knew well what it was capable of. The British-made Venom ROV was a model that was used a lot in the oil industry and would most likely be able to snip each of the cables that were trapping them against the hydrophone array. It might take a few hours to do it, but the equipment was right there above them. All they had to do was hang on, keep calm, and wait for their surface support ship to deploy the ROV. It would not be long before they'd be free to float back up to the surface and open that hatch.

Thursday, 4 August
SS + 2 h 30 mins
19.00 Kamchatka
***Georgy Kozmin*, Berezovya Bay**

Novikov looked down from the bridge on the crews hurrying about the back deck and, for the third time that day, cursed his luck. Not only had he been ordered from on high to take on a job without the proper backup equipment, but he'd given in to emotional pressure from below that now left his position even more exposed. None of the crew – himself included – were properly paid. Since the costly Chechen war, spending on defence had plummeted and the Navy's share of it had dwindled to boot. Five years previously the Navy had got 15 per cent of the budget; now it got between 11 and 12 per cent. Investments in new ships, weaponry, combat training and maintenance facilities were the first to fall away, but now the Navy was struggling to even pay the salaries of the sailors. As a mere Captain 2nd Rank, Novikov had no control over that, but he did have a say in when the men took their holidays. When the only fully trained operator of the new Venom ROV asked to go on leave with his family that week in August, Novikov had agreed.

He ordered the backup ROV team to report to him. To his relief they assured him that they would be able to operate the vehicle. All they needed was for the *Georgy Kozmin* to hold position over the array. They would then guide the robot down to inspect the problem and free *AS-28* from her bonds.

Just as Captain Lepetyukha on *AS-28* had not wanted to involve outsiders until absolutely necessary, Novikov chose not to alert Navy command just yet. The bearer of bad tidings often got the full brunt of the blame. And, after all, there was still a good chance that they'd be able to recover the submersible without help. He carefully checked the current, then ran upstream for 500 metres, dropped anchor in the deep water and allowed *KIL-27* to drift back over the antenna. It wasn't ideal by any means, but it was better than risking the cable drifting into the vessel's spinning propellers.

Soon after the $5m Venom ROV was deployed things started to go wrong. Although she had an anchor out, the *Georgy Kozmin* was not a stable platform. She was swinging on her anchor, forcing more and more umbilical cable to be paid out in order for the ROV to stay in one place. But when the ship swung back, the loops of umbilical – carrying high voltages and all the control signals – began coiling in loops around the ROV and its powerful thrusters. Even with a highly experienced crew it would have been a tricky situation.

It wasn't long before the screen in front of the stand-in ROV pilot suddenly distorted and went blank. The vehicle was dead in the water. The umbilical was reeled in and the ROV recovered. Once everything was on deck the damage – and the culprit – was clear. The umbilical cable – its power lines and the delicate fibre-optic cables – had been badly mangled. With the right knowledge and equipment it could be patched up and made watertight enough to withstand the pressure 200 metres down, but neither was available on the *Kozmin*.

Novikov decided that enough was enough. He picked up the radio to the commanders of 70076 military unit in Petropavlosk and reported the situation.

A large part of the reason the *Kursk* tragedy had become such a scandal was the time it had taken for the bad news to pass up the chain of command. Admiral Vyacheslav Popov, the commander of the northern fleet, took 12 hours after the explosion to declare a fleet-wide alarm. It was 19 hours before President Putin had learnt that Russia had lost one of its most advanced nuclear submarines and over 100 sailors.

Whatever the penalty, Captain Novikov now had no option but to explain the situation as completely as he could. He made his report, confirming that their Venom ROV was out of action but that they would be attempting a survey using their second, smaller Tiger ROV. It was only a mobile video camera, but it should at least give them a better idea of the situation on the seabed.

Once the report of *AS-28*'s predicament reached Petropavlosk headquarters the news rapidly spread to the highest echelons of the Russian Navy. The last thing they wanted was an embarrassing accident now. Later that same month, on 19 August, Russia was joining China in an unprecedented joint military exercise. A full naval squadron – including submarines and 17 long-haul aircraft – would take part in settling an imaginary conflict in a foreign land. It was called 'Peace Mission 2005', but the bark at US Naval power on the other side of the Pacific was thinly veiled.

Russia still wore the costume of a superpower, but it was threadbare and China's economic muscle was increasingly intimidating. But, for now, their tactical alliance suited them both. Oil flowed south from Siberia in new pipelines to China, and Russia's military engineers were some of the best in the world. Every year the Chinese imported millions of dollars' worth of Russian military hardware (although the quantities were beginning to drop as Chinese scientists reverse-engineered the designs for fabrication in their own factories).

There was already enormous disparity between the two navies – hardly surprising, given that China was able to spend $15bn more on its defence than Russia. It was bad enough that China would surely know that Russia had not been able to add a single Navy ship to the Kamchatka fleet for 15 years, but for them then to have to admit to having got one of their rescue submersibles stuck on their own hydrophone array was not an option. While trying to work out its next move, the Russian Ministry of Defence remained resolutely silent.

Friday, 5 August
SS + 18 h 30 mins
11.00 Kamchatka
STS-Kamchatka News, Petropavlovsk-Kamchatsky

It was 11 o'clock the next morning when STS-Kamchatka's Radio 3, Petropavlovsk's most popular station, got a strange telephone call. A woman, in tears, sobbed that she had terrible news that must be heard but that she needed to be anonymous. The producer assured the caller that her number had not shown up on their system, listened for a minute, then put her on to Guzel Latypova, one of the news agency's chief editors.

Guzel Latypova was a veteran broadcaster, born and bred in Kamchatka. For more than 20 years she had worked her way up through the newspapers and on to radio before breaking into TV with her opinionated and popular talk show. Her soft face, bobbed blonde hair and intense, probing eyes were well-known among the 400,000 residents of Kamchatka, but it was her familiar voice which was now calming her hysterical caller.

After being assured once more that her identity was unknown, the woman drew breath. 'There's been an accident in Berezovya Cove. At this moment there are seven men trapped in a bathyscaphe, more than 200 metres underwater,' she said.

Latypova paused. She wasn't really sure what a bathyscaphe was, though she guessed it was an underwater craft somewhat smaller than a submarine. She'd taken the call because it was a slow day with no news about, but she was cautious. Petropavlovsk was a strange town, full of people – especially women – driven to the brink by isolation, alcohol or loneliness. The radio seemed to act as a focal point for the crazies, a voice in the void. But there was something focused about this woman's ranting, and her insistence on remaining anonymous piqued Latypova's interest. This was not the usual story of a fire or a road accident, and the woman obviously wasn't calling just to get her voice heard on radio.

Something about the call made Latypova think that the woman had something to do with the military headquarters, or some close link with it. But before she could ask any more questions the woman began asking once again if the call was being recorded, then suddenly hung up.

Latypova had been a reporter when the *Kursk* had gone down, and had been one of those drafted in to try to fill the insatiable demand for stories on the subject. Petropavlosk was home to Russia's second-largest submarine fleet, and everyone knew someone who worked on board one. The whole city had been gripped with terrified fascination by what was happening at the other end of the country. Vidyaevo, the northern submarine garrison town where most of the victims had lived, was a sister city, and everyone had thought how easily the same thing could happen here. And now it had. Not with a huge nuclear submarine, but the thought of seven men trapped in a tiny metal coffin was almost more tangible. Their frozen, suffocating incarceration was somehow more claustrophobic and human, and easier to imagine.

Latypova thought for a minute after putting down the phone. Her journalistic antennae were tingling. It had taken 32 hours for news of what had actually happened to the *Kursk* to reach the Russian public. If this story were true it would be a big scoop. She picked up the phone to the office of the commander-in-chief of the North-East Military Forces and asked if there was anything to the story.

'No comment,' came the reply, and with those words Latypova knew she was on to something. Within minutes she had the news-flash on air.

'We have learnt from a well-informed source a bathyscaphe with seven seamen aboard is in distress at a depth of 200 metres in Berezovya Cove,' the newsreader said. 'The headquarters of Russian North-East Military Forces neither confirm nor deny this information.'

Latypova quickly typed up a report to send to Interfax, the news-wire agency that she'd once worked for and still fed with breaking news, while her colleague Oksana Guseva sent it to RIA Novosti, the state news agency based in Moscow. Calls soon began to come into the station from various specialists and anonymous members of the military giving other details of what was evidently already a sizeable operation.

Latypova quickly pulled her teams together. She sent a film crew down to the military headquarters and got some reporters to hit the phones and call anyone relevant. Then she began working out how to take the story forward. When she thought back to the *Kursk*, the image that first came to mind was not the interviews with stone-faced Naval commanders, or footage of rescue vessels or of sub-marines tied up on the pier side, but of the desperate wives and mothers.

She decided to take another team to the district of Zavoyko, where many military families lived on a peninsula that jutted out from Petropavlovsk just as Kamchatka protruded from the Russian mainland.

Zavoyko was once wreathed in glory, but those who referred to it as the 'city of heroes' now were being sarcastic. While the early 1990s had not been kind to mother Russia as a whole, it was in her former military strongholds and northern regions – and especially the remote, isolated Kamchatka, that the decay was worst. This stung Latypova, for she was both patriotic and acutely conscious of how much the people of Kamchatka had given to their country.

Zavoyko was named after Captain 1st Rank Zavoyko, who, a century and a half before, had fought off the combined might of the French and British fleets. In late August 1854, the Crimean war had arrived at the shores of the Russian east coast in the shape of four French warships and four British frigates (including one six-gun paddle-steamer, the latest in military hardware). The fleet was bent on capturing Petropavlovsk, then Russia's main Naval facility in the Pacific.

Russia's only substantial warship in this area was the 60-gun *Pallada*, and for her to face the enemy fleet alone would have been suicide. She turned tail and hid far up the river Amur, leaving Petropavlovk's forces to fight alone. The garrison was small and there were no reinforcements available, so Captain Zavoyko roused the general population to man the gun batteries and defend the city themselves. Even then they stood little chance, for they had only 68 cannons to bring to bear against the 212 of the assembled allies. But fortune was on their side. Whether by mistake or on purpose, before the fighting even began the Commander of the British Fleet, Rear Admiral David Price, was below decks in his quarters and shot himself in the head with his pistol.

Under new command, the allied French and British forces landed 70 men but were repulsed. A few days later they returned with almost 1,000 men, and again the hard-bitten Russian resistance fought them back. It was the most significant battle in the Pacific theatre of the Crimean war, and the result was clear. During the siege, the Russians lost a hundred men, but killed five times as many. The heroic defence became a symbol of all that was great about the Russian military: resourcefulness, bravery and the snatching of victory from the jaws of almost certain defeat. Warships were named Petropavlovsk in honour of the event, and Captain Zavoyko was lauded with his own city.

But in Zavoyko district, many of the concrete five-storey apartment buildings were now deserted, their sides streaked with rust and their windows broken. The quaysides of the port were lined with vessels that would never put to sea again. The one road that connected it to the rest of Petropavlovsk was frequently washed by the sea or buried beneath snow, cutting the district off from the city. When isolated from the mainland in this way, officers alighting from their vessels in Zavoyko on leave had to simply return to their ships. The town didn't even have its own bakery. When the people of Petropavlovsk wanted to evoke the poor conditions of life, they would say *It's like in Zavoyko*.

Stepping out of their car – one of the few on the streets there – Latypova and her colleagues walked over to a shop with empty windows and began asking about the families of the submersible's crew.

The journalists had not been sniffing around long when they noticed that a military vehicle was passing from one apartment block to the next, apparently making visits. They walked over in time to see a handful of men in military uniform coming out of the main doors. A man and a woman were standing outside smoking, and Latypova approached them to find out if they knew anything. She struck lucky. It was Slava Milachevsky's sister and her husband. Not only that, the woman had seen Latypova's shows and was happy to help.

Friday, 5 August
SS + 23 h 30 mins
16.00 Kamchatka
***AS-28*, 210 metres beneath Berezovya Bay**

The rasping of men's breath was all that could be heard in the darkness aboard *AS-28*. Occasional metallic noises clunked and pinged, the sounds distorted by the spherical pressure chambers, but mostly it was silence that hissed in their ears.

There was no insulation on *AS-28*'s titanium hull. Other military submarines are covered by a layer of rubbery tiles that serves not only to soften the craft's sonar reflection, making it hard to detect, but also to prevent the metal hull from conducting all the heat away from the living space. Not designed for either stealth or long immersions, *AS-28* had nothing but paint on her exterior. Inside, the men were freezing.

Without the warmth of human bodies, the internal temperature in the forward compartment where one watch member manned the underwater telephone had plummeted to a bone-chilling 4°C, only fractionally warmer than the black water pressing against the outside of the pressure hull. Bolonin's fur-lined jacket was the only consolation, worn by whoever was on that watch.

Not that clothes were helping much. None of them seemed much better off than the one who was without an immersion suit. Condensation was dripping from the curved walls of their prison, the moisture stripping heat away from their bodies even if their clothes were still fairly dry. The heaters and dehumidifiers that normally kept the submersible comfortable lay silent – the machines would suck too much power from the batteries. It was a delicate balancing act for Captain Lepetyukha and Bolonin: if the crew got too cold and started shivering uncontrollably they'd use three or four times as much oxygen as normal. It would be no use if the rescuers found the *AS-28* with battery power remaining but the crew all suffocated.

The only way the men could feel any hint of warmth was by huddling up. They'd laid all of the boat's lifejackets on the floor of the aft compartment and the six of them lay on top of them in a row, sharing their body heat. Like emperor penguins sheltering from the Antarctic winter, they took turns enduring the cold outer edge.

Lying in the huddle, Captain Lepetyukha was trying to think through what was to come. Previously he'd been confident that with this new technology his Navy would have quickly freed them.

But now, through some unspecified technical failure, the ROV was gone. The *Kozmin*'s operator had said it would be back in the water, but hadn't said when.

Bolonin had assured him that the ROV was designed to be repairable on the deck of a ship, that there were often problems with them, but they were often quickly fixed. But Lepetyukha was more familiar with the operational state of the Navy. Even if there had been someone on board the *Kozmin* with the skills to do it, he wouldn't have the necessary tools. Anything moveable had been sneaked off the ship and sold long ago.

During the frantic scramble to rescue the *Kursk*, the crew of *AS-34* had sent a telegram from their mothership, the *Mikhail Rudnitsky*, requesting equipment to fix their craft. On the list were the most basic of requirements: monkey wrenches, socket sets and manual drills – all things that should be carried as standard but that had been spirited away by the impoverished crew.

Tools weren't the only thing being stripped off the rescue ships. Before 1992, some of the Priz class of submersibles used large quantities of mercury in their ballast tanks to help them trim their attitude to match the tilt of a sunken submarine's hatch. Once the mission was complete, the valuable liquid metal was dumped on the seabed to allow the submersible to surface. Only when it turned out that the mercury was seeping into the hull and causing dangerous fumes did the authorities decide to substitute water for the mercury.

In 1994, the *Georgy Kozmin* steamed to Vladivostok to have her tanks drained of mercury and enlarged so that the job could be done by seawater instead. One of the crew, Officer Steshenko, apparently spotted an opportunity and contacted the coastal mafia to offer them the metal. The previously poor officer began spending lavishly in bars, but something apparently went wrong with the deal and a few days later his headless body was found. The remaining mercury was stored upon the *Kozmin* in small cast-iron tanks, but soon that started disappearing as well. Two years later, an inspection found that more than 60 kilos were missing, leading to the conviction of several sailors who had secreted some of the liquid metal in hidey-holes beneath the deck and some in an apartment block in Petropavlovsk.

With rescue from the *Kozmin* looking unlikely, Lepetyukha tried to think further afield. The *Sayany* rescue and salvage ship that carried the Atmospheric Diving Suit was too far away. He knew she was only able to steam at eight knots on a good day, and the *Kozmin* had confirmed that she would not be with them until 9 August, four days away. He'd already rationed the oxygen canisters as much as he dared. There was no way they would survive that long.

Try as he might, he couldn't imagine how help was going to arrive now. And he should know, as a captain of one of the Russian Navy's submarine rescue submersibles. He tried to put these fears out of his mind. Coordinating a rescue was not his job at this stage. His task was to keep his crew – and their hopes – alive for as long as possible.

Friday, 5 August
SS + 24 h 30 mins
17.00 Kamchatka
The Milachevskys' dacha, near Petropavlovsk

Yelena Milachevskaya had spent the day working in the garden of the family dacha. Owned by Slava's parents, it was usually a welcome refuge from the oppression of Petropavlovsk itself. Today she'd been unable to appreciate it, her mind filled with the echoes of the nightmares she'd been suffering.

She'd come in to give the girls their dinner and was standing at the sink in the kitchen, doing the dishes. She had the television on in the next room, but her mind was roaming between the sound of the local news, the noise of the twins playing outside, the clink of the dishes and the evening light on the slopes of the mountains in the distance. When the word 'bathyscaphe' filtered through the doorway from the living room, it somehow wasn't enough to rouse her from her dishwashing trance. Perhaps, coming from a submariners' town, the word was bandied around so much that she didn't feel it applied to her, even given her premonitions. She didn't pay too much attention to the news anyway, and had a healthy disrespect for the media.

When she heard the newscaster say the word '*Kozmin*' it pierced the armour of her inattention. She rushed to the television. *Kozmin* was the name of Slava's mothership. But by the time she got there she caught only the last few seconds of the bulletin, and knew only that something had happened to a submersible from Petropavlovsk, and that it was serious enough for the Naval Headquarters in Moscow to issue a statement. Worse still, she knew that if the *Kozmin* was involved, Slava's submersible was the only one on board.

Panicked, the first thing that Yelena did was call Slava's parents. Slava's father, Vladimir Valentinovich, had worked on the same Priz submersible, *AS-28*, from the beginning of its construction through its commissioning and sea trials, logging 17 years in it before his retirement from the Navy. He'd heard nothing, not even the news bulletin. He said he would call his friends who were still in the service and find out what was happening, and call her back.

Yelena didn't even put the receiver down. She hung up using her finger and dialled the number for Naval Headquarters from memory. She demanded to know what was going on. They told her that they too knew nothing. She should keep watching the news, they said.

'The news bulletins? But they may concoct some untruth! You are the official body!' she cried into the phone.

'We do not know anything,' the operator said. 'We are also watching the news.'

Even Kamchatka's governor, Mikhail Mashkovtsey, was doing

the same. Despite claiming to be an atheist, between bulletins he admitted that he was praying. When a news reporter called him to ask what he planned to do if the men were rescued, he promised them a reward. With admirable self-belief, he said to the reporter: 'I have known for a long time that for many people a small merit certificate from the governor is more important than any material benefits.'

A friend of Yelena's from her university days had been staying at the dacha and stepped in to shield the twins from their mother's worry, but it could not have been long before they realised that something bad had happened. Yelena sat in front of the television, waiting for the next update, with her hand on the telephone ready for when Slava's father called back. Finally he did, and he was unable to hide his despair from his daughter-in-law. His Naval friends had only been able to tell him what the media already knew. *AS-28* was stuck some 200 metres underwater, trapped by fishing nets or other cables, and that so far the rescue efforts had been unsuccessful. But his anxiety was compounded by his experience with the Priz submersibles and with the Russian Navy. He knew that not a single one had ever been rescued, and that no means of rescue were available. What's more, he'd calculated that – if they'd submerged with the standard equipment – there should be enough breathable air to last his son and the other six men only until around midnight on Saturday.

Yelena was starting to feel suffocated herself. She'd peered inside Slava's Priz submersible soon after they'd met. She hadn't gone inside, for the Russian Navy still clung to its superstitions and there remained a feeling that having a woman step on board was bad luck. She hadn't wanted to anyway – it looked so claustrophobic. She could hardly believe that one man could squeeze inside there, let alone seven. Her chest felt tight at the thought of it.

She had no faith that the Navy would bring Slava back to her. She'd seen and heard too much. But how could she survive without him? She remembered when she first saw him, almost three years before, as though it was yesterday. She and some friends had been organising a party for a girlfriend and were on the hunt for nice men. It was around eight o'clock when they'd found him standing in a corridor with a bunch of other officers, smoking and passing cigarettes around between them. The girls had invited them along on the spot. Though Slava always denied it later, he'd proposed that same evening.

When Yelena called Slava's sister, she got the same sense of inevitable doom. The Navy might be saying there was cause for optimism, but everybody that Yelena loved and trusted seemed to be saying something different. There was no hope, she knew. She would not be seeing Slava again. She had to get back to Zavoyko and confront this nightmare. Her friend agreed to drive her back, despite protesting that they would be better off waiting until morning.

Why hadn't Slava just come home like he had said he wanted to? He'd called on Russian Navy Day, on 31 July. He'd just been awarded a merit certificate for 'Good Settings Afloat' by the Commander, and said that he was longing to join them at the dacha but that they'd been called out for a job again and couldn't come.

Without him, she had nothing. They still didn't have legal rights for the flat as they'd just moved in and the licence had not been issued to them yet. She was without a job and had the twins to look after with only 500 roubles (about £10) to her name.

Friday, 5 August
SS + 25 h 30 mins
18.00 Kamchatka
Zavoyko military settlement, Petropavlovsk-Kamchatsky

Tatiana Lepetyukha let herself into the Orthodox church and knelt at her pew, the golden carving of the altar a dull glow in the dark interior. Evening mass was still half an hour away, but she began praying. She'd known something had gone wrong at precisely the moment at which it had happened. Her heart had told her. Now she needed to tune back into that same guidance.

When Father Yaroslav appeared, she talked to him about all that had happened. He counselled her to keep communicating with God and with her husband. Just as she was not alone in her prayers for the men, she must pray also for the other men aboard the craft under her husband's command. She did so, fervently. After all, they might be in dire need of her prayers: she had no way of knowing if the others were all christened or not.

Tatiana had been fiercely religious ever since her father had died in 1992, the same year that her younger son, Roman, was born. She carried her faith proudly, and it helped her get through the long periods of absence from Valery. She now used that same strength to allow her to present a brave face with which to lead the other wives. She shuddered at the memory of Irina Lyadina, the wife of the *Kursk*'s commander, on television five years before, resolutely staying calm as all others around her collapsed. She sank her head and delved further into prayer that things would not turn out in the same horrific way as they had on the *Kursk*, but to be given the strength to act with similar leadership if they did.

Tatiana had been in the third year of her studies at Leningrad's Medical Institute when she met the young Valery, who was attending the Leningrad Naval Academy. He'd waited until International Women's Day, 1983, to propose. That was the happiest day of her life, but it had eventually led her to the opposite end of the country to Kamchatka, and – inexorably – to her desperate prayers in this church.

She'd not yet told the 13-year-old Roman about the danger to his father's life. Unlike his elder brother Anton, a 22-year-old Naval officer, Roman wasn't familiar with Navy service, and she didn't want to cause him unnecessary worry. She did, however, call Anton back in St Petersburg, and told him what was happening. He was stoic, as she knew he would be. He had unflinching confidence in the service. When friends later heard his father was trapped and tried to give him comfort on the street, he laughed and told them that when his father came back ashore he would not understand why anyone was worried. More than anyone on the desolate peninsula of Kamchatka, it was her faraway son who was Tatiana's strength.

Just before Mass began, Tatiana noticed the parents of Slava Milachevsky, the pilot, arrive at the church. Slava's wife, Yelena, was not with them, but they stood through the Mass together, and placed lit candles to mark their prayers.

Friday, 5 August
SS + 26 h 30 mins
07.00 UK – 19.00 Kamchatka
Royal Navy lodgings, Bristol

Commander Riches was already half awake when the radio came on at seven. The thin curtains were ineffective armour against the morning sunlight. He opened his eyes, winced, and closed them again. The newsreader was far too chirpy. Right now all he could think of was the remaining day of drudgery before the weekend.

He'd only been half listening when the voice on the radio announced that a Russian submarine was trapped underwater off the country's Far Eastern coast. He was instantly awake, but there were few other details. She said there were seven people on board, from which he assumed it must be a scientific research submersible, not a full-size military submarine. Still, it was worth finding out more. It wasn't every day that the undersea world made the national headlines.

He swung his legs out of bed, and paused. The Command mobile phone was sitting on his bedside table. It being August, the operational head of the Submarine Rescue Service, Commander

Jonty Powis, was away on holiday, leaving Riches in charge. He stared at the phone for a second. It was supposed to be a key node in a classified international network that instantly came alive in any submarine emergency. It was silent.

The gears in his brain began to turn. Russia's east coast was about as far away as possible. He could think of at least three rescue teams that were better placed to get there than his. But he knew how commanders think, and top brass wouldn't let this chance go. They'd want to use this as an exercise and a test of his team's preparedness. It wasn't as though he'd actually be deploying either the UK's rescue submersible or the underwater robot, but he'd have to go through all the motions.

He needed coffee.

Friday, 5 August
SS + 26 h 30 mins
07.00 UK – *10.00 Moscow* – 19.00 Kamchatka
UK embassy, Moscow

Captain Jon Holloway entered the secure zone in the British Embassy's Chancery section, where all the more sensitive, political matters were discussed. Holloway had been one of the nuclear engineers on board the vessel during Riches' submarine command 'Perisher' trial, and the two men were familiar with one another. He now walked into the meeting room and eased into his chair, laying his file on the table. All the surfaces were the same, light-coloured softwood, a design that was reaching for Cool Britannia rather than old world authority, he guessed. The Defence Attaché, the sturdy Air Commodore Wils Metcalfe, walked into the room and bade good morning to Holloway and the Military Attaché, Colonel Pat Callan, and nodded towards the assistant attachés. Uniforms weren't worn in the embassy, and all the men were in shirts and ties, having left their jackets at their desks on this bright summer morning.

Metcalfe sat back in his chair to listen to updates that he would afterwards be presenting to the Ambassador. One by one the attachés from the three forces gave their briefings, but all knew what the main item would be today. They'd all read the same newswire reports. Filling only half the seats around the rectangular meeting table, the group listened to Captain Holloway's outline of the situation. Usually there were two or three stories of relevance at the morning briefing, reports of activities and key events that they'd plucked from the morning papers – shifts in the military hierarchy, budget cuts, that sort of thing. Today was different.

Holloway could add little to the original Interfax report beyond updating them on the two calls he'd managed to make so far. The first was to the Duty Fleet Controller at the Northwood HQ. They'd been tipped off about the incident through another channel, but were also finding more detailed information hard to come by. The second call had been to the Russian Main Naval Staff, but his contact had been tight-lipped, and had stonewalled him. He'd not been able to get any further before coming to the meeting.

Eyes were narrowed and chins were being stroked. If the UK could somehow assist, there was potential in the situation to aid relations between Moscow and London. Although in relatively good condition at the time, the UK was determined to preserve its coveted Special Relationship with the US, whose encounters with Russia were becoming increasingly strained. Russia stood accused of exporting nuclear fuel to Iran, as well as of supporting the anti-US forces in Syria by selling them missiles. Staying close to the US meant pushing Russia away.

But to a greater degree the problems between Moscow and London were direct. For the past four years, the Russian oligarch Boris Berezovsky had been using the UK as a base from which to attack President Vladimir Putin. Berezovsky, maths genius and a businessman accused by his critics as being the epitome of 'robber capitalism', had helped put Putin in power in March 2000 using the television station he owned, ORT. But, once elected, Putin had thanked him by trying to wrest the station back into state hands. The new president didn't want such power in the hands of others, and used the people's dislike of the oligarchs – who stood accused of stripping the nation's wealth for their own gain – as an excuse. The two men became bitter enemies.

Then, in August of that same year, the *Kursk* disaster unfolded, and Berezovsky used ORT to unleash harsh criticism of Putin. Soon he began to fear for his life. He fled to the UK, where he was granted political asylum, and joined the ever-widening 'London Circle' of Russian exiles. Three times the Russian authorities tried to extradite him on charges of fraud and political corruption, and three times the British refused. There were rumours of assassination attempts. None of this was good for diplomatic relations.

The Naval Cooperation Programme still linked the two nations, one of the fibres preventing the slide towards another Cold War. It had been set up with the aim of trying to bring the Russian Federation close enough to start participating in joint international operations. With a working relationship and regular contact between the two forces, it would become easier to defuse tensions, and harder for misunderstandings to arise and ferment.

Cooperation on submarine rescue had been a major element in the programme. Just two months ago, Russian observers had joined the NATO submarine rescue exercise in the Mediterranean. Navies from around the world came together every three years, usually in either the Mediterranean or the Baltic, to practise rescuing sailors from each other's submarines. That year, the UK's system had plucked crewmen from Italian, Dutch and Greek submarines that were playing dead on the seabed. The training would prepare them to act instinctively when the Naval 'SUBSUNK' signal was received, indicating that a submarine was down.

It was an awesome show of military technological wizardry, deployed for saving rather than ending human lives. The only letdown was the naming protocol. While US exercises came up with pulp fiction titles like 'Cobra Gold' or 'Valiant Shield', this one from NATO's naming protocol sounded like a cheap, watery dessert: Sorbet Royal.

About 44 nations in the world operate military submarines, and only four – Iran, Libya, Taiwan and North Korea – were not included in the rescue community. The exercises began in 1986, and 30 nations had turned up to participate or observe during 2005, including Israel, India, Pakistan and, of course, Russia. Even China would attend three years later.

Initially the Russians were going to bring a ship to join those of France, the US and the UK, but in the end had just sent observers. The simple presence of Russian submarine escape and rescue specialists on this exercise was a major advance. Unfortunately, the programme was extremely vulnerable to being used as a political tool. When the same invitation had been extended in 2000, just prior to the *Kursk* disaster, the Russians had refused to join in at all.

Building such links was Holloway's main mission as Naval Attaché. The *Kursk* disaster had shown the Russian people, and elements of the Navy, that there was an international will to assist when things went wrong. Holloway had worked hard at bringing the Russians to the table in Submarine Rescue planning, developing the framework for how the two nations would work together in case a rescue was needed, and making sure that each was familiar with the other's equipment. On the latter front, Holloway had brought members of the Russian design bureaus (including the Lazurit office in Nizhny Novgorod responsible for the design of *AS-28*) and Russian search and rescue crews over to the UK a number of times.

Holloway closed his briefing by outlining what his next actions were going to be. They'd treat it like any other submarine emergency, in the way that they had practised on exercise so often. No matter if you thought it was likely you'd be called into action or not, you readied your equipment. Firstly he'd call the Duty Fleet Controller at Northwood, UK, and make sure that the UK Submarine Rescue Service (UKSRS) was on alert. They would start working out an estimate of how quickly they could get into action. Only one measure mattered: the Time to First Rescue. Once given a realistic time at which the first men could be taken off the submersible, the Russian Navy would be in a position to decide whether to accept the offer.

A call to the MOD's Russia Policy Desk was next: having the equipment and the team to help out was worthless without the political will to send them. He'd also talk to his American counter-part in Moscow, Captain Mike Morgan, to squeeze out more information. All along, he'd be continuing to try to get in touch with the Chief of Staff of the Russian Navy.

The discussion of how the situation might develop occupied the whole half-hour allocated for the meeting. When the time was up, the avuncular Commodore Metcalfe thanked the assembled attachés and made his way to brief the Ambassador himself.

Friday, 5 August
SS + 26 h 45 mins
***07.15 UK* – 10.15 Moscow – 19.15 Kamchatka**
Edinburgh

Stuart Gold tapped out the beat on the steering wheel as his Ford Focus accelerated away from the last set of lights before the main road. The rush-hour traffic was already queuing up on the other side of the carriageway, but he was cruising in the opposite direc-tion, just the way he liked it. He was tuned to BBC Radio 2, and when the strains of Level 42's 'Good Man in a Storm' started to play, Gold twisted the volume up a notch to get the song to its rightful level. He felt good. He'd just put his partner Susan on to a train at Waverley station – she was off to her last day of work, finishing a two-year stint ringing the changes at a shopping centre in Newcastle. That night they'd be celebrating in the best way possible – with a takeaway, a DVD and a bottle of wine. The fancy parties were all done and dusted, thank God, and now they could just go and slouch on the sofa. Perfect.

He'd just passed Hermiston Gate before getting on the motorway when the news had come on with the announcement. A submersible trapped off Russia. That got his attention, alright, but all the newsreader said was that seven Russian sailors were trapped in a mini-submarine off Kamchatka. Poor bastards, he thought. He'd no idea where Kamchatka was, though he had a vague memory of it being the one place you had to conquer if you were going to invade the United States, at least as far as the board game Risk was concerned. The Pacific coast of Russia sounded an awfully long way away. He wondered if they'd have any more information by the time he got to work an hour or so later.

Gold knew better than most what being stuck on the seabed would feel like. He'd spent years working in tiny submersibles during the early 1980s, exploring routes for new transatlantic cables and other pipelines in the North Sea and the North Atlantic for a company called British Oceanics. It was exciting work for the young electrical engineer, but after his youngest son was born backwards with both hips dislocated, suddenly the long periods away became difficult. Knowing that his baby son was struggling in a leather-and-metal cage was too much. When a six-week deployment to the South China Sea came up he'd resigned, and taken a job with a local computer company instead.

Ten long years he'd worked there, until he'd got a call from his old boss at British Oceanics. Martin Bully was now working at a small company in the Lake District that had a big mission – running the UK's Submarine Rescue Service – and wondered if Gold fancied a change.

Although commanded by the Royal Navy, the UK's Submarine Rescue Service was run by a private contractor, James Fisher Rumic. It was a good way for the Navy to harness the experience of the offshore underwater industry. Navy recruits would have been rotated out every two years, while many of the guys at Rumic had spent their lives working with the type of gear the rescue service operated. Gold had never had a serious accident during his time on submersibles, but he'd spent plenty of time imagining what it would be like to be trapped on the bottom. During long dives he and the pilot would often settle the vessel down on the seabed to take a lunch break. One by one they'd shut down the non-essential systems. First the whine of the thrusters would die away, then the noisy sonar would stop its metallic rasp and they'd be left sitting in darkness on the cold floor of the ocean with only the sound of the carbon dioxide scrubbers whirring. Though he was in the window-less stern looking after the submersible's electrical systems, his only view of the surrounding sea via a monitor, the silence seemed as pressurised as the water around them. They'd eat their sandwiches without much talking, just exploring the sensation of being in that alien world that so few humans have been able to experience. It was only natural that the mind wandered into the realms of horror, of wondering what it would be like if something went wrong, if that was where they'd remain, slowly freezing, starving, suffocating to death while the indifferent ocean swirled past the portholes.

As the road rolled on beneath him, heading west towards the base at Renfrew, Gold thought about the day ahead and the final preparations for Exercise Northern Sun, a series of submarine rescue scenarios about to be run off Norway. LR5, the rescue submersible, was on the trucks already, and Scorpio – the underwater robot that was his baby – was boxed up in its containers. He just needed to double-check things and make sure nothing was missing – after all, he wouldn't want to go through the embarrassment of having to ask if he could borrow tools off the Norwegians or the Swedes. It should be an easy enough day, and an interesting one, too. Even so, he'd definitely be keeping an ear to the radio to hear how those Russians were doing.

Friday, 5 August
SS + 27 h
07.30 UK – 10.30 Moscow – *19.30 Kamchatka*
Petropavlosk-Kamchatsky

Yelena Milachevskaya was almost out of the dacha in her chaotic rush to return to Zavoyko, when another news report came on to the television. Captain Igor Dygalo, the aide to the head of the Russian Navy, came on the state-run RTR channel. As her friend turned the volume up both of them stared desperately at the screen.

'The *AS-28* has enough air for one day,' Dygalo said. 'We have a day and will continue our intense efforts to save the *AS-28* and the people in it. The crew's activity is being kept to a minimum.'

Yelena began a low moan. There had been nothing but contradictory accounts of how much time her husband had left to live. Naval Headquarters had said many days, and initially Captain Dygalo had said five. Though Yelena did not know it, Dygalo was the same officer who had first broken the news of the *Kursk* disaster to the Russian people, more than a day after the accident when the lifeless *Kursk* was still lying undiscovered on the seabed. *Rescuers have established contact and are supplying air and no casualties have been reported*, he had said at the time. None of it was true.

Tatiana Lepetyukha's faith had so far kept her strong. She'd spurned the military's offers of psychologists for her to talk to, preferring instead to rely on the Lord. That didn't mean she was passive. She had installed herself at the local headquarters, where she could be kept immediately up to date with the progress of all aspects of the rescue operation. There she was also shielded from the rumour -mill that was raging outside. She'd already developed a dislike of the local journalists, especially the pushy women.

She'd left her 13-year-old son at home and had been shocked

to get a panicked call from him saying that a woman was trying to get inside to ask him questions. Tatiana told him to say that it was the wrong door, that no one lived there any more. When that failed to send the insensitive journalist away, she'd said, 'Tell them to go to hell.' Roman followed her instructions and the woman had left, leaving Roman surprised at the power of popular Russian language.

When Yelena reached her flat in Petropavlovsk, she hadn't been able to stand it inside. Although they'd just moved in, it already held too many memories of Slava. Boxes of his things still lay unpacked, and in the living room was a big model of *AS-28* that he'd carved out of wood. So they drove on to Yelena's sister, Svetlana, who lived up the road in Zavoyko.

Soon after they arrived Svetlana called the Naval Headquarters on Yelena's behalf. There was no news from Bereyozova Bay, but they asked about Yelena's whereabouts. The Department of Moral Welfare of the Forces wanted to send around a military psychologist to help her through these difficult times. Svetlana thought it sounded like a good idea, and encouraged Yelena to agree.

An hour or so later the psychologist arrived and began a brief physical examination of Yelena. He had not yet asked her any questions, but as he was strapping up her arm to test her blood pressure he started to muse.

'I wonder how they can still survive down there, when they have reportedly no air left to breathe,' he said.

Yelena whipped around and snarled, 'How can you say such a thing? You, a doctor?' she raged.

The psychologist's only defence was to claim that such counselling was not his normal job, that he specialised in suicides.

Furious, she pushed him out of the flat as fast as she could. 'Do you want me to hang myself?' she shouted after him.

'Pray,' said the doctor as she slammed the door in his face. 'There's nothing else you can do.'

But the anger had focused Yelena and lifted her from her

hysterical state. She began calling the staff of the Moral Welfare of the Forces department every few minutes. She'd only called a couple of times when there was another knock at the door. Yelena tore it open, expecting the psychologist again, but was instead confronted with a blonde woman whose face was vaguely familiar. The lady introduced herself as a reporter and offered brief condolences before coming quickly to the point. The only way to get the Navy to act would be to get the story out, the woman said. Yelena might hold the key to rescuing her husband. Yelena didn't trust journalists as a rule, but when she realised this was Guzel Latypova, she decided to let her in.

Latypova was a good listener, and talking was what Yelena needed to do. Their conversation began broadly, but soon they were talking about Slava's family and their long, proud history with the Navy's submarine fleet and the harsh realities of modern Naval life. The more Latypova heard the more her heart bled for this woman, an innocent victim of the government's neglect of Kamchatka's proud people.

Together they watched the television news. It was another Naval official, Alexander Koslapov, the head of the Pacific Fleet's press service. His words added lead to Yelena's heart as she felt the terrible inertia of the Russian Navy. 'The situation is atypical,' Koslapov said. 'But it's not worth dramatising.'

Friday, 5 August
SS + 27 h
07.30 UK **– 10.30 Moscow – 19.30 Kamchatka**
Bristol

Riches was on the way to the Ministry of Defence's Abbey Wood complex when the Command hotline mobile phone finally rang. It was the Duty Submarine Controller at Northwood.

'Commander, there's been an incident involving a submersible,' he began.

'Off Russia's Kamchatka Peninsula with seven men on board,' Riches cut in. 'Fat lot of good a hotline is if the BBC get the news before we do.'

There was a pause. 'We need a TTFR as soon as possible,' came the level reply. The all-important estimate of the fastest Time To First Rescue they could offer.

'I'm just getting into the office now. I'll let you know when I've worked it out,' Riches said, and hung up.

Abbey Wood was the support and logistical headquarters for all three of the Services: the Army, the Navy and the Air Force. Only from the air did the complex exude any Pentagon-like sense of power; as you swept up to the security gate it looked more like a snappy retail park than a military facility. It was created in 1996 over the scar of an old coal mine, and now fountains sprang from lakes that hugged white buildings with huge, sparkling windows. If it weren't for the Ministry of Defence policeman on the gate and the occasional military uniform, there would be nothing much to indicate the military significance of the place.

Once inside Riches strode through the deserted, sunlit atria towards the part of the building that had been christened 'Cedar Neighbourhood'. He made his way through the labyrinth of unmanned desks belonging to the 250-person Submarine Support Integrated Project Team, until he found his own. While 245 of the desks housed people dedicated to keeping the Royal Navy's submarines loaded with enough supplies, spares and equipment to keep them out there doing their job, only five belonged to Riches' team – the ones responsible for trying to bring men back if anything went wrong.

His first move was to get on to the restricted website of the International Submarine Escape and Rescue Liaison Office, based in Norfolk, Virginia. ISMERLO had been established in the wake of the *Kursk* to help communication and coordination in the event of a similar disaster. Almost every submarine-toting nation used

ISMERLO as its primary information node during an emergency, as did all of the top people in the field, both military and civilian. If anyone knew anything, it would be there. But the updates screen was barren.

Riches thought there must be something wrong. He called Commander Trond Juvik of the Royal Norwegian Navy, who was in charge of the site, clean forgetting that it was 02.30 in the morning on the east coast of the USA. Juvik had heard nothing, he said in a sleepy voice before hanging up.

This wasn't how things went during exercises. Even when they weren't physically participating in an exercise they'd get involved on ISMERLO, calculating and presenting realistic timelines to get their equipment to the scene. They'd never thought of practising without it.

He picked up the phone and called Moscow. Captain Holloway was still trying hard to get official information from the Russian Ministry of Defence, but so far was having to rely on media reports like everybody else.

A string of other calls followed, to diplomats, the Defence Transport and Movements Agency, to James Fisher Rumic. Riches was working down the standard checklist to establish just how fast he could get his equipment into play. Only the faintest prickle of warning on his skin warned that this might be different.

The knowledge that men were trapped underwater had reawakened something inside him. It wasn't often that, sitting in that bright, airy office, he felt like a submariner any more. As is true for everyone who has served in those steel coffins, the sensation of cruising silently through an alien world, invisible but all-seeing, had lodged itself deep in his soul and now he could feel it stirring.

There's a kinship between those who travel or fight on the high seas, sharing the risks of tempests, rogue waves and unseen rocks. Most sailors can expect to survive hours or sometimes days clinging to floating wreckage even if no lifeboats are launched when their ship goes down, but submariners have no such comfort. For them, death is always pressing close around the hull.

Even the deepest-diving hunter-killer submarines can go no deeper than around a thousand metres (except for one experimental Russian boat, the *Komsomolets*). That gives them enough scope for finding hiding places on the seabed or cloaking themselves between water layers of different temperature or salinity while keeping the engineering constraints manageable. But the average depth of the ocean is more than 3,500 metres. In most places in the world, if a submarine gets into trouble and starts to sink, it will be crushed like a discarded Coke can long before it reaches the seabed.

For the Submarine Rescue Service, this enforced a certain morbid economy. LR5, the UK's rescue submersible, could operate only to a depth of 500 metres. It could be built stronger and therefore penetrate deeper, but the continental shelves – the skirt of relatively shallow water that surrounds the continents – are mostly less than 200 metres deep. At their edge lies a steep drop to the abyssal plains and hadal depths. If a submarine sinks somewhere off the shelf – as did both the USS *Thresher* in 1963 and USS *Scorpion* in 1969 – there is no point in sending a rescue craft. Beyond crush depth, there is no hope for those inside.

The standard Royal Navy procedures for a submarine incapacitated on the seabed were still clear in his mind. No amount of desk-bound duty could erase the charged atmosphere of putting a crew through the drills. The first move is a mayday alert – just as in other emergencies at sea or in the air – letting potential rescuers know that you're in trouble and where you are. Seawater is dense enough to stop bullets and radiation, let alone radio waves, so an emergency indicator buoy is released. The brightly coloured marker shoots to the surface hauling up an antenna from the submarine. A coded signal flashes out to orbiting satellites, giving the submarine's position and identity to friendly ears. When rescuers arrive, all being well, they have a marker that will help guide them to the vessel on the seabed.

Next a transponder is dropped on the seabed. Just as the buoy above is transmitting a homing signal, the transponder gives a regular sonic ping. If something happens to the emergency indicator buoy on the surface, this pinging will still act as a beacon for rescuers. Finally, an ECB699 – a submarine-to-shore communications buoy – is loaded into one of the submerged signal ejectors and fired up through the water. Once on the surface the battery-powered transmitter begins sending its coded message to passing satellites, giving the submarine's position and status, and the number of people on board.

Only once all beacons have been deployed will an escape be considered. It wasn't always so. Until the 1960s, Royal Navy submariners didn't expect to be rescued from the surface. No technology was thought to be reliable enough; your best chance was to save yourself. Given an alternative of certain death, the Royal Navy felt a gamble was worth it. Riches, however, knew the Russians did not agree.

The Rush Escape was the last resort, only used if the hull had been damaged. If seawater was forcing its way in, even slowly, the pressure of the air inside the submarine would begin to rise, changing the physical properties of the atmosphere and turning perfectly breathable air into a poison gas. The men were trained to line up beside the exits, breathing from masks attached to air pipes that ran along the gangways, then all hatches were opened and the sea was allowed to flood in. It took enormous discipline to stay in line, moving from mask to mask as the freezing water crept higher and higher and eventually over their heads. Submerged, the men would shuffle towards the exit one by one, progressing along the line of masks as though they were stepping stones. Every 10 to 15 seconds a man would shoot for the surface from the hatch, propelled by the air in his survival suit.

There were many risks, especially for those towards the back of the line. If the submarine was deep the water would be close to freezing – it doesn't matter if you're in the tropics or at the North Pole, beyond the reach of the sun's warming the sea's temperature hovers around 4°C. With the hull no longer keeping out the pressure, every breath of air from the mask forced dissolved gas into the body's tissues, gas that would soon be forming bubbles as it rapidly depressurised on the way to the surface. An ascent from anywhere below 60 or 70 metres would most likely result in the Bends, an agonising affliction suffered by divers, caused by gas bubbles getting trapped in the joints. Whoever survived this ordeal then faced all the challenges of a mariner whose ship has been lost and who is floating alone on the empty ocean.

The equipment and some of the methods had changed substantially since the Rush Escape was first introduced in 1929, but the Royal Navy's training for it hadn't. Until well into the 21st century, every British submariner since had the necessary self-control imposed on them at the bottom of a 30-metre-deep training pool housed in a tower in Gosport on the south coast, where Britain's first submarine base was located. In the early days, escaping sailors were equipped with the Davis Submarine Escape Apparatus. It consisted of an airtight bag containing barium hydroxide that would strip carbon dioxide from exhaled air while fresh oxygen was provided in a cylinder. The concept was identical to that used on German submarines in the First World War and to the re-breather diving systems used by some technical divers today. Escaping sailors using the Davis Apparatus would pinch a clip over their nose, pull a pair of leather goggles over their eyes then launch themselves towards the surface, their ascent slowed to a manageable speed by a canvas drogue that dragged behind them like an upside-down parachute.

By 1980, when Riches had done his escape training in Gosport's pool, the latest version was an orange survival suit fitted with an oxygen-filled hood. But by then the preferred method of escape – if conditions allowed – was the controlled method. One crewman climbs into the escape chamber, shuts the hatch below and opens a valve to let the sea in. Only once the chamber is full and the pressure in the tower equalises with the sea can he open the top hatch and escape. While in the tower he plugs his escape suit into an air outlet which pushes air into a collar around his neck that will later provide him with buoyancy. At the same time, excess air escapes into the plastic hood over his face, allowing him to breath normally. When the automatic hatch pops open, the sailor begins shooting to the surface, the expanding air in his suit streaming past his face and allowing him to keep breathing as normal. Those left on board then shut the hatch again and vent the water from the chamber to take the next sailor. Although safer, with less risk of exposure or decompression sickness, the controlled escape could take as much as 10 or 15 minutes to evacuate each person, despite a planned allowance of only four minutes per person.

But if the hood tears or doesn't work then the sailor is back to the Rush Escape technique. To stop the lungs from bursting when shooting up from the pressurised depths, sailors are taught to shout as hard as they can all the way to the surface in a bellowing exhale that can last a minute or longer as the air expands as fast as it can be expelled.

It was all too obvious at the time that the warm, clear water of the 30-metre-deep training tank was only faint preparation for what it would be like escaping from a submarine flooding with freezing, oil-stained seawater that was probably far deeper.

Thinking about the trapped men while sitting in that empty office, the silence became a roaring in Riches' ears. It reminded him of being in his escape hood, and of the brutal noise of his own everlasting scream.

Friday, 5 August
SS + 28 h 28 mins
08.58 UK – 11.58 Moscow – 20.58 Kamchatka
Ministry of Defence Abbey Wood, Bristol

Finally, shortly before nine in the morning, a message appeared on the ISMERLO site. It was posted by Commander Trond Juvik, using Zulu time – the international standard, the equivalent of Greenwich Mean Time.

07:58:45: Russians are asking for international assistance ref phonecall from [Command Task Force] CTF 74. Vehicle has to be rescued / salvaged from the seabed and ROV / ADS resources are required to do the disentanglement from the net / cables. Eventually cable for lifting arrangements if she cannot come to the surface by her own power.

This was new. The fact that the vehicle – whatever it was – had got into trouble was one thing. But the fact that the Russians had called CTF 74 – the US submarine force based in Japan – and asked for help was another. Somehow the Russians were unable to solve this on their own and seemed willing to bring in outside help.

More messages added other clues. The Russians had despatched the specialised rescue ship *Savany* from Primorye, but it wouldn't reach the area until 9 August, at least three days away. Riches didn't know how much air the men on the submersible had, but three days was a long time – probably too long.

Twenty minutes later another message came up, this time from the US Navy's Admiral Michael Martin of CTF 74. He posted a rough translation of a fax sent to Admiral Wachendorf at the US embassy in Moscow by Admiral Vladimir Masorin, the Head of the Main Staff in the Russian Federation Navy.

Russian Federation Navy
To: Admiral Wachendorf

On 4 August in Berezovya Bay near the coast of the Kamchatka Peninsula while conducting underwater operations a bathysphere AS-28 encountered an emergency situation. At the depth of around 230 metres the bathysphere lost the ability to rise to the surface with an 18mm steel cable wound around its propeller and its hull.

There are seven people on board. There is reserve high pressure air for breathing and food and water on board.

Our specialists have determined that we do not have the means in this region to effect a rescue.

Therefore, the Commander in Chief of the Russian Navy urgently requests that the US Navy examines US capabilities to provide assistance by flying in deep submergence rescue vehicles capable of carrying out a rescue operation to free AS-28 from its cable and to raise it to the surface.

Please respond to me as soon as possible.

With respect,
V. Masorin

Riches picked up the phone to Sam Sampson at James Fisher Rumic to discuss what the UK's response should be. If they were going to respond to this situation, what would they do? The incident might be on the other side of the world, but all nations with Submarine Rescue assets that were involved in ISMERLO would be pondering the same problem, as they did in every exercise. Riches and Sampson agreed that LR5, the UK's Rescue Submersible, was probably not the tool for the job. No one knew much about the Russian Deep Submergence Rescue Vehicles (DSRVs), but they did know that the *AS-28* was a Priz-class rescue vehicle, otherwise known as Project 1855. Because she was designed to mate with stricken submarines herself, she didn't have the now-standard hatches to enable another rescue submersible to mate with her.

She was too deep for the men to try to free themselves without escape suits; even if they had the very latest versions with all the extra floatation and oxygen they provided, 200 metres was at the very outer limit of what was survivable.

'The only solution is to cut the cables and free the submersible,' said Sampson. 'Scorpio's cutter should do it. And if it's too thick for that, we'll bring along LR5's. The guys can adapt it to fit the ROV.'

'Okay. How about timescales? How long to get to Prestwick

6060

60606060

airport?' Riches replied. Although Glasgow's international airport was the closest to the UKSRS base, Prestwick was better for military heavy lift access. Together with the RAF transport division's estimate of how long it would take from there, this would largely determine their projected 'Time To First Rescue', leading to a list of options from which the host nation could choose the best. That was the most crucial factor in determining which rescue team would be asked to help. In the case of submarine rescue, the best almost always meant the fastest.

Making the offer also made the diplomats happy. Riches had phoned the MOD's Crisis Management Cell and they were keen to make the most of the situation, so gears began to turn at a high level.

Once Sampson had told him the good news about Scorpio's state of readiness, Riches made another couple of calls, including to the Duty Submarine Controller. Riches spoke to Captain Holloway to let him know what he was proposing. He didn't want to risk the offer getting delayed by a bureaucratic snag. Finally he posted a message on ISMERLO.

08.24.51 – Scorpio currently sat on lorry awaiting transportation for Exercise Northern Sun. Available at Immediate Notice for assistance subject to UK MoD approval. Estimated time to Intervention approximately 36 hours.

This was all looking good for his report. The theoretical response time of 36 more hours would get them there around 64 hours after they estimated that the submersible had become trapped; the Submarine Rescue Service aimed to reach a stricken submarine within 72 hours. He might not be allowed to command his own submarine, but at least his superiors would see that he could still run a tight team and that their reaction times were good. If this kind of thing ever happened closer to home, they'd be ready. He could see the day developing with a few more phone calls followed by the inevitable order to stand down. They'd been through this too many times for him to get excited about an actual deployment. They were too far away to be considered a good option. But looking on the bright side, he might even make the evening flight back home for the weekend.

The ISMERLO Command site was filling with chatter. The Japanese had responded immediately to the news; three ships were already underway. Riches smiled. The news signalled a diplomatic triumph for the concept of international submarine rescue, for Russia and Japan were locked in a territorial dispute. At the end of the Second World War, both nations had claimed the Kuril islands, strung between the Kamchatka Peninsula and Japan, for themselves. Neither had yet won the argument, and both still refused to sign agreements.

Japan's deep-ocean capabilities were arguably the best in the world. As an island nation, Japan takes the sea very seriously. Its best Remotely Operated Vehicle could reach the very bottom of the deepest part of the ocean, the Mariana Trench, far beyond what any other nations could achieve at the time (Japan's ROV has since been lost, and a US vehicle is now the only one able to reach the Challenger Deep). Its Navy boasted two impressive Deep Submergence Rescue Vehicles. Each of the submersibles had its own dedicated mothership that was fully outfitted with decompression facilities, diving bells and ROVs, and both of these vessels, the *Chiyoda* and *Chihaya*, had been despatched to Kamchatka.

But there was a critical problem. Neither had been out at sea when the alert came out, and Japan was a full three-and-a-half days' sailing from the incident site. No one believed the crew of *AS-28* would survive that long.

Friday, 5 August
SS + 28 h 30 mins
09.00 UK – 12.00 Moscow – 21.00 Kamchatka
Cowes, Isle of Wight

While Riches was working the phones, Roger Chapman was coiling the mooring rope of his cherished ten-metre, gaff-rigged sailing boat, squinting across the water into the morning sun to see how the previous race in the regatta was faring. It was Cowes Week, the highlight of his sailing year. He was in heaven; as yet he had no idea that his weekend was going to be turned upside down, and that the whole of his professional life was about to be put to the test.

It was Chapman's love of sailing that had made him keep his base in the Lake District when most of the offshore opportunities had moved to Aberdeen as part of the Great North Sea Oil Rush. He hadn't fancied swapping the beautiful lakes for the dour grey of Scotland's east coast, no matter how glittering the pay packets. There was more to life than that, so his company, Rumic, had remained based in the Lake District.

Chapman had always done things for the passion of doing them, not simply for the money. He'd joined the Navy because of his feeling for the sea, and submarines had felt a natural choice. As a Lieutenant, he'd worked all the way up to the position of Navigator of HMS *Swiftsure* before they'd discovered a flaw with his eyesight and told him that he wouldn't be allowed to drive the new nuclear boats. They offered him freedom or an office, and he'd decided on freedom. As he saw it, there was no point in staying in the Navy if he didn't get to be out at sea.

Luckily, in 1971, submersibles were the hot new thing in the offshore oil and underwater-cable-laying industries, and Barrow-in-Furness was the centre of the world for subsea vehicles. On leaving HMS *Swiftsure,* all he had to do was walk over the jetty to the offices of Vickers Oceanics, an offshoot of the company that had built *Swiftsure*, and straight into a job. It had recently started operating submersibles commercially and was looking for pilots.

Two years later, in August 1973, Chapman was in the North Atlantic on a cable-laying job when the accident happened. He and his co-pilot, Roger Malinson, had just surfaced in their Vickers Oceanics *Pisces III* after a long survey dive. The sea was rough, but the North Atlantic was rarely calm and they were used to operating in bad conditions. A swimmer was in the water attaching the lifting hook, and both men were looking forward to a cup of tea and a bacon roll back on board the mothership. But, as they were being reeled in towards the vessel, Chapman and Malinson were suddenly flung across the tiny confines of the submersible's interior. Although they did not yet know it, the cable that had been towing them back to the mothership had somehow wrapped around a hexagonal nut and loosened it, causing a hatch to pop open and the aft buoyancy tank to flood with water and pitch the submersible backwards. The stern was sinking rapidly.

Confused and disoriented, it took them a couple of seconds to realise that their worst fears were coming true. Outside the porthole, the shallow, sunlit scene was rapidly darkening. The submersible was plummeting back down to the bottom: 480 metres down, they finally crashed stern-first into the seabed.

The two men lay in their upturned steel coffin, trying to conserve their air and endure the cold while sister submersibles owned by the company were scrambled from hundreds of miles away to search for them. *Pisces III* was designed to support them for two days, but the craft had landed in a dip in the seabed and was hidden from the probing sonars of the searching submersibles, and it was 76 hours before the *Pisces II* submersible finally found them and managed to attach the line that would bring them to the surface. It was the deepest rescue anybody had yet pulled off, and it inspired in Chapman a lifelong interest in saving those trapped beneath the sea.

A decade later, Chapman's company designed and began operating the UK's Submarine Rescue Service, centred around the LR5 submersible. The company had been running the 365-day-a-year contract – worth between £2m and £3m a year – for 18 years now, but the closest they'd got to seeing action was during the *Kursk*. Yet none of their equipment had even got wet, and now the chance for his team to prove themselves was fading.

Rumic's contract with the Royal Navy was about to come to an end. The UK had signed up for a new rescue system that would be shared with other NATO countries. The idea had been kicking around as long ago as 1990: with submarine accidents a rarity, why not pool the resources of submariner nations into a single rescue system? The concept of the NATO Submarine Rescue System was born, but it soon became apparent that not all nations were equally enthusiastic. France, Italy, Norway, Turkey, the UK and the US were all interested at one stage or another, but when it came time to sign up in 2003, only France, Norway and the UK remained in the group. It was enough, however, and plans began to be drawn up.

Chapman had fought hard to win the contract. On its own, Rumic didn't stand a chance of being thought capable of building and operating the £47m project, so he'd allied his company with shipping giant James Fisher Ltd in order to make it appear big enough to compete. It hadn't worked. In May 2004 Rolls-Royce was awarded the contract, beating subsea engineering firms Slingsby and Global Marine. In under two years' time, in March 2007, the UK's Submarine Rescue Service would cease to exist, and there seemed a good chance it would never have been used other than in exercises. Much as he loved spending time on his sailboat, he would much rather retire having shown the world what they were capable of.

That morning Chapman's thoughts were on the surface of the sea, not its depths. When his phone went and the rescue team manager Sam Sampson told him what was happening on the other side of the planet, his mind snapped back underwater.

Rumic's contract with the Royal Navy stated that rescue teams had to accomplish the first rescue intervention within 72 hours of the call, wherever in the world the accident had happened. As the chairman of Vickers Oceanics had said during Chapman's accident, 'The history of submarine accidents is the running out of time.'

Chapman left his boat with his crew and began making his way north. The clock was already ticking.

Friday, 5 August
SS + 29 h
09.30 UK – 12.30 Moscow – *21.30 Kamchatka*
***AS-28*, 210 metres beneath Berezovya Bay**

Through the persistent, bone-aching cold the crew of *AS-28* were now beginning to feel the effects of the foul air, their heads throbbing from the combination of oxygen deprivation and carbon dioxide build-up. Captain Lepetyukha was holding out as long as possible before opening each new V-64 cartridge, all too aware of the limits of his supply.

The canisters – each the size of a five-litre tin of paint – contained soda lime to absorb carbon dioxide and potassium superoxide to generate oxygen. Once opened, they were usually placed in a metal unit on the wall that contained a fan to circulate the air. But they couldn't risk using up power to run the fan, so the V-64 canister currently open was perched precariously above the main motor. To try and coax more life-giving gas from the canisters, Bolonin had suggested that the crew sprinkle a little of their precious water on to the chemicals. He knew from experience that the water would begin a chemical reaction that could coax an extra hour or two from each can.

It was a risky move: such chemicals are notoriously volatile. Add too much water and the potassium superoxide would explode. Two years later, in 2007, contamination of oxygen-generating substances was the chief suspect in a blast on board the Royal Navy submarine HMS *Tireless* en route back from the North Pole.

The challenges of operating beneath the ice had created problems for *Tireless*. Normally a Low Pressure Electrolyser on board uses high voltages to strip breathing oxygen from seawater, discharging the unwanted hydrogen gas back to the ocean. But Arctic water can drop to temperatures of minus two or three degrees Celsius, and is prevented from freezing only by the salt it contains. At certain depths, the hydrogen vents were prone to freezing. It was a known issue with operating beneath the ice, and for the last 11 days beneath the ice the submarine had been using Self-Contained Oxygen Generators (SCOGs) – or oxygen candles – instead.

The SCOGs on *Tireless* used sodium chlorate instead of potassium superoxide, with a .410 shotgun cartridge to ignite them. Two crewmen were in the Forward Escape Compartment towards the bow of the submarine activating a new SCOG. One of them inserted an ignition cartridge and triggered it with a tap, but unbeknown to him some hydraulic oil or grease had apparently leaked into the canister.

The ignition began with the usual hiss as the iron filings and barium peroxide began to burn, creating the heat that would transform the sodium chlorate into common salt (sodium chloride) and oxygen. But the contaminant changed the chemistry of the reaction – investigations into exactly how have been inconclusive – and the slow burn became uncontrollably fast. Seconds later, a loud blast was felt through the whole submarine.

Both men who had been replacing the SCOGs were killed. A third crewman was badly injured and was only saved by the skill of his crewmates and rescuers. The captain managed to locate an opening in the ice pack above, while a helicopter from an Alaskan US Navy base made a daring moonlit flight to rendezvous with the submarine and pick up the wounded man.

Every half an hour the men on *AS-28* would take readings of the atmosphere inside the submersible and relay them to the crews above. The crew were having to rely on manual measurements rather than the usual electronic ones to conserve their battery power. The old batteries were bad enough when operating at normal temperatures; Lepetyukha was not sure how well they were going to last so close to freezing.

Every now and then their status reports to the surface would be answered with medical advice from the specialists aboard the *Kozmin*, even though Lepetyukha already knew what to do: keep still, keep warm, and don't panic.

There was little talking. Lepetyukha had ordered as much. Speaking used energy, and energy meant breathing more air. As Roger Chapman wrote of his time trapped on the seabed in *Pisces III*, 'Every un-needed word spoken would mean so many fewer seconds for the rescue, while every wasted movement might cut off minutes. Even thoughts and worries could steal survival time.'

Gennady Bolonin looked around at the gloomy Naval men. They were so young. He was already 60 years old, and most of his friends were dying anyway. But these sailors were at the very start of their lives. He looked over at Milachevsky's 25-year-old face. Bolonin could only imagine the storm of emotions going on inside the pilot as he faced the growing possibility that he'd never see his two daughters again. Bolonin determined to do all in his power to prevent that from coming true.

But trapped down here, there wasn't much that he could do. His efforts to calm their fears by reminding them about the ROVs had been scuppered when the Venom from *Georgy Kozmin* had disappeared so suddenly. Someone had then reminded him that another of the robots bought after the *Kursk* had disappeared while investigating the loss of the submarine *K-159*.

The whole *K-159* saga was too depressing. The submarine had been decommissioned in 1989 and was one of almost 200 sitting rusting in Naval dockyards. When a coalition of foreign nations decided to encourage the Russian government to begin defuelling the nuclear reactors, storing the radioactive core and dismantling the rest of the submarine with a fund of £130m in the summer of 2003, there was a rush to take action. The rusting remains of *K-159* were prepared to be taken from the Naval base in Gremikha 200 miles up the coast to Polyarny, a closed Naval town on the northern coast of the Kola Peninsula where the scrapping was to take place. Rather than putting her on a transport ship, the Navy had simply lashed her between four ageing pontoons for the journey. But even when *K-159* had been in service she had a reputation as an unseaworthy vessel, and after over a decade of sitting abandoned her hull had corroded to the extent that some areas were reported to be as thin as foil.

The ten men put aboard to monitor the boat as it was towed had a last picture taken of them smiling on the dockside and then set off, a Russian flag flying from the submarine's fin.

Early in the morning on 30 August, *K-159* sank. Although there was no bad weather reported in the area, the authorities later blamed it on a storm that snapped the tow-rope and detached one of the pontoons. Whatever the truth, *K-159* went down so fast that only three men managed to get out, two of whom died of exposure on the surface. The other seven remained trapped inside at 238 metres, still with three quarters of a tonne of nuclear waste on board.

By the time rescuers arrived, there were no signs of life. The fancy new Venom robot was only deployed later during the investigation, but its fate didn't inspire confidence. The pilot had managed to suck the Russian flag that still hung from the fin into one of the thrusters, and in the end the brand-new machine had been lost.

Bolonin's drooping eyes were drawn to a movement at the edge of the huddle of damp, freezing bodies. Sergei Belozerov was starting to stir. His hand reached into his top pocket and fumbled in slow motion with numb fingers until he produced a cigarette. All the men were looking by this time, their blank stares now with a flicker of interest. They watched Belozerov as he stared longingly at the half-crushed, drooping grey stick. Each and every one of them would have traded a cigarette for almost anything in the world at that moment. A match would have lit, just. But a cigarette would have burnt through their valuable remaining oxygen, reducing their life expectancy far faster than even the most pessimistic of the service doctors warned. Belozerov didn't need to light it. He drew the cigarette beneath his nostrils with a long, passionate inhale, his eyes closed in rapture. Weak smiles broke out all round, and the wilting cigarette was passed from one man to the other without a word.

Friday, 5 August
SS + 29 h 30 mins
02.00 Pacific Standard Time **– 10.00 UK – 13.00 Moscow –**
22.00 Kamchatka
Tuhula Vista, San Diego, California

Commander Kent Van Horn of the US Navy's Deep Submergence Unit (DSU) had just climbed into bed when his Command mobile phone started ringing on his bedside table. He shifted his massive frame towards the edge of the bed then raised himself up to answer it. A call at this time of night was unusual, and normally wasn't good news. Either something had broken during an equipment overhaul, or one of his men had got himself into trouble. The US Navy had been working hard to de-glamorise the use of alcohol, but a lot of the guys were young and away from home for the first time. The DSU were a good bunch, but the divers did tend to have a wild streak that would emerge every now and then. Van Horn was fully expecting a report that someone had got into a fight, or had been stopped for driving under the influence.

But the tone of this call was different from the start. There was no apologising for disturbing him at this time of night; there was simply an instruction to call a guy at Submarine Group 7 on the coast of Japan. He did so, and was told that a Russian craft had become trapped in the western Pacific and that US help had been requested.

Van Horn was out of the door in 15 minutes and in his Toyota Lexus streaking towards Naval Station San Diego on North Island. He was on the phone constantly, making and receiving calls to try to clarify the situation and determine what the US Navy's response was going to be. It was only when he got the call from SubPac in Hawaii (the US Navy's Pacific submarine command) that he dialled a code into his phone to initiate a recall of his team. A computer at the base received the code and then sent a pager message out to all of the 130 men in Van Horn's team. *Emergency Recall. Get to DSU immediately*, they were told. All were Navy personnel, not subcontracted to a civilian outfit as is the case in the UK, and training runs told him that 80 per cent of them would reach the base within an hour.

The only other time the DSU had been fully mobilised while under his command had been six months previously when the Los Angeles-class nuclear submarine USS *San Francisco* had smashed into an uncharted seamount south of Guam at full speed. The crew managed to surface and make an emergency call before beginning frantic efforts to discover the extent of the damage. The only things that really mattered were the buoyancy tanks. If they were punctured they'd shortly be sinking back to the seabed.

Van Horn's crew had assembled rapidly at the DSU, but before they'd been deployed the *San Francisco* established that the tanks were holding and that she was going to be able to stay on the surface unassisted. His team had been stood down.

Some of the men were already at the base when Van Horn arrived. In the end, 90 per cent would arrive within an hour of the pager message going out, thanks to the clear, night-time roads. On taking the position in December the previous year, Van Horn made it his mission to speed up the deployment of the Deep Submergence Rescue Vehicles. He'd felt the crews weren't drilled enough on how to load an aircraft rapidly, so he'd been working them hard to change things. He never wanted his team to be the slowest element in a situation, and as a former defence linesman for the Navy American Football squad he knew something of how training speeded up a team.

The Deep Submergence Unit was home to the newly modernised US Submarine Rescue Service, and had a wide-ranging suite of equipment available for different situations. Alongside the Atmospheric Diving Suits – pressure-resistant exoskeletons with life support that were able to take humans to a depth of 300 metres – were two or three different breeds of ROV. The deep-diving rescue submersible *Mystic* was at the core of the system, and differed from other DSRVs because it could be docked with another submarine, not just a surface-going mothership. That meant rescues were possible when conditions on the surface – weather or geopolitical – were hostile.

Also under Van Horn's control at North Island's Deep Submergence Unit was the 'McCann' Diving Bell. Essentially an outsized, upturned steel barrel that could be bolted over the submarine's escape hatch, the device was the brainchild of Charles 'Swede' Momsen. Its simplicity was due to the fact that it had been designed more than 70 years before, when it was the first device ever to allow outsiders to rescue sailors trapped inside a submarine. Until that point, the unspoken code of the submariner was that if anything went wrong, you knew you either saved yourself or died with the boat. It took heretical thinking and a healthy disrespect of authority to break that presumption, and these were qualities that Momsen had in spades. Unfortunately, they didn't endear him to the Naval authorities, who chose to name the bell not after the inventor but after the man who modified it for operational use, Allan Rockwell McCann.

Momsen, whose Scandinavian looks earned him the nickname 'Swede', was an insatiably curious engineer, as well as a submarine commander. He'd been in charge of the US Navy's S-1 – the first of 51 S-class boats built between 1918 and 1925 – when he'd received a Mayday call. The S-1's sister ship, S-51, had collided with a passenger ship and sunk without trace. Momsen raced to the scene and immediately began a search for the submarine using grappling hooks and wires dragged between boats. Only when he followed the track of the passing ship that had sliced through her hull did he find at last the haunting markers of their fate: a patch of oil surrounded by breaking bubbles. But despite finding their location there was nothing he could do for the trapped men. As Peter Mass, Momsen's unofficial biographer, wrote in *The Terrible Hours*, 'Months later he would witness the horribly contorted faces and flesh-shredded fingers of those in the S-51 who had not drowned immediately, who instead spent the final minutes of their lives trying to claw their way out of a steel coffin.'

When another S-class submarine, the S-4, sank in 1927, Momsen vowed to find a solution. Like S-51, S-4 had collided with a surface vessel – this time a coastguard cutter chasing a prohibition rum-runner. All 40 crewmen had survived the accident and were only 33 metres below the surface, but despite 'a score' of vessels circling above, nothing could be done to save them. For three days those on the surface could only listen to the crew hammering against the hull, the blows growing weaker with every hour. A storm eventually chased the ships from the scene, but when the wreckage was finally recovered, notes were discovered on the bodies of the sailors. 'Please hurry,' read one.

With the optimistic clarity of an engineer Momsen saw a simple solution. The concept of diving bells had been around for centuries. In the same way that an upturned glass in the bath does not fill with water, a steel bell can be used to take life-supporting air beneath the surface. If the bottom of the bell could be sealed against the upper hatch of a submarine, the crew should be able to transfer from one to the other without even getting wet. All it required was a suitable flange to be fitted around all submarine hatches to allow rescuers to get a watertight seal with a bell, but the Navy's Bureau of Construction and Repair refused, saying it was 'impractical from the standpoint of seamanship'.

Momsen wouldn't be put off, and by 1928 had come up with a

way to escape the steel coffin that wouldn't involve the conservative Bureau of Construction. The prototype 'Momsen Lung' was a lung-sized rubber bag made of car tyre inner tubes. Unlike the Davis Submarine Escape Apparatus used by the Royal Navy, there was no cylinder of oxygen. Instead the bag was pre-filled with oxygen together with granules of soda lime to absorb carbon dioxide. Two hoses protruded from the top; one took exhaled air, the other delivered recycled air for inhalation, enabling a trapped man in a drowned submarine to gain precious extra minutes with which to make his escape. Momsen demonstrated the effectiveness of his device by testing it personally on the wreckage of the ill-fated S-4. With the hull towed and re-sunk in safer waters, Momsen went back down inside and made a simulated escape from the same motor room in which eight people had died just 14 months before.

Following the success of his artificial lung, Momsen was finally allowed to go ahead and build his rescue bell. In June 1939, an air induction valve to the engine room of the submarine USS *Squalus* failed to close while starting to dive off Portsmouth, New Hampshire. The rear three compartments of the vessel flooded, and she sank to the seabed. When the craft was eventually found – the position of her last dive had been somehow misreported – Momsen and his bell were brought to the scene. Heavy weather made the work difficult, but the seal between the hatch and the bell worked.

Lift by lift the crew began to be recovered, in batches of eight, but the sea was growing rougher. The wire cable holding the bell was unable to take the strain of being jerked taut by the building waves, and it began parting. It was only when the captain left the *Squalus* – the last man to do so – and had climbed into the bell that someone noticed that it was dangling from just a single strand of wire. If that broke, there would be no chance of finding the bell again before the looming storm was upon them. They had to chance it. They filled the bell with just enough air to make it buoyant, and the deck crew gingerly took in the line, terrified that an unseen wave would cause the ship to lurch and snap the remaining strand. Foot by foot the bell drew closer to the surface, until finally a swimmer could jump in and secure another line to the top of the bell. All 33 survivors of the original flooding survived. From that day on, submariners were no longer expected to save themselves or die quietly. They now had hope of rescue from the surface.

The type of rescue bell that had saved *Squalus*'s men 65 years before was still an active part of Commander Kent Van Horn's arsenal of equipment – Turkey and Italy still used it as their main rescue system, after all – but it wasn't right for this job. And although all NATO submarine rescue craft could, with delicate handling, just about mate with Russian submarines using the system that Momsen had devised, *AS-28* did not have the special hatch required.

Van Horn rapidly came to the same conclusions as the UK had done about what equipment the Kamchatka situation required: a Remotely Operated Vehicle. It would be quickest to deploy, and would be better able to make the tight movements that might be required to disentangle the stricken submersible. The decision made, he pulled together an equipment list, and it totalled around 78 tonnes of kit. Now he needed to get it to Russia. While Air Support services began tracking down aircraft for him, he began planning the later stages of the deployment.

In every exercise speed was the critical element. Now, in a real-life situation, Van Horn was pulling out all the stops to shave off the minutes. He decided to separate his teams into three different groups that would work in parallel to offload the aircraft and mobilise it on the vessel they were assigned. Thinking ahead to mounting equipment on the deck of the Russian ship, he noted that if welding was taking too long he'd be prepared to lash the kit in place with grips and tie-downs rather than the usual welds. Anything to save precious time.

Friday, 5 August
SS + 29 h 30 mins
10.00 UK – 13.00 Moscow – 22.00 Kamchatka
Workshops of Rumic Defence Ltd, Renfrew, Glasgow

Stuart Gold was going through the spares kit of the UKSRS Scorpio ROV, double-checking the replacement circuit boards, cables and Duck tape supplies, when the phone went in the small office in the corner of the workshop. He made a last mark on his checklist, then paced over to the desk.

It was Martin Bully, his long-time boss. 'Looks like you'd better get yourself at least thinking about mobilising Scorpio, Stuart. There's a possibility that you'll be off to rescue the Russians. Best get on the phone, see who's about,' he said.

No problem, thought Gold. Scorpio was never more than a few hours from being operational, and right now she was fully ready. Six weeks before she had been out in Italy for the main NATO exercise. A couple of tiny problems had cropped up there, and since then he'd been firing her up every couple of days as normal, checking the electrics and the hydraulics, and everything was shipshape and ready for playtime with the Swedish and Norwegian navies.

Just as the US Navy had taken time to accept that submariners could be rescued, the existence of the UK's Submarine Rescue Service was not a given. In fact, when the British submarine HMS *Poseidon* sank in the North China Sea in 1931, the Royal Navy created a hard-set policy that submariners should save themselves, not rely on others.

Poseidon was on exercise on the surface in perfect visibility when she somehow collided with a Chinese vessel. Half of the crew managed to scramble out before the submarine sank to the seabed 40 metres below, but the rest remained trapped inside. Knowing they were far from help, eight men had donned their Davis Submarine Escape Apparatus and opened the hatches to the sea. Two of the men never made it to the surface and one died soon after reaching it, but the other five were proof that self-rescue could work. The fate of the men who remained inside is not clear, although the Chinese Navy may now know more: in 1971 they secretly salvaged the *Poseidon*, but have yet to respond to the UK Ministry of Defence's inquiries for information about what was found.

The successful use of the DSEA equipment instilled a firm belief among Naval commanders that self-rescue was the best chance for submariners. All British submarines were modified to include escape hatches with fast-flood valves, and crews were ordered not to wait for outside assistance in the event of an accident. Until then, submarines had been built with external valves so that high-pressure air could be injected inside by surface salvage vessels, but, in line with the new policy, these were now welded shut.

It was eight years before the strategy faced its first big test. In June 1939, just one week after the successful rescue of the crew of USS *Squalus* with Momsen's bell, the newly constructed HMS *Thetis* made her way into the middle of Liverpool Bay for her test dive. Some of those who'd built her, from the company Cammell-Laird, had been invited to come along for the historic journey. Instead of her design crew of 53, she had 103 on board. The spectators were supposed to disembark on to a waiting tug before the submarine submerged, but when things were deemed to be going well, they were invited to stay for the show.

Thetis herself seemed reluctant to dive, however. Her captain, Lieutenant Commander Bolus, ordered the front torpedo tubes to be flooded to encourage her nose to sink, but this seemed to make little difference. Puzzled, he ordered the torpedo room to check that the tubes had in fact flooded.

Torpedo tubes have two doors, one on the inside through which the torpedo is loaded, and one that opens to the sea through which it is fired. One or other must be shut at all times to keep the seawater out. When the crewman checked the indicator for the outer door it showed open, but it was possible that there was a fault.

Owing to the obvious danger of mistakenly opening both doors at once, the designers had included a small valve which could be used to test if there was in fact water inside. A crewman opened this 'test cock', but there was not even a dribble of water. The outer door indicator must be faulty, he concluded. Since the tube was dry the outer door must still be shut. There was no way he could know that a fresh coat of enamel paint inside the torpedo tube had blocked the inlet for the test-cock. He opened the interior door and Poseidon made his entrance.

In seconds tons of seawater had flooded the forward compartment, seconds that coincided with a surge of power from *Thetis*'s engines and a full-down setting on the dive planes as the captain tried to get his craft to dive. This time she responded dramatically and *Thetis* plunged downwards. The crew at the bow couldn't get the watertight doors of the first compartment shut in time, and the sea had crashed through into the second compartment before they finally managed to contain it. Seconds later, *Thetis* hit the seabed 48 metres below.

Thetis was designed with two escape chambers and emergency air for 36 hours. But, like *AS-28*, she had twice the number of crew she was designed for, and the air would only last for 18 hours. What's more, she'd hit the seabed a mile from where she'd been seen leaving the surface, night had set in, and she could not be found. The only positive was that they had packed enough DSEA kits to go around.

With the forward two compartments irretrievably flooded, the captain blew the ballast water from the aft torpedo tubes and the stern broke free of the mud. It kept on rising, the 275-foot hull pivoting on its nose until the stern rose out of the water like a tombstone. Although there was chaos inside the submarine, the aft escape hatch was now only twenty feet below the water. They were so close to freedom, but escape would most likely mean drowning unless they knew that a rescue ship was on the surface waiting to receive them. It wasn't until an hour after dawn that the protruding stern was spotted – 18 hours after the accident and at the limit of the boat's air supply. Soon afterwards, the first two men made their exit using their DSEA sets.

With more than a hundred men to get out of the submarine and all of them starting to suffer from too little oxygen and too much carbon dioxide, they needed to speed things up. It was decided to try putting four men at a time in the rescue chamber rather than the usual two. The first four crammed inside and pulled the hatch up behind them. Pulling leather goggles over their eyes and nose clips over their noses, they opened the valves of their DSEA oxygen bottles and turned the valve that would flood the tiny escape chamber with seawater. Once it had filled, they opened the outer hatch.

Quite what went wrong is unknown, because all four men had drowned by the time they reached the surface. At least one had been together enough to close the outer hatch behind them, allowing those still stuck inside the submarine a chance, however. The chamber was drained of water, and two more men climbed inside, but the men were now too weakened by the foul air to close the hatch behind them properly. When the valve to flood the escape chamber was opened, the sea flooded not only into the escape chamber, but into the submarine below. As the water filled the submarine the air pressure inside built, increasing the effect of the carbon dioxide. One by one the remaining men passed out, then passed away.

Ninety-nine men died with their escape route only six metres from the surface and within sight of land, a disaster made worse by the contrast with the successful rescue of the USS *Squalus* just one week before. Even Adolf Hitler sent a telegram expressing his condolences, just three months before the outbreak of the Second World War. HMS *Thetis* had more in store. A Navy salvage diver, Henry Perdue, was helping raise the wreck when he became entangled in something in the murky water. He struggled to break free, but when he finally did so it was unexpected and he was too buoyant. He shot to the surface without any constraint. The gases that had been forced into his muscles by the pressure bubbled into his veins as gas, then became trapped in his joints. He died in agony later that evening, the air bubbles eventually blocking the flow of blood to his brain. *Thetis* had claimed her 100th victim.

Despite the damning parallels between the outcomes of USS *Squalus* and HMS *Thetis*, the Royal Navy stuck to its ethos that when things went wrong beneath the surface, escape was the only route to salvation, not rescue. It was a position that wouldn't change for another 30 years.

While some tools of Gold's trade had remained essentially unchanged since those early days, the Scorpio ROV was not one of them. It relied on the latest electronic engineering, a subject in which Gold was entirely comfortable. He was the sole full-time member of the Scorpio team. The other 11 members of the UK's Submarine Rescue Service all looked after the LR5 submersible.

But while he could maintain the robot on his own, deploying her was another matter. He needed a pilot, a co-pilot, a winch-man and an umbilical-tender at the very least. If the job was going to be round the clock – as most offshore work was – he'd need double that to run two shifts.

Like all offshore engineering companies, Rumic kept a database of trusted ROV operators. Good crewmen were valuable commodities, and Rumic leased theirs to companies all over the world. Piloting the things could be tricky – like flying a plane, it required you to keep a lot of different variables in your head and make a constant stream of decisions. A mistake might not have such disastrous consequences or happen so quickly, but it would definitely be costly. There were plenty of multi-million-pound robots stuck in hard-to-reach places around the world, or cut loose and drifting across remote seabeds.

Engineers often made the most useful pilots because they understood how the machine worked and could repair it when it didn't. Salt water, electronics and crushing pressures made an uneasy combination, and things often went wrong. When they did, it was up to the team on the water to diagnose the problem quickly and fix it, fast. Offshore operations cost upwards of £20,000 a day, and you didn't want to be the ones causing the hold-up.

Tommy Calvert was, in Gold's opinion, the best pilot in the business. He'd been everywhere, done everything, and always came out grinning. Just thinking about Calvert made Gold smile. Gold was halfway through dialling his mobile number when he remembered: Calvert was hundreds of miles away in the Mediterranean. Rumic required a 12-hour mobilisation, and there was no way he was going to make it in time. That's if Calvert would have come in the first place; he was on what must be the cushiest job in the business, working on Paul Allen's superyacht the MV *Octopus*, indulging the Microsoft billionaire's penchant for underwater exploration.

Gold didn't need to pull out his list of pilots to know who to call next. He knew Pete Nuttall was in town. Nuttall had been trained up by Calvert and was already a sought-after pilot in his own right; after seven years with Rumic he'd now decided to go it alone and had handed in his notice.

When Gold called, Nuttall was in his back yard in Ramside, Barrow, hosing down his Royal National Lifeboat Institution storm gear.

'Where are you?' said Gold.

'Barrow. What's up?' replied Nuttall.

'Fancy a trip to the far end of Russia?'

'Siberia?' said Nuttall with a smile. 'Who've you pissed off now, Stuart? I like you, mate, but you can do your hard labour on your own.'

'No, seriously, Pete. Are you free?'

Nuttall paused. As a member of the RNLI he was used to dropping everything in an emergency. He was also used to false alarms. He'd had two or three of them already with the Submarine Rescue Service, and this one seemed a bit of a stretch. The Russian Far East? The thought entered his mind that Gold was messing with him. Gold knew that he was going to a wedding this weekend.

Was that it? Whatever, Nuttall decided to play along.

'I'm supposed to be going away this weekend,' he said. 'But if it's desperate . . .'

'Great. Tommy's off on the *Octopus*. Don't go anywhere – I'll give you a call in a wee while if things get serious.'

Gold hung up, and started dialling the next number on his list. The first stage in getting the ball rolling was to establish who was available, nothing more. He hadn't finished all the digits when his mobile phone rang. It was Susan, his partner.

'I've heard you're going to Russia,' she said.

Gold blinked in astonishment. 'You what? How did you hear about this? I've only called one person!'

'It's been on the news. I thought you were getting me a takeaway, not getting taken away!'

Gold laughed. 'Honestly, Susan, I really don't know what's going to happen,' he said. Mobilisations almost invariably ground to a halt before anything came of them. Once or twice he'd been through a couple that weren't for an exercise. One Saturday morning about nine years ago, one of Her Majesty's submarines had missed a scheduled report. He'd raced out of the house to get to the base, but had only got about halfway to Glasgow when Martin Bully had called him to say the submarine had called in and that everything was okay. The same sort of thing had happened when the Russian November-class submarine *K-159* had sunk in August 2003. She'd been under tow on the surface with ten crew on board when she'd flooded and sunk. His team had scrambled to get ready, but before long it turned out, thanks to delays in reporting the incident within Russia, any action they could have taken would have been too late.

But Gold was now aware that there were things happening further up the chain. The fact that the BBC was reporting that his team were being despatched started to make him think that this might be serious.

Friday, 5 August
SS + 30 h 10 mins
10.40 UK – *13.40 Moscow* – 22.40 Kamchatka
Moscow

In the back of one of the British Embassy's black Volvo S70s, Captain Jon Holloway cursed. The White Ensign mounted on the front right wing hung limply from its pole. It wasn't even two in the afternoon yet already Muscovites were piling out of the city for the weekend, clogging the roads with traffic. The journey to the Russian Ministry of Defence wouldn't take more than five minutes on a normal day, but he'd already been in the car for twice that. The ministry closed at one, and though he'd called ahead to tell them to stay open, he didn't want to keep them waiting. Impatiently he tapped his leg with the plain buff envelope containing the diplomatic note that was the object of his trip.

Holloway understood the workings of the Russian Ministry of Defence better than most, and knew that much depended on who he managed to get through to. Earlier in the day when he'd called to test the water and see if there was a chance that an offer of help from the UK would be accepted, he'd been stonewalled. He was not at all confident that his message had got through to the right people, and when he'd reported back to London he'd given the chances of being welcomed in by the Russians at only 20 per cent.

Improving relations with the Russians was his job. His Naval career as a submariner had taken a twist after he'd accepted a position on the Royal Yacht, when someone found out that he'd studied Russian. Some years later he was offered a shift into the diplomatic side of things. At first he found it strange. He'd been acutely aware that to his old shipmates being a Naval Attaché meant one long round of cocktail parties. He'd trained in the gritty, down-and-dirty elements of submarine engineering, and the delicate nature of diplomacy felt a world apart.

But now something real was happening. Submariners were

trapped deep underwater, and diplomacy represented their best chance of seeing daylight again. Plus the value of a real-life rescue would do far more for future relations than the few Russian observers despatched to join international submarine rescue exercises. There were political risks, of course. They might be invited along but prevented from coming too close, as had happened with the *Kursk*. Or, worse, they might be allowed to help but set up to fail.

Much would come down to smooth communication. Even before they'd had ministerial clearance to make the offer, Captain Holloway had got his office to call and check availability on the evening's Aeroflot flight out to Petropavlosk. Though economy class was full, he was told, there was plenty of space in business class. Weighing up the chances of things moving forward, Holloway decided to be prudent with Her Majesty's Purse and wait to see how the UK's offer was received before making the booking.

At last the embassy car took the right turn into the New Arbat road. At the imposing 1970s block that housed the Russian Ministry of Defence, the driver turned left and was waved through the security barrier, the diplomatic vehicle and plates enough to persuade the guard to let them pass without even stopping. They pulled up outside the worn-looking, Tsarist-era building that stood opposite the ministry, where the nation's military foreign relations department was spread across three floors.

Holloway stepped up smartly to the front door and pushed inside, where he showed his diplomatic identity card to the sentry and said that the Duty Officer was expecting him. The sentry made a call, spoke a few words and hung up. A few minutes later the Duty Officer appeared and escorted Holloway up a flight of stairs to the first-floor meeting room. Weak sunlight filtered through old, tobacco-coloured windows. The photographs of Russian military might on the dark, wood-panelled wall looked similarly faded. Holloway's gaze flicked across the boxy lines of the Russian tanks and missile-launchers that they pictured.

'*Gospodin* Duty Officer,' said Captain Holloway. 'We have heard reports that one of your submarines has become trapped under-water off Kamchatka. The government of the United Kingdom has a rescue system that your Navy is familiar with, and which can be on site within thirty-six hours. All we require is your government's permission to help, and assistance with a vessel from which we can launch our rescue system. Our Scorpio robot is ready to leave at 11 p.m. tonight. It can be in Kamchatka eleven hours later, but what happens after that is up to you – we would rely on your equipment to get us from the airport out to the accident site.'

The officer – a major whom Holloway had not seen before – listened solemnly. He was evidently used to pushy foreign attachés, and knew that their stated intentions were often different from their real goals. But his duty was not to judge, just to listen and relay. He nodded curtly and said he would return shortly.

For 15 long minutes Captain Holloway sat in the gloomy meeting room before the officer finally returned.

'*Gospodin*, Attaché,' the Major said. 'Thank you very much for your offer. It is being given serious consideration personally by the Minister of Defence. We will contact you very shortly.'

With that he was shown back down the stairs and out of the foreign relations department. Whatever happened next would be a vital indication of how the Russians were treating the incident, and if anything had changed since the *Kursk*. When the UK had offered to help during that disaster it had been met with only a bewildering silence. It had taken four days for Putin finally to accept international offers of help, and even then they had hardly been welcomed. Holloway got back in the car and told the driver to head back to the UK Embassy. They'd hardly reached the end of New Arbat when his phone went. It was the head of the Operational Department of the Russian Naval Staff, Vice-Admiral Avdoshin – a man Holloway had got to know well.

'Jon,' Avdoshin said with no preamble. 'Thank you for the British offer of help. I need to clarify one thing. What thickness of cable can Scorpio cut through?'

Holloway leafed through the specifications that he held in the folder he was carrying. '*Do semyi-desyati,*' he said.

'Damn,' said Avdoshin. 'We need to be able to cut through cables of eighteen millimetres, Jon.'

Holloway frowned. The Vice-Admiral sounded as though he was writing off the British offer of help after all. Then he realised. 'Seventy' in Russian sounded much like 'seventeen'. Holloway clarified what he meant and the Vice-Admiral's voice relaxed momentarily. Then he dropped his bombshell.

'Is there anything you can do to accelerate the timescales?' Even in Avdoshin's thick Russian, the tone was clear. It was as close as the man would ever get to pleading.

Despite the placatory information being given to the hungry press corps in Kamchatka about the amount of oxygen left on *AS-28*, the estimated Time To First Rescue of 36 hours given by the Scorpio team was clearly not fast enough.

Friday, 5 August
SS + 31 h
***11.30 UK* – 14.30 Moscow – 23.30 Kamchatka**
Renfrew, Glasgow

Stuart Gold had just about found himself a core team when Martin Bully called back. Things were progressing higher up the chain, Bully said. It was time for Gold to start a second round of calls, this time telling everyone to assemble at Prestwick airport as soon as possible. Scorpio herself was just about to be despatched.

First up Gold called Charlie Sillet, the team's long-time mechanical wizard. On his last call Gold had caught him at home in Edinburgh and told him not to go anywhere. Gold hadn't wanted Sillet getting any further from Edinburgh because he needed someone to go round to his house and pick up his passport. Now Gold told him to go ahead and make his way to Prestwick, stopping at Gold's house on the way. His kids were home, enjoying their summer holidays, and would let him in.

Next he called back the ROV pilot Pete Nuttall at his home in Barrow. When Nuttall put the phone down he scowled. He hadn't been expecting things to escalate. How was he going to break this one to his wife? Sue was at work, and he was supposed to be picking up his youngest daughter from tennis school. Even if Sue was free, an illness prevented her from driving long distances. Then there was the weekend. He was supposed to be an usher at his cousin's wedding, and he wouldn't be popular for missing that.

After 17 years together she was used to his sudden departures, even if she didn't like them. Whenever his RNLI pager went off, Nuttall would be out of the door in seconds. All he needed were his shoes to get him to the lifeboat shed – everything required to do his job as a crewman on the boats was there. Things were slightly different with a Submarine Rescue alert. Apart from the exercises, which would mean someone calling him out of the blue and asking where he was and if he was available, real alerts had only come through two or three times in the years he'd been on the team. They meant a bit more thought, planning what to take. After all, you didn't need a passport to rescue a yacht in trouble up the coast.

Within half an hour Nuttall had managed to talk his sister into picking up his daughter, had packed a bag and was on his way to Broughton where he picked up two other members of the team, Nigel Pyne and Will Forrester. They both had a bit of packing up and organising to do, but before midday they were heading north on the M6, all crammed into his little diesel Rover 200.

Will Forrester had been Gold's winchman for 15 years, but when not wearing his Scorpio cape he owned a travel agency in Barrow-in-Furness. While a lot of his business came from getting guys out to their offshore jobs in foreign lands, he got to sea himself only occasionally. Like most of the guys in Gold's team, he was a contractor, brought in by the day when he was needed and available for exercises.

Gold jumped into Sillet's car when he got to Renfrew and together they headed to Prestwick. In Gold's mind the whole thing was still an exercise; he knew that there were still a lot of hurdles to clear. The fact that the Foreign Office had approved the UK's offer of help didn't mean that his team would be able to get there in time. Who knew which of the reports of remaining air on board the submersible was accurate? And who knew if the Russians would even accept the help?

The news reports were quoting a Russian Admiral saying that the waters off Kamchatka were stuffed with military secrets, and that no foreigners should be allowed in. Gold didn't like the sound of that.

He remembered all too clearly this time five years ago when he'd spent three days helplessly watching news reports on the BBC, glued to the events on the *Kursk* along with the rest of the world. Eventually they'd got permission to mobilise and steamed up to the Barents Sea with LR5, Scorpio, the whole kit, hoping against hope that the Russians would let them in to help. For another whole day they'd listened to the reports of knocking sounds against the hull – that was pretty chilling, even though the sounds ended up being diagnosed as only the clanging of fenders on the side of rescue ships.

Back then the Russians had been paralysed by fears of revealing their military secrets, which they seemed to value far more than the lives of the 118 sailors on board. This time there were only the lives of seven men to weigh against those secrets, not a hundred.

If the Russians did relent this time, there was plenty of help on its way. The Swedes had just offered, the Americans were mobilising, the Japanese were on their way, and he'd just heard that the Australians had diverted an oil exploration vessel that was on charter off nearby Sakhalin Island for Shell. With two powerful ROVs on board, they looked like a good option, but their ETA was still unknown.

Friday, 5 August/Saturday, 6 August
SS + 31 h 30 mins
12.00 UK **– 15.00 Moscow – 00.00 Kamchatka**
RAF Brize Norton

Squadron leader Keith Hewitt bounced along the path between the
barrack buildings at Brize Norton airbase, making his way towards
the Operations Room. Strictly speaking he was still on leave for
another few hours, but he thought he'd come in to check what the
evening had in store for him. The weather for the last few days
had been glorious, and he'd been making the most of it. Yesterday, along with two old friends from his earliest days in the force
35 years earlier, he'd been to watch England's cricketers beat
Australia during the second Test match at Edgbaston. That had
been a welcome reprieve from the long flights he'd been pulling,
flights whose beginning or end always held a little more tension
than coming or going from a normal airfield. Even before checking the roster, he knew that tonight would see him lifting off
under the cover of darkness, headed into the maelstrom of either
Iraq or Afghanistan.

Ops was busy as usual. Hewitt noted that there was a Special on
– a non-standard transport flight that usually meant an aeromedical
or coffins bearing servicemen killed in action. He didn't bother
trying to find out more – Specials happened all the time, and he had
his own flight preparation to deal with. He checked the lists to see
what time slot he was slated to fly, scanned the weather reports and
caught up with the news.

He still had the rest of the day before beginning the two or three
hours that it would take to complete all his flight planning and
pre-flight inspections, so Hewitt made his way back towards his
quarters. He needed to get in a bit of rest before nightfall to be legal
for the flight, but as soon as he'd got there his mobile phone rang.
It was the Operations Room.

'We need you back here now. Come in your greens, and pack

88

a bag,' the Ops Controller said. Hewitt frowned. He was already wearing his tan-coloured desert flightsuit out of habit. That was the one certainty. With so much action in Iraq and Afghanistan, you pretty much knew you'd be headed into the desert. A green suit meant he was going somewhere else entirely.

He hurried back to the Operations Room and inside bumped into the Station Commander, an old friend. Hewitt began telling him about the magnificent batting and tumbling of wickets he'd seen yesterday, but was cut off rather sharply when the Group Captain appeared. It was rare to see them both at the same time and place, and, short of receiving a medal, doing so wasn't usually good news.

The Station Commander handed over a Flight Authorisation Form on a clipboard. 'You sign it, I'll sign it. We'll sort out the details later,' he said.

Hewitt blinked. This was most unusual. He began to protest, but the officer cut him short. 'You need to get out to the aircraft, Keith. Right now. There's a crew warming it up as we speak.'

Now Hewitt knew something big was up. Fighter aircraft might get scrambled, but not a huge, cargo-transporting C17. One of the fundamental rules of flying, drummed into any pilot from the very start of their training, was that you do your own pre-flight checks of the aircraft and flight planning. But this time the necessary two hours apparently couldn't be spared. Whoever was warming up the aircraft probably didn't have enough crew hours remaining to take on the mission, whatever it was.

His clearances signed, Hewitt headed out of the door and jogged over to the C17 that was standing on the apron, engines running. He clambered up the port side steps into the crew door, and took two practised paces up to the left on to the flight deck. As he'd been told, the other crew had already done the pre-flights and warmed up the aircraft. It was a strange feeling, to get into the pilot's seat and have to take it for granted that everything had been done properly. His eye skimmed over the gauges, looking for any signs that it hadn't.

Minutes later Hewitt's co-pilot, Flight Lieutenant John Mac-intyre, turned up and together they were handed command of the aircraft. There was none of the usual verification of diplomatic clearances, checking of charts or consideration of the many other aspects crucial to a successful flight – such as information about the final destination. The station commander simply said 'First stop Glasgow Prestwick. You just go. We'll think about the rest later on.'

The rest of the crew had been on standby for the Special flight. They didn't know much, but they did tell Hewitt more than he'd known up until then: they were on a submarine rescue mission.

Originally the C17 was to fly to Prestwick, pick up Scorpio and the rescue team, then tack back to Brize Norton to pick up a second aircrew. That would have allowed the aircraft to depart at around midnight. Then word had come back from Moscow that time was already becoming critically short, and if they were going to be of any help they'd need to arrive faster than that.

Friday, 5 August/Saturday, 6 August
SS + 33 h 45 mins
14.15 UK **– 17.15 Moscow – 02.15 Kamchatka**
RAF Nimrod: maritime patrol flight, Irish Sea

Two hundred feet above the Irish Sea, Squadron Leader Dan Gray was trying to keep his cool while flying his Nimrod maritime reconnaissance aircraft in a tight search pattern above the water. While his eyes flicked between altimeter, airspeed, heading and the sky ahead, the six analysts in the back were scouring the sea below for the enemy submarine. At that altitude there was no room for error, and Gray had to keep the aircraft on rails so as not to miss out any patches of sea where the boat might be hiding. They'd never find it, of course. They were on a training exercise.

Flying a search at this altitude wouldn't ordinarily have caused Gray any discomfort but for the presence of the man standing behind him on the flight deck. The Standards and Evaluations team were on board, checking that everything his crew did was up to scratch and as per training. All through the aircraft, inspectors were shadowing each of the tasks being performed. So far things seemed to have gone fine. Before the submarine search they'd run through a couple of Anti-Surface Unit exercises, doing radar scans at a thousand feet to identify targets – in this case hapless fishing vessels – before dropping down to 200 feet for a close pass in which to take photographs. It wasn't a move used in combat situations, but secure identifications were a likely request in the run-up to escalations, and were a vital part of their tactical quiver.

Back at the navigation panel, Flight Lieutenant Simon King was feeling on top of things too. The navigation was going according to plan, and that's the way he wanted it to stay. Four hours into the flight, they were coming towards the end of the search phase. Soon they'd be turning for home.

Back in the main body of the aircraft, amid the banks of equipment used by the 'wet operators' – those who scan beneath the sea for enemy submarines – and the above-water radar and ESM modules, the Radio Officer turned to the telex machine that had started clattering. It might be 1970s technology, but for clarity nothing quite beat an order coming through in printed form. This one was from OPCON, the Operational Controller.

IMMEDIATE RETASK IF FUEL PERMITS. YOU ARE TO LAND AT BRISTOL TO PICK UP PAX FOR KINLOSS

The Radio Officer tore off the paper and immediately relayed the message through the hardwired audio link forward to the nav room and flight deck.

King swore to himself. This was the last thing they needed on a STEV flight. All his careful pre-flight planning would go out the window. With the inspector watching his every move in silence,

King immediately started working with his co-navigator, Squadron Leader Martin Williams, to plot a route to Bristol, and up to Kinloss as the first stage in deciding whether they would have enough fuel to take the assignment. Making the trip itself would be fine, King could already see. The problem was the diversions. For every intended landing, he had to make sure the aircraft had enough fuel to divert to a different strip, just in case there was a problem with the first choice.

There were two airfields near Bristol, the International Airport at Lulsgate and the strip at Filton. Lulsgate was often shrouded in fog – it was so notorious that Second World War fighter pilots were sent there for low-visibility training. King made inquires, discovered that the passenger was coming from Abbey Wood, and decided to plan for the one that was closer by, Filton.

Neither of the navigators had landed at Filton before, so they pulled out the Terminal Approach Procedures manual and checked that the runway was long enough. It was – in fact, in April 1969 the second Concorde had taken its maiden flight from that very runway. British Aerospace still had factories there. Thanks to the residential houses nearby the approach was strictly controlled by Noise Abatement Procedures, but otherwise there didn't appear to be any problems with landing there.

Williams began calculating distances, windspeeds and altitudes. King took detailed readings from the fuel tank gauges, then pulled down the thick Operating Data Manual and started running through the decision trees and many lines of calculation required to estimate the fuel burn for the trip.

It was no simple matter. Ascents and descents used different amounts of fuel depending on how heavy the aircraft was, which in turn was largely determined by how much fuel remained on board. The weight of the aircraft also affected how much braking was required to stop it on the runway. The hotter the brakes after landing, the longer they'd have to wait before take-off. Shutting down the engines during the wait was out of the question because of the time-consuming start-up processes, but keeping them idling also bit into the fuel calculations further down the line.

Some of the boys weren't going to be happy about the changes to their Friday night plans, thought King, but he reasoned that OPCON didn't issue a change of plan like this for no reason. The pressure was to get it right in front of the STEV team. If they screwed up, they could get bumped off Combat Ready status to Limited Combat Ready or even, if things went really awry, Non-Combat Ready.

Twenty minutes later the navigation calculations were complete. It was close, but they could do it. The pilots had already got clearance for a route into Filton and had turned on to that heading in anticipation. It would not have been difficult, given the presence of the examination crew, to play cautious and decide there was not enough fuel on board, but they didn't. The decision saved the submarine rescue mobilisation a solid four hours.

Friday, 5 August/Saturday, 6 August
SS + 34 h
14.30 UK – 17.30 Moscow – *02.30 Kamchatka*
***AS-28*, 210 metres beneath Berezovya Bay**

Gennady Bolonin grunted with effort as he shuffled from the middle of the huddle to take his turn at the outer edge. He'd barely begun to feel the warmth of being sandwiched between two bodies and it felt too soon for it to be his turn in the cold, but he refused to allow any ill-temper to show in his face. With his long experience it was he, more than anyone else, who should be leading by example. And if anything was going to save them from this situation it was discipline and strong character. Without that, those canisters of V-64 had no hope of seeing them through.

It was dim in the chamber. Was it dimmer than it had been?

Were the batteries giving out already? Or was this carbon dioxide poisoning starting to make his senses fade? He forced himself to concentrate, and that's when he noticed that there were only five men on the floor beside him.

Bolonin hauled himself upright and on to one of the steel shelves that served as seats. He waited for five minutes until the heaving of his lungs subsided, then made his way slowly through the hatchway to the forward compartment. Inside he found the pilot Milachevsky manning the underwater telephone, and beside him one of the junior midshipmen. Both were scrawling on notepads, which they blearily attempted to put out of sight when they noticed he'd appeared.

Writing farewell notes wouldn't go down well with the Captain, but Bolonin put a hand on each of their backs. He didn't speak, but they knew what his touch meant. What he'd seen would go no further. Not that his old comrade Captain Lepetyukha looked as if he'd have the energy to object even if he had seen them. He was slumped in the aft compartment, his chest heaving. It was an open secret that their captain had lost a third of his lung in surgery, and now all of the younger crew members were looking concerned about him.

Seeing the men pen their last words on damp paper was an awful reminder of the notes written by those who had survived the *Kursk*'s explosions, only to be discovered when the wrecked hull was recovered months later. Captain-Lieutenant Dmitriy Kolesnikov had written the names of all 23 survivors, and a brief, stoic message:

Olichka, I love you.
Don't suffer too much. My regards to
GV and regards to mine.
Mitya

'GV' were the initials of his mother-in-law, while Mitya was the shortened, familiar form of his own name. Later, in the cold darkness, he'd estimated their chances of survival at between 10 and 20 per cent, and concluded:

Regards to everybody; no need to be desperate.
Kolesnikov.

Another note had been found among the bodies of those exhumed from the recovered wreckage of the *Kursk*, this one from Senior Midshipman Andrei Borisov:

If you are reading this note this means I am dead. But your lives will carry on and I am asking that my son becomes a true man, like I used to be.

Bolonin didn't try to stop the crew writing letters to their loved ones. Why shouldn't they? They were already putting up with a lot. The cold, the damp, the thirst, the hunger, and the claustrophobia of the body's screams for fresher air. The stink did not help. This was a rescue submersible, designed for a maximum of six hours beneath the water. A sailor was expected to hold his bowels for that amount of time. But not 30 hours. With no facility on the vessel, the crew were making do with an empty V-64 can, which they sealed as best they could with a rag.

When it came to urine, the boat was better prepared: there were a few sealable polyurethane bottles on board. Bolonin was watching them fill with a drugged curiosity. He'd been put in charge of rationing out the precious drinking water that remained, and he estimated that ten times more fluid was coming out of the men than was going in. Slowly but surely their bodies were drying up. The cold might be terrible – made more so by not being able to deploy the traditional defences of a Russian against the winter, beating your arms, smoking and vodka – but it was the thirst that was foremost in his mind.

Bolonin had made his own calculations of how long the seven of them might be able to survive on the V-64 canisters, and from there decided the water ration. Three times a day he passed a plastic mug between them, with the words 'I declare time for watering.' Each man was allowed just one gulp.

Watching the men's desperate eyes as they followed the mug from mouth to mouth – both before they'd drunk and afterwards – made Bolonin's spirits sag. He'd spent his life designing some of the world's best underwater technology for the Russian Navy, but they were now trapped aboard one and were threatened by the most ancient of the dangers that mariners face: thirst. *Water, water, everywhere, nor any drop to drink.*

Never had the two faces of the Russian Navy been clearer to him. As an engineer, he knew how beautiful the nation's best technology could be. When the plans for the great battlecruiser *Yuriy Andropov* were first announced in 1986 their splendour was undeniable. Yet it took ten full years for her to be launched, by which time battlecruisers had gone the way of the battleship, and become an outmoded weapon in naval warfare. After the Soviet Union collapsed, the ship (renamed *Peter the Great*) was declared the pride of the Navy and the flagship of the Northern Fleet (indeed she was the target that the ill-fated *Kursk* was supposed to have been firing upon when the explosion had occurred), yet just last year she'd been laid up in the drydock. The Commander-in-Chief of the Navy, Vladimir Kuroyedov, had announced she had been badly maintained and could 'explode any moment', adding that she was especially dangerous owing to her nuclear reactors. If this was the fate of one of the country's most prestigious vessels, what hope was there for the humble *AS-28*?

Friday, 5 August/Saturday, 6 August
SS + 34 h 30 mins
15.00 UK – 18.00 Moscow – 03.00 Kamchatka
Royal Navy Lodgings, Stoke Gifford, Bristol

The walls of Commander Riches' staff lodgings near Bristol began to reverberate with the distinctive roar of a Nimrod's Spey turbo-fan engines. Riches threw a pair of waterproofs into his bag – his staff had said the weather would be just like Scotland – grabbed his passport and headed out of the door.

The Shell oil exploration vessel from Sakhalin Island was still 48 hours away. Airlifting Shell's ROVs had been discussed, but dismissed as unworkable: none of the Russian vessels in the area could take a helicopter transfer. The French Ministry of Defence was also offering an ROV that could be flown at six hours' notice, but the ISMERLO team still regarded the US Deep Submergence Unit as the best option. It would be tight. Their estimated Time to First Intervention was roughly equal to the pre-dicted survival time as could best be calculated from the confusing Russian reports.

Thanks to the *Squalus* rescue 70 years beforehand, the US Deep Submergence Unit's Rescue team liked to wear T-shirts that boasted of being 'The Only Proven System'. Smug bastards, thought Riches. If he got a chance, he'd like to consign those shirts to the bin. He wanted to prove what he strongly believed – that the UK's Submarine Rescue Service was the most effective rescue unit in the world. If it was, it was largely thanks to a dramatic change that had occurred since the tragedy of HMS *Thetis* and the days when submariners were expected to save themselves.

In 1971, HMS *Artemis* was moored up in the safety of Haslar creek opposite Portsmouth on the south coast of England, prepar-ing for a mission. She'd just been in for repairs on the other side of the dockyard, and although she was trimmed with her buoyancy tanks to be low and stable in the water, her fuel tanks had been emptied. Some small jobs were still being done on board, and an electrical shore supply cable ran from the jetty and snaked through the submarine, preventing any of the hatches between watertight compartments from being shut.

The water of the estuary lay only inches beneath one of the open deck hatches. Fuel tanks on submarines have any empty space filled not with air – which would compress with depth – but with seawater. A-boats like *Artemis* also used one of their ballast tanks to carry more fuel, the usual hole in the bottom having been plugged with a special 'Kingston' valve.

Before refuelling the tanks, it was necessary to 'first fill' them with seawater. One of the crew was ordered to do so, and took a water hose from shore. The submarine settled lower and lower in the water as he filled the fuel tanks. Very soon seawater began to flood into the open deck hatch. The duty Senior Rate managed to evacuate a party of Sea Cadets who were visiting the submarine, but within 60 seconds the water had filled the submarine enough to sink her stern into the bottom of the creek nine metres below. Three men, including the duty Senior Rate, were trapped in an airpocket inside.

The Navy scrambled to assemble a rescue team, but by dawn the next morning they still hadn't reached the men. Eventually the submariners took matters into their own hands, donned their escape suits and launched themselves out of the forward torpedo hatch and to freedom.

Although the men had saved themselves, just as the Navy procedures expected they should, the incident shook the submarine establishment. The first nuclear submarines had been commissioned just nine years before, and a foolish series of errors had allowed one of Her Majesty's Ships to sink while still at her moorings. What's more, despite now having hundreds of sailors fighting beneath the waves, there was no provision to rescue them when things went wrong. As a result, the Submarine Rescue Service was born.

★ ★ ★

This might just be the Service's first live deployment. Riches was excited, but also felt a nagging doubt. The reputation of the Royal Navy felt like it was in his hands. As commander, any mistake would be on his head. With the front door open, he unzipped his bag and checked he had a couple of clean white uniform shirts. Some things about the Navy were burned deep in the brain; a crisp uniform was one of them. If he was going to screw up, at least he'd do it without a dirty shirt.

Ten minutes after slamming the door he was handing his bag up to an RAF crewman and being showed up the ladder into the waiting Nimrod by the Captain. All of them were very sombre and polite. The Captain showed Riches to the cockpit and sat him down in one of the seats next to their antisubmarine warfare equipment, turning it so that he was facing forward and could peer out of a porthole.

As the aircraft began to roll out towards the holding point, Riches pulled on the headset they'd handed him.

'Don't worry, sir, we'll have you in Kinloss in an hour and a half,' said the Captain.

'Kinloss?' Riches replied. 'I don't want to go to Kinloss . . . I need to get to Prestwick.' Sitting at the holding point at the end of the runway, engines running, the pilot and co-pilot looked at one another. Speaking as clearly as he could despite the hurry, he told them what was going on. The co-pilot pulled out a mobile phone and filed a new flight plan.

The sombre atmosphere evaporated. It turned out that the RAF crew had not been told anything other than that they were to take a Navy commander 'up north'. Although such scant information could sometimes signify a top-secret mission, more often it meant a compassionate case. And if someone had just lost a loved one, they didn't want to be coming out with the usual banter.

While the new plans were being calculated by the Navigator someone came up from the back with some rudimentary in-flight catering. Riches hadn't eaten all day, and wolfed down a cold chicken fajita and Coke. Before he'd even finished eating, the

Nimrod's engines started to roar again. The tension in his veins ebbed; at last he was moving.

The noise didn't please everyone, however. One of the local residents, apparently upset about the noise of the Nimrod taking off, called the airport and reported that they'd seen something falling off the aircraft as it passed overhead. Twenty minutes later, the news came through on the VHF. The pilots did a full check of the instruments while other members of the crew looked out through the bubble windows to see if they could see anything hanging off the aircraft, or missing. No one could spot anything wrong.

The Nimrod crew told Riches it was not an unusual tactic by those living near airfields, in retribution for flights that disturbed them. It was an effective, if unfair, punishment. The crew would now be forced to do a full shut-down and system check at Prestwick rather than simply dropping their passenger and continuing on, adding at least another hour and a half to their already delayed Friday-night plans.

Friday, 5 August/Saturday, 6 August
SS + 35 h 45 mins
16.15 UK – **19.15 Moscow – 04.15 Kamchatka**
Prestwick International Airport, Glasgow

Four minutes after the Nimrod took off from Filton, Squadron Leader Keith Hewitt touched down at Prestwick in the scrambled C17. Other members of the team were being assembled further south. An RAF tactical team and a Russian interpreter had been picked up from Henlow airbase in Bedfordshire and taken in a Merlin helicopter to RAF Lynham near Swindon, where they would be joined by the backup C17 aircrew. A Hercules was coming to pick them up and deliver them to join the gathering rescue forces at Prestwick.

The logistical jigsaw that Hewitt had avoided in his rapid departure from Brize Norton caught up with him on the tarmac apron of Prestwick. As aircraft commander of the C17, Hewitt was responsible for all aspects of delivering the Navy crew to their destination. As soon as the engines were shut down he despatched his crew like a tactical bomb, the multiple warheads homing in on different targets: route details, weather predictions, destination data and flight clearances.

The loadmaster concentrated on the containers on the back of Rumic's lorries that would be making up their payload, the co-pilot took charge of programming the flight computer with the course and working out the fuel equations, and the second flight crew began to hunt for up-to-date meteorological reports for the 11-hour flight, aviation charts and any information at all on Petropavlosk's landing strips.

Stuart Gold had arrived at Prestwick half an hour before the enormous Boeing C17. He'd never seen one before, and was awestruck by its size as it dropped out of the sky. He watched, fascinated, as it taxied over to his containers and slowly opened its back gate to reveal its cavernous interior. For the first time he realised that this might actually happen. They might actually be going to Russia.

Flight Sergeant Andy Macintyre, one of the two loadmasters, strode up and introduced himself and nodded at the assembled shipping containers containing the Scorpio rescue equipment.

'We need to get the weights of your kit,' the RAF man said.

'Sure thing,' replied Gold. He looked over at the three containers and took a breath. 'Well, that's six tons right there,' he said, drawing a finger at the furthest to the left. 'That one there is also six. This one is about five. And the umbilical cable there, that's about two tons.'

Macintyre paused for a second as if waiting for a punchline. None came. 'Er . . . no, I'm sorry, I'm going to need those weights accurate to the last, well, more or less to the last pound,' he said. 'We're going to need every drop of fuel we can get on board. The last thing we want to do is run out.'

Now it was Gold's turn to pause in disbelief. But Macintyre was serious. The 4,500-mile run to Kamchatka was at the outer edge of the C17's range. To calculate how much jet-A1 fuel they could load, they needed to know how much the submarine rescue system weighed.

'I'll get on it,' said Gold, and hurried off to the command container. He should have seen that request coming. Both Scorpio and LR5 were designed to be air-transportable – in fact they were lighter than the rescue systems of many other countries, making this was one of the major advantages of the UK system. But aside from one trip to Sweden in an Antonov a few years back, all the exercises had involved loading the system straight on to a mothership from a lorry, so he'd forgotten just how exact the requirements were.

He pulled out the data file and ran through the weights. All had been taken within the last year, and no major modifications had been done since then. Just to be sure, he compared notes with the crane driver that Prestwick airport had supplied upon their arrival. While picking each of the containers off the flatbeds, the driver had taken down the readings on the crane's strain gauges. The figures tallied, so Gold passed them on to Macintyre.

The loadmaster passed on the total weight to the co-pilot for the fuel calculations, and moved on to the next phase of his job: to work out where on the plane he should load each of the pieces of kit. When flying fully loaded, the enormous C17 needed its centre of gravity in exactly the correct spot. If the cargo was placed too far forward the nose would never lift off the ground. Too far back and the freighter would take off only to stall and fall back to earth. It was the loadmaster's job to make sure everything was secured in exactly the right place in the cargo bay.

Most of the equipment being carried out to the UK's overseas campaigns had been air-freighted before, and even then it was not taken at such short notice. At Brize Norton the Joint Air

Transport Evaluation unit had a full-size mock-up of the C17's cargo bay where all cargoes could be accurately weighed and their ideal load position worked out. All the loadmaster usually had to do was to follow the instructions and plug the resulting figures into the on-board Michigan computer. Supplied with the weights and their position in the cargo bay, the computer gave the final confirmation that the aircraft would fly.

But they'd never loaded this equipment before, and Macintyre and the other loadmaster found themselves beginning a high-pressure test of their training. Word had spread fast that this was no exercise, and that Russian sailors were trapped beneath a freezing sea on the other side of the world, hours away from dying, and that these containers might hold the key to their survival. The growing fleet of press vans only added to the tension. The newshounds had been kept well away, just inside the perimeter fence, but it was obvious that cameras were already rolling. The loadmasters tried to keep such things out of their mind, concentrating on getting each container in the right way around (their internal weight distribution mattered, too) and then shifting it left a couple of inches, right a bit, back or forward until it was in exactly the right place. What with all the effort going into loading the aircraft, the process of unloading it again seemed a distant concern.

They were not privy to the ongoing conversation on the ISMERLO website, where it had emerged that Petropavlovsk airfield did not have the capability to offload either the US or the UK's equipment. Neither team had room for the requisite K-loader inside their aircraft, so the Naval attachés began to request that the equipment be sourced in Russia and waiting for them there on arrival. A rolling teleconference was established by ISMERLO to resolve the issue, along with a steadily mounting number of others.

As the loadmasters were worrying about how to load the rescue kit while keeping the C17's centre of gravity in the right place, Hewitt and his co-pilot were trying to work out if they could actually make it all the way to Kamchatka with the fuel they were able to carry. Stopping to refuel would cost them valuable hours, hours that Russian officials had tacitly admitted they didn't have. But it would help no one for the UK's rescue effort to make it nine-tenths of the way to the incident site and then run out of fuel.

The C17's maximum take-off weight was 585,000 pounds – around 260 tons. The rescue equipment wasn't that heavy, compared to the tanks and artillery they sometimes carried, so much of their payload could be fuel, which would burn off as the journey progressed. The jet plan would have to juggle the greater efficiency of flying high with the fuel cost of getting up there – a decision whose crucial factor was the strength and direction of the winds. They'd be flying the path of the polar jet stream, where winds could vary between 52 and 215 knots. For that reason, today's jet plan for the route could be very different from tomorrow's.

Flying at the extreme edge of an aircraft's capability presented other problems too. Weather forecasts were wrong only slightly less often than they were right, and on a long-haul flight such forecasting errors could mean hours being added to the journey time – airborne hours that an aircraft with just enough fuel might not be able to afford. Such uncertainty – together with the risk of equipment malfunction – made planning good diversions an integral part of flight planning.

The unfamiliarity of the territory only made things worse. Not only had Hewitt never flown over any of this territory before, but the most detailed charts anyone could find were 1:1,000,000 – 50 times less accurate than they would normally use. On this chart, 50 centimetres got you halfway around the world. Hewitt tried various combinations as a backup airfield, but he was continually coming up short. The enormous swathe of eastern Russia was barren of airfields, at least on that chart. He couldn't find a route to Kamchatka that would give a workable diversion. Without one, if the wind blew even slightly in the wrong direction, the C17 – and its 29 crew and passengers – would create an emergency much worse than the one they were trying to resolve.

Friday, 5 August/Saturday, 6 August
SS + 36 h 45 mins
17.15 UK – 20.15 Moscow – 05.15 Kamchatka
Prestwick International Airport, Glasgow

Just over an hour after leaving Filton, the Nimrod turned on to final approach for Prestwick airport. Riches peered through the cockpit windows trying to spot where his team had congregated, then finally saw the enormous grey bulk of the C17. The white tubes of the airliners nearby looked like twigs next to a tree trunk. The thing was huge.

After touch-down the Nimrod rumbled down interminable taxiways until suddenly the C17 appeared again, its bulk filling the view. During the isolation of the flight, Riches had been convincing himself that the crisis would suddenly have been solved or his team stood down, but crews were bustling all around the aircraft.

Two hundred metres away the Nimrod rolled to a halt and airport steps were brought up to the door. A crewman opened it to reveal a red van at the bottom of the steps, with two men in suits standing alongside.

Riches took his bag off the crewman, walked down the stairs and shook their hands.

'Kind of you to offer a lift, but I'll walk it,' he said.

The men both nodded and ushered him into the van anyway. Riches now recognised one of them; he was from the Navy Public Relations office at Her Majesty's Naval Base Clyde. All three men sat down inside, but the engine was not started.

'Of course, you should go over there and talk to the team, and get the latest sitrep,' said one of the welcoming committee. 'But we need to have a chat first. Because as soon as you're up to date you're going to have to face those boys,' he continued, nodding his head towards the perimeter fence.

Riches' stomach lurched. He'd been so keen to get to the team that he hadn't seen the throng of vans, satellite dishes and people positioned just inside the wire. There was as much activity going on there as there was around the C17, with technicians setting up lights and tripods, satellite dishes rotating from the roofs of the network vans and photographers wielding huge lenses to get images of the loading.

'They're hungry for interviews as soon as possible so that they can make the six o'clock news.'

Riches cursed himself. He hadn't even thought about the media. He should have done – he'd heard about this thing through the BBC after all. And he hadn't considered that as the Naval officer in charge of the team he'd be the one stuck in front of the cameras. He suddenly regretted the fact that he'd turned down the media-training course that he'd once been offered.

'We just need to have a chat about what you should say, and what you shouldn't,' said one of the suits.

They kept it pretty clear. The mission was a humanitarian one to help fellow submariners, and the Royal Navy would do everything in its power to ensure a successful outcome. The fact that they were Russians was irrelevant.

'Don't say anything about politics or be drawn into speculating on how it might have happened. And don't whatever you do talk about the competence or incompetence of the Russian Navy,' he continued.

Standing in front of the television cameras 20 minutes later Riches tried to project all the confidence he could, but was all too aware how much of it was bluff.

'We understand that the sailors have only one day's worth of air left. Do you think you can get to them in time?' asked the first anchor.

'We all hope that by the time we get to the scene the Russian sailors will have been rescued. But we are deploying so that the ROV can be in place as a contingency if required by the Russians,' Riches replied, picking his words carefully as the wind buffeted around him, whipping his tie around as though it were an indicator on a wildly fluctuating gauge.

After a couple of rounds with different stations he began to get the hang of it. They asked the same sort of questions, and he was starting to know what they wanted to hear in reply. He walked away all puffed up, convinced that his earlier nerves were simple stage fright.

By the time Riches had finished playing the media monkey, the real work was almost done. Meanwhile, a C130 Hercules had thundered into land, carrying an RAF translator, the backup flight crew for the C17 and the aircraft security team. To get everybody on board, the submarine rescue squad had been trimmed. There were only eight from Rumic, including a naval architect to help assess and rig the equipment on the Russian mothership. A Naval architect was not a usual part of the team, but Gold had requested him, warning that they had no idea what vessel they were going to be given to work from.

The loading was close to completion, but the team were still awaiting their final flight clearance. Squadron Leader Keith Hewitt came and introduced himself to Riches, bringing the news that he'd received a fax detailing their permission, and grinned that they'd been granted humanitarian status. Normally clearance could take days or even weeks to arrange, but now they had the right to overfly any countries they wished without the bureaucratic headache of getting diplomatic permission.

As the hatch sealed the fuselage of the C17 from the darkening tail-end of the day in Scotland, the first glimmers of sun were appearing on the horizon over the sea east of Kamchatka.

Friday, 5 August/Saturday, 6 August
SS + 37 h 30 mins
18.00 UK – 21.00 Moscow – *06.00 Kamchatka*
Headquarters of 70076 military unit, Petropavlovsk-
Kamchatsky

The sun was already high in the northern sky when, at six in the morning, the headquarters of 70076 military unit – to which the *Georgy Kozmin* and its Priz submersibles belonged – found itself under siege from a platoon of local journalists. An ordinary building on the bay shore, it was not designed for such an assault. Its only defence was the hill on which it was sited – there was not even a fence, just a fringe of overgrown weeds sprouting at the base of the walls.

Guzel Latypova was there, waiting in the cold. She knew it was going to be tough to get anything out of the authorities on this. Yesterday she'd been met with nothing but walls. When she'd first arrived this morning, the Officer of the Watch had summoned help to try to chase them away. They were highly agitated at the presence of journalists, and didn't hide it. But, eventually, a man stepped out of the door, in a uniform but without epaulettes on his shoulders that might indicate his rank and so help deduce his identity. He didn't say his name, but confirmed that there was indeed an emergency event. Then, without giving any more details, he disappeared back inside, shutting the door on the pack of newshounds. Far from quenching their curiosity, the mysterious official's admission had only added fuel to the fire.

Later, Oleg Kashin, a reporter for Moscow's *Kommersant* newspaper, managed to engage the guard in conversation. The guard confided that the usual commander of *AS-28* – Vladimir Cheremukin – had gone away on vacation a few days before the incident.

'He did the right thing,' the guard told Kashin. 'He is such a big guy that if he'd stayed he would have taken the oxygen of seven men.'

The press pack was baying for blood by the time the military spokesman, Deputy Chief Petrov, finally emerged from the military headquarters to address them. He soothed them by admitting that there had been an incident, and that their efforts to assist had taken all their attention so far. However, now that things were going better, he could spare the time to share some information with them. The rescuers had succeeded in raising the temperature of the submersible from five to ten degrees, he said. It was a partial truth, after all. By moving crewmen back from the frigid forward compartment into the warmer second compartment, the temperature around them did indeed rise by four degrees. But that four degrees was generated by the warmth of the men inside, not by any actions from the surface.

Petrov also announced that the rescuers had managed to shift the stricken Priz submersible 30 metres from the accident site using grappling hooks dragged from vessels searching the area. There was no way that the journalists could know that the hooks had yet to snag the submersible at all, let alone drag it anywhere. Russian rescue planes were on their way, he added, although they would never arrive. But what everyone really wanted to hear was how long the sailors could survive on the air supplies that they had on the seabed. Here Petrov continued the long and distressing sequence of mis-information that would keep the families on tenterhooks for the next three days, as estimates of remaining air in official press releases swung between two and 48 hours.

Because of the building media frenzy, Vladimir Kuroyedov, head of the Russian Federation Navy, was on high alert. He'd recently suffered a string of embarrassing incidents. In January 2004, he'd invited President Putin on to a Typhoon-class nuclear submarine to witness two ballistic missile launches from Delta IV-class subs. Television news crews had been on board, cameras rolling, to record the great event. But the launch time came and went with no action, and for 20 minutes they waited, Putin seething. Both launches had failed entirely.

Then, just last month, the day before the Navy Day celebrations on 26 July, Kuroyedov had suffered the embarrassment of having the lead ship in their festival parade – the *Neukrotimy* ('Indomitable') patrol boat – sink right in the middle of St Petersburg. Officials had planned to demonstrate the blowing up of a dummy mine during the traditional Sunday ceremony. The device had 30 kg of TNT inside, less than the amount packed in a normal mine but still enough to make a splash that would to reach the spectators on the river bank. The ship had sailed up the River Neva, which cuts through the city, to prepare for the big event, but as the sailors were laying the dummy mine the current swept it up against the vessel's hull, where it exploded with enough force to rupture a weld and send water flooding into the engine room. The vessel was promptly retired from the line-up.

With such a catalogue of recent humiliations, the last thing Kuroyedov needed was something else to go wrong.

Friday, 5 August/Saturday, 6 August
SS + 39 h
19.30 UK – *22.30 Moscow* – 07.30 Kamchatka
Sheremetyevo airport, Moscow

Thick in the chaos of Moscow's Friday afternoon traffic, Captain Jon Holloway glanced at his watch for the fifth time that minute. The embassy's black Volvo wasn't even moving and he needed to be at the airport. He wasn't just late for the flight – he didn't even have a ticket yet. As soon as he'd taken Admiral Avdoshin's hint that the Royal Navy's offer would be accepted, he'd asked the office to get him on a plane to Petropavlosk. The reply had come back that the flight was now full.

Holloway knew that the mission might depend on his ability to smooth the communications between the Russians and his own people, but in order to help he had to be there. He needed to be in Petropavlovsk to meet the UK rescue team, and this evening's Aeroflot flight was the only way of making it. Every time he closed his eyes he saw an image of the business class cabin, newly filled with journalists hungry to broadcast the drama and the attempted rescue – a rescue that might fail for the lack of a diplomatic middleman. His one hope of getting the flight had been to reach the airport early and try to talk his way on board, but his day had become an endless rolling barrage of diplomatic notes arranging flight clearances, visa facilitations, and requests for personnel and equipment. And now, finally on his way to the airport, the traffic. It was Friday night, and the whole of Moscow, it seemed, was decamping to its dachas.

With only an hour and ten minutes before the flight was due to depart, Holloway's car pulled into Moscow's Sheremetyevo airport. Victor, the small, moustached driver who'd been with the embassy since the end of the Cold War, drove past the turning for the flashy international departures building and turned towards the 1970s concrete of the domestic terminal instead. Dumping the diplomatic car in a loading bay, Holloway and Victor hurried upstairs to the Aeroflot ticket office, easily identified by the long queue that stretched out of the door and along the corridor.

Holloway marched straight to the door and up to the desk, where a harassed-looking woman was dealing with some distraught customers. He barged the queue, ignoring the grumbling and resentful stares. There were no objections. In a curious mix of Old Soviet and New Russian mentalities, the very fact that someone was trying to barge a queue was usually assumed to mean that the person had the authority to do so.

'*Dyevyshka*,' Holloway said, interrupting with the formal address, 'Girl', while passing his dark pink diplomatic card in front of her. She glanced down at the photograph and the

Russian inscription saying the bearer was a diplomat and must be accorded every assistance.

'I must have a ticket for the flight to Kamchatka. The British Navy is assisting in the rescue operation of a submarine. I must be there to act as liaison.' A flicker of recognition passed behind the clerk's eyes. The news had been all over Russian television all day, though Holloway had only had a chance to glimpse the reports in passing.

The lady raised her eyebrows, and turned to her computer, her shoulders already shrugging. 'I'm sorry, sir, I think the flight is full.' A few seconds later she nodded. 'There are no more seats, I'm afraid.'

'I understand that. But seven Russian sailors are trapped on the seabed and are running out of air. You have to let me go and help them.'

The lady behind the desk looked at him for a moment, then shook her head again. There were no more seats, she insisted. The flight was full, but there was another one in the morning. Holloway did not budge, and repeated the situation in stronger terms. He hadn't mentioned the *Kursk*, but the memory hung in the collective Russian unconscious and he was banking on it to convince her to pull some strings.

She began checking her computer again, and Captain Holloway felt the knot in his stomach loosen a fraction. He knew that when an Aeroflot flight was full it didn't necessarily mean all the seats were taken. Although they may have stopped selling tickets to the general public, a few places would be kept back for emergency flights by state officials.

Finally the lady looked up.

'Well, sir, I have in fact found you something,' she said. She scribbled a message on a scrap of paper. 'You must go immediately downstairs to the cashier to pay.' She pushed the note over to Holloway, and turned to the other customers who were already pressing in behind him.

* * *

As Captain Holloway hurried towards departures, Dmitriy Podkapayev of the Russian Navy's Search and Rescue service was pacing the hall in front of the gate. He'd been travelling all day, making his way from the Scientific Research Institute in St Petersburg, home to the deep sea diving and rescue unit at which he was based. Beneath a squall of white-blond hair, his normally jovial face was tense. He'd been among the crew of one of the Priz submersibles that had tried to mate with the ninth compartment of the *Kursk*, where the survivors had clung to life for perhaps three days after the explosion. If they'd succeeded, a few of the crewmen might have still been alive. But for some reason they'd been unable to lock on to the hatch – either the seal was somehow obstructed by damage, or weak batteries on the submersible cut short their attempts.

Podkapayev had been a member of Russia's delegation to the recent international submarine rescue exercises, and when news about *AS-28*'s situation had come in he'd helped the Scientific Research Institute's Calculation Post decide to contact foreign rescue teams. A key lesson he'd taken from the NATO exercises was the importance of mobilising all resources as fast as possible in order to provide backup in case anything went wrong. Now that their recommendations had been taken seriously, Podkapayev had been despatched to liaise with the foreign rescue teams when they arrived in Kamchatka.

Podkapayev was not the only one being pulled into the action. At that moment, the Defence Minister, Sergey Ivanov, was just leaving an emergency meeting with President Putin. He was the first non-military man to have been appointed Defence Minister. In explaining the distinction some have pointed out that Ivanov was at college with Putin.

Putin's father had been a submariner, but that hadn't been enough to push him into asking for foreign help in the critical early stages of the *Kursk* disaster when it was clear that assistance was needed. It was only late on that help was requested. This time, however, he was reacting promptly and sending his most senior officials to the scene. The last thing he wanted was to feed his enemies in the independent press and television stations another public relations disaster.

Friday, 5 August/Saturday, 6 August
SS + 39 h 15 mins
19.45 UK **– 22.45 Moscow – 07.45 Kamchatka**
RAF C17 Globemaster

With the last of the crew now on board the C17, Squadron Leader Hewitt nodded to the rest of the cockpit crew of flight Ascot 6564. They immediately began to run through the start-up checklist. In the back, the RAF support squad were already settled in for the ride while the submarine rescue team were still getting used to the uncomfortable seats.

Hewitt had 29 people on board. A trip this long meant twin flight crews were essential. That gave him the advantage of having four pilots up front if they got into any hairy situations, each fully qualified and capable of taking control of the aircraft. Their presence made Hewitt feel a little more comfortable, given how many corners he'd had to cut to be in a position to begin the take-off this soon. Their flight plan still didn't have a useable diversion; after all, there was barely enough fuel to make the destination. But making tough, tight decisions was what he was trained for, it was his bread and butter. As an ex-tanker pilot he was used to having fighter pilots harassing him in mid-air, wanting every last ounce of his reserves in order to continue with their missions. His personal risk aversion radar was on a different setting from commercial airline pilots; if he stayed on the ground any time there was a risk of not coming back, he'd never get airborne. Not that he was pretending the fuel wasn't a problem. Fuel was something they were going to have to keep a very close eye on. But the lack of a diversion airfield was not going to keep his wheels on the ground.

Hewitt was strapped into the co-pilot's seat as the C17 swung its broad nose around at the end of runway 31. So much for his regular sortie out into the jaws of Iraq or Afghanistan. He was about to fly into the unknown.

Sitting beside Hewitt was Flight Lieutenant John Macintyre – no relation of Andy, the loadmaster – who would be handling the takeoff. Macintyre ran through his last checks, including a last look at the windsock – a habit born of his training that he hadn't let wear off, despite the fact that it took a howling 30-knot crosswind to worry the 260-ton plane. Macintyre held the enormous aircraft's brakes while he slowly pushed each of the four throttles to maximum thrust. Fully loaded like this, they couldn't afford to waste runway with a long take-off roll. Just as the aircraft began shuddering he released the brakes, and the C17 started to edge forwards.

When the aircraft neared rotation speed, Macintyre gently pulled back the yoke to lift the nose into the air. The designers had done a good job of leaving just enough feedback in the highly automated fly-by-wire; he could sense the aircraft's reluctance to rise.

Roger Chapman, the Managing Director of James Fisher Rumic, was on the tarmac watching the aircraft accelerate down the runway. Despite being in and around the Globemaster for the whole afternoon, he was still taken aback by the size of the thing. He only wished he could be inside it. In a very real sense the whole of his professional life had been building up to this point – at least everything since his own submersible accident back in August 1973. A huge rescue effort had gathered on the surface back then, with a fleet of ships and aircraft converging on the featureless sea above them. For interminable hours, days, he and his co-pilot had tested the drips of water on their tongues, dreading the taste of salt that would mean not condensation but a leak. The splitting headache from the foul air was bad, but worse still was the damp cold.

He wanted to be there on the scene in Kamchatka to try to save the trapped Russians. There had been so many people involved in rescuing him that he felt a little strange not to be there to pass on the favour. But he had bowed to the aircraft's weight issues, conceding that out there he might have been one manager too many.

All he could do was watch as the Globemaster shrank into the distance. It seemed to go on and on, and was a tiny speck in the distant twilight when at last it lifted into the sky.

As the C17 circled over the North Atlantic, working slowly upwards through the layers of low stratus cloud to gain enough altitude to cross the Scottish highlands on its way east, Commander Riches looked down the line of faces of the team. He'd met almost all of them before – some had been part of the squad on the recent NATO exercise in the Gulf of Taranto in June.

Gold, Nuttall, Sillet, Forrester and Hislop he knew, but he hadn't met Nigel Pyne, another winchman and general fixer, or Marcus Cave, the naval architect that Rumic had insisted on sending. Gold had told him that both were as good as they get. At the end of the row of seats was David Burke, an ex-submarine officer who had been with Rumic less than a year. He wasn't wearing a uniform, of course, but he was still the only other one on the Submarine Rescue Service side of the aircraft with military bearing.

The rest of them were obviously civilian. These guys formed one of the best submarine rescue crews in the world, but they wouldn't have looked out of place in a dark barroom. Nuttall was a case in point – with his untamed hair and scruffy jeans, Riches would once have written him off. Now he knew better. Nuttall had a level of expertise that was hard to replicate anywhere, military included.

The canvas padding on the fold-down seats was already feeling thin. He dreaded having to sit in it for the next ten hours – there'd be little chance of sleeping in it. The din from the engines was unrelenting, the lights glaring. Just then a chill began to creep into the cabin. Before the aircraft had finished climbing, the RAF boys, most of whom were sitting across the fuselage from the team on the facing row of seats, began to dig into the rucksacks they'd carried on board. They pulled out warm clothes, sleeping bags, bed rolls, eye-covers, ear defenders and even portable DVD players, then began making themselves beds on the free pallets and on any other bit of spare deck. The rescue squad all looked at one another. All they had besides their rescue equipment was their passports, a change of clothes and their toothbrushes.

Up in the cockpit, the four pilots were still poring over the charts they'd managed to gather at Prestwick, trying to work out how to make it safely to Petropavlovsk. Their planned route followed a 'great circle', arcing over the northern tracts of Siberia more than 80 degrees north, coming within a few hundred kilometres of the North Pole. Although the shortest distance between any two points on the surface of the earth, following a great circle route involves constant adjustment of course because you are flying in a curve relative to the North Pole, the anchor of all navigational systems.

No matter how efficient the route, the pilots were still unable to track down a workable diversion if Petropavlovsk's airfield was for some reason not operational. In the end Hewitt had to turn to his last resort: the Ascension Clause. Wideawake airfield, the joint UK-US base on the British-administered, mid-Atlantic island of Ascension, is so remote that it is impossible to fly there and have workable diversions. Once you're past your point of no return you have no choice but to land there, whatever the problem. Using the Ascension clause was far from ideal, but if they were going to reach Petropavlovsk the rules regarding diversion had to be relaxed.

The crew had collected all the latest information about Petro-pavlovsk Elizovo airport before departure, and would keep asking for regular updates all the way up until their point of no return. The airfield was receiving commercial flights and the weather was good and forecast to remain so. The one consolation was that even if the conditions changed dramatically once the aircraft was fully committed, the airfield data sheet listed an Instrument

Landing System that would be able to guide the aircraft down even if there was thick fog.

As Macintyre levelled the Globemaster off on a heading for their first waypoint above Norway, the second crew settled into their off-shift. They'd each be spending two hours in the single bunk, keeping themselves as fresh as possible for the long flight over. They'd need every minute of rest they could get. Unbeknown to them, the first tendrils of cloud were beginning to gather around the sharp volcanic peaks that guard the approaches to the runways of Elizovo airport, and the Instrument Landing System at the airport that they were banking on was out of action.

Friday, 5 August/Saturday, 6 August
SS + 40 h 30 mins
21.00 UK – 00.00 Moscow – *09.00 Kamchatka*
Petropavlosk-Kamchatsky

Watching the television news on the Rossiya channel in her sister's flat in Zavoyko, Yelena Milachevsky jerked herself upright. Pacific Fleet Commander Viktor Fyodorov appeared from his headquarters in Vladivostok to announce that *AS-28* was being towed to shallower waters, where divers would be able to disentangle any remaining nets and cables. 'We have hooked on a cable,' he said. 'Our ships are raising and towing the submersible to shallow waters. We will carry out this task using our own resources and will raise (the submersible) to the surface.'

Yelena called the headquarters to find out more, and was told that her husband's craft had been towed for 30 metres. An hour and a half later, the Navy announced that it had managed to raise the temperature inside the submersible to ten degrees. But when Yelena called Slava's father, her hopes started to wither once more. Why, Vladimir Valentinovich Milachevsky asked, if they'd managed to tow the Priz at all, did they not tow it all the way to the surface? And how were they increasing the temperature inside? Milachevsky senior could think of no mechanism with which this could be done.

He was right to be suspicious. On the *Kursk*, the last surviving sailors had survived for ten long hours after the initial explosion that had sent the submarine crashing to the sea floor. Unable to reach the wreckage because of repeated failures of both procedures and equipment, the Russian rescue teams had not known what the situation on board was, but a full three days and ten hours later, official sources were still saying they could hear tapping from the hull, and that there was enough oxygen on board for another five to six days.

Igor Dygalo, the aide to the head of the Russian Navy, whose wildly varying estimates of the breathable air remaining on *AS-28* had so spooked Yelena earlier in the day, had also been among those releasing information during the unfolding *Kursk* scandal. Four days into that drama, he'd claimed that *Kursk* had settled at a severe angle on hitting the seabed, while terrible visibility and strong currents were hampering rescue attempts on the sea bottom. The international rescue effort, including Commodore David Russell, who had led the UK's team, had heard the announcement and fretted. Those conditions – particularly the angle at which Dygalo said she lay – would confound anybody's technology. But some with experience of the Barents Sea were suspicious: the shallow shelf seas that dominated the region rarely felt currents as strong as were being claimed. They were right. When Norwegian divers were finally allowed to reach the site, they found the conditions benign and – what's more - the submarine was only listing at a very manageable four degrees.

Guzel Latypova had already paid a visit to Yelena that morning, sitting with her and discussing the situation with her and her family as it developed. Latypova kept a special ear open when Yelena's friend at the Naval headquarters rang. This, she'd realised, was a far more regular and reliable source of information than the official press statements. Every half-hour or so, Latypova would discreetly file a short update to *Interfax*.

Friday, 5 August/Saturday, 6 August
SS + 42 h
14.30 San Diego – 22.30 UK – 01.30 Moscow –
10.30 Kamchatka
Naval Air Station North Island, San Diego, California

Commander Kent Van Horn was tearing his hair out. Despite all the drills he'd put his men through in the past nine months to speed up the loading process, things were moving like cold treacle. There was a C5 sitting on the apron at North Island, but they weren't being allowed to use it, and it had taken until four in the morning to get even an ETA for a replacement aircraft. His men were ready and waiting, but they were being held up by other elements.

He had all crews and equipment standing by ready to load the moment that the C5 arrived. The short journey across the airport had been one of Van Horn's concerns when looking out for trouble spots where his unit might lose time in loading. Since they were reliant on trucks that weren't under their direct command, there was a chance that they would be delayed by other obligations. To cut out that risk, Van Horn had installed wheel systems on the bottom of his equipment containers, so that the Deep Submergence Unit's pickup trucks could tow them over to the loading area if the usual heavy-hauling trucks didn't show up in time. But he'd had hours to get his equipment in place while waiting for the aircraft to arrive from Travis Airbase, outside San Francisco. It hadn't got there until 12.30 Pacific Time.

When the loadmasters emerged from the C5 they had bad news. The tail-section door was not functioning properly, and they would only be able to load through the nose of the aircraft. Although that was just as big as the aft doors, using only one end was going to slow them down. Van Horn gritted his teeth. The C5s had been around since 1968, and though the type had been through some major refits – including new sets of wings in the 1980s – they were still notoriously temperamental.

A Reliability Enhancement and Re-Engining Program (RERP) was being planned, but for now the C5 crews knew their aircraft by another acronym, FRED, standing for 'F***ing Ridiculous Economic/Environmental Disaster'. On top of its enormous fuel consumption, for every hour of flight the C5 required an average 16 hours of maintenance. Some of Van Horn's precious cargo space was occupied by entire pallets full of spares for the aircraft, forcing the DSU to break apart some of their carefully pre-packed pallets and store them loose in order to get them on board. Once again, Van Horn's carefully rehearsed drills were going out the window. First the plane was late, now the loading was taking far longer than it should.

An hour before takeoff the C5 was the only aircraft that was scheduled to be making the trip, but the US response was escalating. Other elements of the Navy had become convinced that Atmospheric Diving Suits (ADSs) were a better bet than an ROV in this situation. Because they carried a human operator they only required a crane to put them in the water and recover them, rather than the additional complexity of running umbilical cables and installing a command cabin on board a foreign ship. This simplicity meant they could be airlifted straight from the airbase out to the ships that were on site, potentially saving many valuable hours. Preparations began to send a second aircraft, a C17 Globemaster, with two ADS suits.

After all the delays, it wasn't until 14.22 Pacific Time that the C5 began rolling down the taxiway, and it finally lifted off eight minutes later. According to his first projection of the US team's Time to First Rescue, his Super-Scorpio ROV should be tapping against the side of the trapped submersible in just ten hours' time.

But now he suspected they'd still be in the air, and would certainly not have offloaded, been transported to the vessel, then have loaded, set up and steamed into position over the incident site. Even with the 31 enlisted men, six officers and three civilian dive contractors he had on board, he'd be pushed to make it in even 16 hours.

Van Horn badly wanted to get to those men. Not only had he spent years of his career on nuclear submarines – and qualified as an Executive Officer – but he'd always worked with craft that were involved in rescue operations. There weren't many submarines that could act as motherships for rescue submersibles, but he'd served on two. Equipped with the right onboard chambers and hatches, they were able to transport rescue submersibles to an accident site and take delivery of sailors from the distressed craft without any support from the surface.

But the bulletins on ISMERLO as he left were not sounding good. Thanks to all the delays, the Australian oil exploration ship was now regarded as the best hope for the trapped submariners.

Ominously, the principal scientist from a UK defence contractor called Qinetiq, was on the message board offering to analyse the crew's chances of survival if they attempted a Rush Escape. Even if they'd been equipped with the latest survival suits with buoyancy, breathing apparatus and protection from the near-freezing water of the depths, the chances of survival coming up from that depth would not be good. Two hundred and ten metres was beyond the design limit of the suits, but not by much. As the scientist pointed out, with timescales for rescue looking very tight, it was worth projecting if such a drastic solution might result in a lower loss of life.

Saturday, 6 August
SS + 43 h 30 mins
00.00 UK – 03.00 Moscow – *12.00 Kamchatka*
AS-28, **210 metres beneath Berezovya Bay**

Just past midday, the Russian Navy's Pacific Fleet spokesman announced that *AS-28* had now been towed for 90 metres.

On the seabed, Slava Milachevsky lay half frozen in the forward compartment, his head pounding and his lungs labouring. He had to strain to hear what the voice was saying on the underwater telephone. His hearing was fading as the level of carbon dioxide in his blood crept slowly upwards.

Surface vessels were dragging grappling hooks through the water to try to clear the obstructions and free the submersible, he was told. *AS-28* must report when one of them made contact with the hull. But aside from occasional clangs – presumably from the hooks striking somewhere on the huge flank of the array – there had been no sign of them whatsoever. At one point the *Kozmin* operator had called excitedly, saying that a hook had caught. But *AS-28* never moved. Whatever the grapple had snagged was not their steel coffin.

The Pacific fleet's media arm was not the only one relying on comforting deceptions to keep morale high. Sergei Belozerov – the 34-year-old mechanic in charge of the engine room – had been put in charge of dispensing the only food on board, the dry crackers. At breakfast, lunch and dinner times, he would haul himself upright out of the huddle and hand each man a cracker with great ceremony, announcing that the handouts were being given compliments of Belozerov's café.

But Belozerov's other innovation was far more important to the men than crackers made almost inedible by their lack of saliva. For a Russian sailor the smoke break is a sacred ritual; a moment for pause, comradeship, contemplation and humour in their day of grind. Every few hours Belozerov would declare another smoke break, and the sailors would share out cigarettes. They took them hungrily, and took them to their mouths. After a couple of unlit, and unsatisfying hauls on the cigarette they began smelling, licking and even chewing the tobacco – anything to get a tiny taste of normality.

Saturday, 6 August
SS + 44 h 30 mins
01.00 UK – 04.00 Moscow – *13.00 Kamchatka*
Petropavlovsk-Kamchatsky

Every time Yelena Milachevskaya closed her eyes she saw the cramped inside of the submersible with Slava inside, gasping for breath. When she opened them again she would be frantic with worry.

All night she had been answering the telephone, hearing different updates from the Naval headquarters. She'd got up to sit by the phone at six in the morning, but she'd stopped hoping for news. The estimates of the amount of breathable air changed so often that Slava's father had gone to the headquarters in person to try to get to the truth.

Her sister was growing concerned. Yelena kept saying that she felt like her heart was failing, that she couldn't feel her hands and feet. Her sister called headquarters once again, this time requesting that paramedics come with tranquillisers.

Five years before, the wives of those lost on the *Kursk* had sought solace in the same way. As the full horror of the tragedy started to leach out from reluctant Russian leaders, wives and families streamed out of the conference rooms and into the arms of medics. But not all injections were taken voluntarily. When the Deputy Prime Minister, Ilya Klebanov, was trying to sooth families at a tense meeting, Nadezha Tylik, the mother of one of the submariners, leapt to her feet and shouted, 'You're a swine! They're dying down there in a tin can for $50 a month! And you don't care! Do you have children? Do you?'

Soldiers surged towards her, but the woman continued her tirade. 'I will never forgive you! Take your medals off and shoot yourself! Bastards!' She had become surrounded, and the television footage clearly showed a female medic plunging a hypodermic needle into the woman's thigh. The commotion had drawn security attention away from the Deputy Prime Minister, who suddenly found himself faced with another distraught sailor's relative who had climbed up on to the podium. She had wrapped her hands around his neck and was trying to throttle him before his minders managed to pull her off.

But Yelena was in despair, not fury. When the paramedic arrived she took the drug without struggle, and was soon in a dazed, muted state, lying on her bed. She was still conscious enough to keep one hand on the telephone, but her eyes were glazed. Aside from her sister, the only person she'd let help with the twins was Slava's old friend Artyom. He came around to help look after her and the kids.

She had not eaten since she'd first heard the news. The tranquillisers had transformed her panicked grief into a blank-eyed hollowness. Yelena's brother in-law tried to gently push a spoon of broth between her lips, but most of it dribbled from the side of her mouth.

Yelena had not seen Slava since June, when they'd had a few days in the countryside together. The time before that they'd only been together for a day before he had to go back to work. Over and over she was imagining the moment when she would have to tell the girls that their Daddy was not coming home. She couldn't think how she could ever say those words.

Maybe everything was her fault. Wordless guilt crushed down on her as she blamed herself for every quarrel they'd had in the last three years, and she cursed herself for having fought with him the last time he'd come back. There was no way for him to have known that she was only fighting with him because she loved him, because she wanted him to come home. How could he understand? For most of his life he was surrounded by men, but when he was home he was surrounded by girls – his girls, as they were always known in the text messages they sent to each other's phones.

Occasionally, Yelena's thoughts would brighten and she'd daydream of her handsome husband climbing up a ladder to a high window in which she was perched, and sweeping her off her feet, just as he'd done one day when she'd been in hospital and visitors had been barred. They were laughing together, she joking that he was too small to lift her. But every time the darkness would return, and Slava would start getting smaller and smaller, as he was crushed inside the impossibly tiny submersible.

With their mother helpless in bed, Artyom fed the twins and then took them out for a walk around the streets of Zavoyko to give them some air.

Though today the clouds were starting to roll in, on a good day the view back towards Petropavlovsk was framed by the majestic peaks of the twin volcanoes Koryaksky and the smaller Avachinsky, while on either side the horizon was serrated as far as the eye could see. Artyom walked with the girls, telling them stories to try to cheer them up.

They weren't the easiest streets for lifting gloomy spirits. Somehow the rugged natural beauty of the surroundings only made the town's decay more depressing. Artyom knew the situation only too well, but these streets made it all seem bleaker still.

Saturday, 6 August
SS + 45 h 30 mins
02.00 UK – 05.00 Moscow – 14.00 Kamchatka
RAF C17, over the Russian Arctic

Pretty soon all activity had ceased in the back of the C17. Trays of food had been handed out by the loadmasters, and the RAF boys were all settling into their sleeping bags, looking warm and comfortable. Just seeing them made the cold feel even worse.

Unable to sleep, Riches tried to distract himself by visiting the flight deck to see if any operational updates had come through on the radio, but there was nothing. His mind began playing out various scenarios of what lay ahead. Most likely, he thought, their help would turn out not to be needed. After all the fuss, they'd be sent home with nothing to show for the effort and expense of getting there. He wondered about the wildly varying estimates of remaining air that had been given by the Russian authorities. All they had were the Russian assurances that the men inside were still alive. Given the time they'd been trapped, there was a good chance that they were already dead. Were they being set up as a distraction to draw fire away from a failed Russian rescue, or worse, as a scapegoat?

Then the real demons began to arrive. What if they were needed and he wasn't up to the job? Suddenly, unexpectedly, his chance had finally come to accomplish something tangible and win respect from the submarine community that he so valued. Yet he'd shelved his ambitions of command so long ago and with it the total confidence that was an essental part of the job. Even with familiar ships in known waters there was so much that could go wrong on this kind of operation. In the wilds of Russia, it would surely be a lot worse.

He tried to rein himself in by summoning back the training that he'd had to leave behind when his genetic heritage had forced him from the operational fleet. He began thinking the problem through step by rigorous step, breaking everything down into manageable chunks that could be accomplished with effective logistics and a good team. He'd done it in exercises dozens of times. Everything would come automatically. How much could really go wrong?

Sitting on his canvas seat in the C17, Stuart Gold was huddled up in all the clothes he'd brought with him, trying to clear his mind and get some sleep. He'd tried lying on the floor using a foul-weather jacket as a tent, but that hadn't worked. There was adrenaline running through his veins. After ten years of training, he badly wanted to get the chance to prove that his equipment could actually do the job. But it also seemed impossible to him that they would be the first team to get there, what with the proximity to Kamchatka of both the Americans and the Japanese. Both nations were superbly equipped with underwater rescue equipment, with everything from ROVs like Scorpio to saturation diving systems that allowed men to work for up to a month in water as deep as 300 metres.

Unable to rest but aware that he needed to, Gold stood up to take a look if there was anywhere slightly darker, warmer or less noisy where he could lie down. Walking towards the front of the aircraft he squeezed between the Effer Crane and the 1,000-metre drum of umbilical cable and found the converted shipping container that made up Scorpio's tool shed. Alongside was the 20-foot control cab. When he saw it, Gold smiled. Inside was the cushioned bench that was always fought over on exercises during teabreaks by those wanting a lie-down. He opened the door, letting the light spill in. There was a groan from inside. There on the cherished bench, huddled up in a waterproof jacket, was Charlie Sillet sprawled out beneath a jacket. Gold apologised, but was grateful to hear Sillet say that he'd give it up for Gold in a couple of hours.

Pete Nuttall was used to the cold from his lifeboat work. He should be used to the nerves too, but this job was different. He was confident that he knew what he was doing when the boat got called out. There were uncertainties, sure, but at least he knew what they were. The weather could be worse than it had looked from the shore or from the forecast, or the state of the stricken vessel could be worse or the crew injured in some way. But here they were stepping into an unknown world where everything was a mystery. There wasn't even a local forecast.

He wished Tommy Calvert had not been luxuriating on Paul Allen's yacht in the Mediterranean but here on the plane. He was glad to be going out on this mission, but he would have loved Tommy to be there with him. Not only was there a distinct lack of information on what they were about to face, making their planning difficult, but he'd seen the TV crews at Prestwick and was all too aware of the spotlight of the world's media that was on them. Then he caught himself. Tommy always told him to stop caring so much. *Why do you care?* he'd ask. *Stop it.*

It would have been interesting to see Tommy out here, he thought. Tommy always boasted that he only did things that were to his own advantage. If you were on a sinking boat with him and there was only one lifejacket, you wouldn't be the one with the lifejacket, he'd say. The thought made Nuttall smile, before he snapped back to his current situation. Even Tommy would care about this one, with seven men slowly suffocating.

Nuttall tried to think about the cables that had snagged the submersible. What else was down there? It would be all too easy to get himself tangled, especially in an unpredictable environment. Get caught up badly enough and he could end up losing the Navy's £5m rescue system.

In the back of his mind, impossible to banish, was a dark pit of recent memory. Just a few months ago the lifeboat had been called out to Morecombe Bay, on the west coast of the UK above Blackpool, where a father and a son had been out fishing. The previous year 23 Chinese people had been killed when out on the sands picking cockles, caught by the tide which can come in as fast as a galloping horse. The south side of the bay was less treacherous, and 'fishing the tide' was a popular pursuit. You'd throw out a hook on a long pole, then keep ahead of the rising tide with a brisk walk. Usually it was easy to know which way to land – just put your back to the water – but that day a thick fog had rolled across the bay. With visibility down to a few tens of metres, occasional sandbars could cause confusion; the water could creep around out of sight, then appear to be coming in from all sides. With his footprints disappearing in the stalking sea, the father had become disoriented. As the water crept higher he had managed to make a call on his mobile phone, and soon the lifeboat's inflatable was screaming out across the flats towards their estimated position. But when the rescuers had arrived and cut the engine to a low idle and listened, they could hear no shouts of distress. Within the hour they found them, both but it was too late. Both had drowned.

The team estimated they'd been within half a mile of reaching them in time. Just those few minutes had separated life from death. Now there was a family ripped apart by the tragedy, without husband, son, brother. Was there something they could have done to get there faster? It was so easy for people to misjudge the sea, and it took so little time to be overcome by it. Now there would be seven people relying on him to get them out in time, each of them with families and loved ones.

With two hours to go until the C17 reached Petropavlovsk, a call came through on the radio, having been relayed from the UK by other operators. Flight Lieutenant Macintyre came to pass the message to the Navy boys in the back. He needed to stretch his legs. He was already feeling the tug of tiredness, accentuated by not having had enough rest prior to the flight.

'Just got word that the Americans are on their way, but are an hour or so behind us. Thought you'd like to know,' Macintyre said.

Only snoring came from the RAF side of the aircraft, but a small cheer went up from the sleepless civilian rescue team. Macintyre made his way back to the cockpit and reported to the other pilots that they looked pretty glum.

The pilots, on the other hand, were enjoying themselves. They were about to do what few RAF or USAF aircraft had done – land at a Russian airbase. Although their aviation charts were far from accurate, the Russian air traffic controllers whose zones they were flying through all knew who they were, and did not seem bothered by the fact that the RAF flight was constantly having to estimate when zone boundaries were being crossed, rather than calling with the precision usually expected of aviators.

An hour out of Petropavlovsk, Squadron Leader Hewitt asked Elizovo ATC three times to confirm their last transmission, before turning to the other pilots.

'Elizovo ILS is down,' he said flatly.

The others turned to look at him, to check he wasn't messing with them. As one, they realised he wasn't. The Instrument Landing System was their only crutch in making the decision to go ahead without a diversion airfield. If they got there and the weather was terrible, they'd have no way of accurately guiding themselves to the airstrip.

'Are they hoping to fix it?' one asked.

'It's been out of action for days, they say. So I doubt it. Cloud base is at 3,000 feet. They're advising NDB.'

Every pilot learns how to home in on an airfield's Non Directional Beacon, but very few ever use it again after that. The technology had hardly changed since the Second World War. The wobbling needle of the NDB gauge was squeezed in towards the edge of the C17's instrument panel more because of historical precedent and inherited legislation than by necessity. The instrument was the same as could have been found beneath the windshield of a Spitfire 60 years before. Once you were within around ten miles of the airfield it could give a rough bearing, but that was it; because the NDB couldn't give the range, navigating with one meant making calculations using a stopwatch. But Second World War pilots had managed to guide themselves home through fog with the NDB system, so it was possible. And while those pilots had had the advantage of familiarity with their destination, their home airfield, Hewitt's crew had the advantage of their Global Positioning System. Although often used, GPS was not certified for use in aircraft navigation by authorities – it was still classed as experimental. In the same way as the loadmasters had been forced to go back to basics while loading the aircraft in Prestwick, running centre-of-gravity calculations from scratch, the pilots were being forced to reacquaint themselves with how to use an NDB beacon.

Two hundred and sixty tonnes of the very latest in Western military hardware were now hurtling towards Russia's Elizovo airport at 500 miles an hour, into a black hole where normally critical elements of their aircraft's technology were useless. The pilots had no idea how much they could trust the expertise of the Russian Air Traffic Control personnel to guide them in, so the entire descent and approach now had to be planned out by the crew themselves, using whatever they had at hand.

Over the Sea of Okhotsk, Ascot 6564 passed its point of no return. There was now no longer any option but to land at Elizovo airport. If the weather was too bad to allow landing, the aircraft would have to circle the runway and hope for a break in the cloud. If nothing had cleared in two hours, then the aircraft would be forced to ditch.

Hewitt glanced around at his three fellow pilots. They were all feeling less than fresh. Ten and a half hours of continuously recalculating diversions and fuel performances had taken their toll, along with trying to estimate control zone boundaries and the challenge of deciphering the radio calls from Russian air traffic controllers. English might be the language of international aviation, but out over the wilds of Siberia it seemed that a new dialect was evolving.

By all their calculations, they were in the right place. All of them had been trained not to trust GPS for navigation, but it was a comfort that the multi-coloured readout also showed them where they should be. Everything seemed right, but beneath his cool, collected exterior all of Hewitt's senses were screaming caution. The enormous Globemaster was sinking fast towards the carpet of cloud that stretched in front of them. Piercing the whiteness like blackened teeth, the tips of Petropavlovsk's 13,000-foot volcanoes were smoking. They'd last erupted 15 years before (and would again three years later in 2008), but for now the lava was not flying. But rock didn't need to be molten and hurtling through the air to cause them trouble. A cloud unexpectedly filled with cold, hard granite was similarly effective. Hewitt was having to take it on trust that the airfield was where it said it was and that the terrain had been accurately surveyed, and it didn't feel good.

Elizovo Air Traffic Control now said that cloud base was at 500 feet above ground level. That meant a 10,000-foot descent through cloud before popping out and finally getting visual contact with the runway. Only then would Hewitt breathe more easily. Until that point everything was theoretical. Aviation charts and flight computers didn't show rogue vehicles crossing the strip or other aircraft taxiing lazily across it. Coming in on a precision approach, that moment of clarity could occur just ten seconds before landing, 200 feet above the ground, only two-thirds of a mile from the runway threshold. But without an operational ILS he needed twice that. He'd have to break cloud 450 feet above ground, a mile and a half away from the strip, in order to be sure his approach was good.

On the plus side, Elizovo strip was 3,400 metres long, enough to take a fully laden 747. Even at maximum weight, thanks to the ability to reverse the thrust of its engines, the C17 would only need around 820 metres, and by now almost all of its weighty fuel had been burnt.

It was raining, Air Traffic Control said, and the light was beginning to deteriorate. Hewitt's one consolation was that they had now located a military airfield on the southern Siberian coast where the weather was passable. It was the diversion they'd been searching for all along, close enough for them to be able to run one trial approach at Petropavlovsk, abort and still reach a safe haven. It would be the end of the British rescue mission, but at least the disaster would not be compounded with a wrecked transport aircraft and its human cargo.

Hewitt had programmed the C17's flight computer to guide the aircraft on to its final approach, and was now in the hot seat as the pilot in command. He watched the sweep of the ground radar as it illuminated large swathes of high ground ahead. There was a calm silence on the flight deck. All four of the men were methodically scanning the screens and gauges, watching for the first sign of trouble.

Suddenly a red light started flashing on the instrument panel, accompanied by a sharp buzz. The autopilot had disconnected itself. Hewitt cursed. Something had gone wrong in programming the approach. Almost immediately afterwards, Elizovo ATC started talking them in, reading off their approach heights. While one of the co-pilots started trying to trouble-shoot the autopilot programming, Hewitt concentrated on trying to decipher the air traffic controller's incomprehensible accent. It didn't help that the heights were being given in metres, not feet. No country in the world had decided to go metric for aviation altitude measurements except for Russia. And the C17, for all its technological wizardry, worked in feet and had no instant conversion feature.

The opaque grey of cloud filled the cockpit glass. Instrument-only conditions are famously deceptive and disorienting, convincing unwary pilots to believe their plane is rolling upside down when it is in fact flying straight and level. Flying by instinct becomes a lethal urge. The pilots of the C17 were blind to the outside world, reliant on instruments calibrated to a different scale from the one the voice guiding them through the cloud was using. The presence of steep granite mountainsides lurking in that same cloud did not make it any more comforting.

Everyone in the cockpit felt the same ratcheting up of the pressure, and all four of them began giggling. While Hewitt and the lead pilot from the second team concentrated on flying the

C17 on the path they'd plotted on their atlas, the two co-pilots worked on translating the altitude instructions from Elizovo's Air Traffic Control. A mistake here would be fatal. One pilot was taking the readings from a conversion table himself before the other cross-checked the figure and double-checked on their topological chart to make sure that they weren't being directed into a volcanic crater.

In 99 Squadron they'd become accustomed to evaluating reports from ground-based commanders before landing in Baghdad or Kabul, weighing up threats from machine-gun fire and rocket-propelled grenades. Now they were having to weigh up an altogether different risk, and it felt good. They were pilots, after all. This is what they lived for.

'Nine hundred feet,' one called out against the murmur of cockpit activity.

'Eight hundred.'

The blank greyness that filled the windshield flickered briefly, then returned. Ten seconds later it flickered again then disappeared, revealing dark fields and brooding mountainsides. All four pilots began urgently searching through the gloom. The C17's head-up display projected essential flight data such as airspeed, attitude and heading on to the windshield and so their attention was not focused simply on the cockpit immediately around them, but flying on instruments and flying by looking out at the real world still used different mindsets, and it took them a second or two to adjust. Squinting through the exploding raindrops and the sweep of the windscreen wipers, all at once they saw the tiny lights ahead.

'Elizovo ATC, Ascot 6564 has runway in sight,' Hewitt said into his mike.

Hewitt nudged the huge aircraft's rudders, making final adjustments to the drift to take account of the wind, and 15 seconds later they were over the threshold, RAF rubber bouncing on Russian concrete. The time was 0521 Zulu, or twenty-one minutes past six in the evening local time. The Americans – having started over a thousand kilometres closer – were an hour and a half behind.

Saturday, 6 August
SS + 50 h
06.30 UK – 09.30 Moscow – *18.30 Kamchatka*
Petropavlosk

'The British rescuers have landed.' The words floated through the fog of Yelena Milachevskaya's tranquillised mind. She'd been drifting without hope, but the news suddenly anchored her. She felt that at last she had been given something solid to hold on to.

All of her worst fears about the Russian Navy were coming true. Admiral Fyodorov had just been on the television saying it had decided to use explosives to free the craft. The obstructions trapping the submersible would be targeted, he said, blowing the link to the two 60-tonne anchors that held the array in place, in the hope that the entire array would float to the surface together with *AS-28*.

But now the Western rescuers had come. No matter that Slava despised foreigners. They would rescue him and bring him back to her.

Saturday, 6 August
SS + 50 h 05 mins
06.35 UK – 09.35 Moscow – *18.35 Kamchatka*
Elizovo International Airport and Military Airbase,
Petropavlovsk-Kamchatsky

Once the aircraft finished a long, slow taxi and at last rolled to a final stop, Commander Riches made his way forward to take a look. From the cockpit windows, he had his first glimpse of Russia. Beyond the taxiway were trees and, through the drizzling rain, the vague shapes of distant mountains. He couldn't see any terminal buildings – not even a hangar. Hewitt explained that the control tower had directed them to park here in a distant corner of the airfield. It was a bleak scene. Puddles of water stood on the cracked slabs of concrete that made up the runway apron, and tufts of grass were growing up between the grey reflections of low hanging cloud.

Sixteen degrees and raining in Kamchatka, the team had told him back in Abbey Wood. *Just like Scotland,* they'd said. *You'll feel right at home.*

Then the loadmaster opened the aircraft's passenger door on the port side, and revealed just how far from home they were. A reception party had gathered beside the aircraft to meet them, a mix of soldiers wearing huge, fur hats and Air Force officers with the high-fronted, small-peaked military hats that added almost a foot to their height. Clustered behind them was a group of civilians wearing bright waterproofs. After some orders were barked out by an officer, one of the civilians explained in halting English that they were not to come down from the aircraft, but instead to hand over their passports while their situation was assessed. An officer climbed the ladder and took the documents. This wasn't the kind of welcome they were expecting.

Riches asked the interpreter – who turned out to have been a student of English recruited from the local university – to explain that they were there to save Russians, military men like them. The translated version of his words seemed hardly to register. The British team were soon back inside the aircraft, the minutes ticking by as the Russian officers leafed through their passports and had long conversations over a handheld radio. Riches could feel his blood rising. There was still so much to do, and every minute mattered. The sailors had already been in their freezing coffin for 60 hours, and his team still had to offload the aircraft, get to the port, set themselves up on the ship and steam out to the site before they even started the business of trying to cut the submersible free.

A quarter of an hour later he was about to escalate the

situation and demand to see a senior officer when he caught a glimpse of something familiar outside the aircraft. He turned to see a Royal Naval uniform coming up the ladder. When he looked up he immediately recognised Captain Holloway, Naval Attaché to Moscow.

'Hello, Ian, fancy meeting you here,' he said. 'What seems to be the problem?'

Riches' scowl eased as Holloway explained the hold-ups. 'We'll get this cleared up, we've just got to play the game a little,' said Holloway before turning to his companion, a Liaison Officer from the Pacific fleet.

The customs and immigration staff had their own procedures to follow, and didn't feel the same sense of urgency. When Holloway had arrived an hour and a half ago he'd been told he would be taken back to his hotel to rest after the flight. He'd refused and insisted on being taken directly to the military side of the airfield to meet the C17 on landing – a process that had taken him the entire time.

After several minutes of discussion, Holloway told Riches that nothing could be done until customs had been cleared. His eyes warned Riches to be patient. Later he recounted the bureaucratic nightmare he'd been through when trying to clear musical instruments for a Royal Marine band into Moscow for a performance. Many tonnes of military-grade submersible hardware was a different league entirely.

Eventually the customs officer stepped on board, his face a caricature of an officious, poisonous character. He stepped around the inside of the aircraft, prodding and poking Scorpio and her supporting equipment, before demanding a manifest that listed the value of each item. Although equipment lists existed, they weren't in one document, and certainly not with a value assigned. Seething, Riches scrawled a list out by hand on a scrap of paper, conferring with Gold to help make estimates of value.

Neither of them knew what it would be used for, but muttered under their breath that the Russians may be calculating the benefit

of keeping it for themselves. When Riches handed over the completed – and barely legible – manifest, the customs official began
making an announcement. Riches found himself staring incredu-
lously as the interpreter finished the translation. If the team left
anything behind on Russian soil once they had finished their business, he said, they would be fined based on the value of the items.

As the customs officer laboriously went through the manifest
ticking off the items one by one, Riches called Neil Hopkins, one
of his team at Abbey Wood, for an update. It was two thirty in
the morning and Hopkins answered with a bleary voice, but he
was up to date. Nothing much had changed: the submersible had
not been rescued, and wildly different estimates of remaining air
aboard *AS-28* continued to pour out of various parts of the Russian
military machine. Finally, he confirmed that the US Rescue Team
were on their way and due in at about 20.15 local time, nearly two
hours behind them.

While Riches was struggling with the customs officials, the loadmasters had been anxiously scanning the airfield apron around
the airport looking for the lifting equipment they'd been promised
by the Russians. To get Scorpio, its umbilical reel and the control
cabin out of the C17 they needed a K-loader – a heavyweight version of the Atlas loaders that carry cargo containers at commercial
airports. Designed as a flat bed covered with rollers whose height
can be precisely adjusted, the K-loader could take the heavy equipment straight from the back of the C17's cargo hold. Without one
there was no easy way to unload without risking severe damage.

All they could see on the apron was one small crane, five flatbed
trucks and a forklift. The crane was no good – the plane's fuselage
would prevent it from being able to reach anything inside. James
Fisher Rumic kept a database of airports and airstrips with details
of what equipment was available where, but in Russia the true
state of facilities was hard to ascertain. Russian military transport
aircraft like the Antanov 124 come equipped with an internal crane
and gantry so that cargo can be offloaded at remote airfields with

limited ground-based assistance. With a 1.5-metre drop between the back of the C17's cargo bay and the concrete below, that suddenly seemed like a very good idea.

By 19.00 local time customs had finally been cleared, but there was still no sign of progress on finding a K-loader. Captain Holloway interrogated the ground crew, who shrugged. They had no K-loaders. There were Atlas-loaders over on the commercial side of the airport, but they are rated to less than a ton and would have collapsed under the weight of the containers. They claimed there was one around four hours away and it might be possible to send it up, but Holloway was doubtful that anything so far off could be achieved so quickly.

Rather than wait doing nothing, Gold suggested making a start by unloading Scorpio. It was closest to the back door and since it weighed only one and a quarter tons, the forklift should be able to get it out. It seemed a good idea, so the loadmasters slid it to the lip of the back door while Gold and the interpreter arranged for the forklift to receive it.

The yellow-and-red forklift was moved into place, its wheels were chocked, and the arms clattered upwards. Gold's face was taut. As the pallet bearing Scorpio was rolled backwards and on to the arms, the forklift began sagging forwards. Then, just as it seemed to be holding the load, one of the side windows popped out and smashed on the concrete below. The Rumic crew all jumped in shock, but the Russians hardly blinked and Scorpio remained in the air. The drama over, the ROV was slowly lowered to the ground with a juddering motion and then moved close to the crane.

But as fast as they'd started, they stopped. There was nothing more they could do without a K-loader. The loadmasters – their pride at stake – began working up a plan to offload the containers straight on to the flatbed trucks using an improvised system of ropes and pulleys. Riches was in no doubt they'd get everything out, but any damage to the equipment and the mission would be over. Squadron Leader Hewitt also had reservations: if the cargo door of his plane got damaged they might be stranded in Petropavlovsk until spares arrived, and that might take a very long time.

They'd flown 5,000 miles only to find that they couldn't unload their equipment. Riches had told his superiors – and the press – that they could pull this off, but their timeline relied on the assumption that they could get hold of the equipment they needed. But they couldn't and now they were stuck.

Riches called Neil Hopkins again, looking for any solutions to the problem. That's when he was told that while he'd been in the air the US Navy had escalated its response. It had four aircraft currently inbound. Alongside the enormous C5 with the main crew, one C17 with two Atmospheric Diving Suits had been launched from Phoenix, Arizona, while another had been despatched from Andrews Air Force Base outside Washington DC carrying a Deep Drone ROV and a generator in case of electrical issues. Both of these C17s were still several hours away from arrival.

Crucially, the US Navy had also discovered from a Russian aeronautical company that there was no equipment at Petropavlovsk airport that would be able to handle their containers, so they'd sent yet another C17 from Osaka, Japan, carrying the K-loader they needed so badly. This last C17 was only 20 minutes or so behind the C5 from San Diego.

The huge scale of the US response was impressive. The true significance of the rescue as a diplomatic mission was becoming clear. On the Russian side, they were evidently so desperate to avoid the political fallout from another underwater tragedy that they were willing to hand their oldest foes the chance of the glory of rescuing their own men, in their own waters.

All the team's hopes were now pinned on the imminent arrival of the US aircraft. If Riches could persuade their commanders to let his team use the US K-loader first, the head start might still be used to good effect.

Saturday, 6 August
SS + 51 h 32 mins
08.02 UK – 11.02 Moscow – *20.02 Kamchatka*
Petropavlosk-Kamchatsky

Even though he knew Russia well, a part of Captain Holloway was still reeling from the fact that he'd flown for nine hours through the night, across nine time zones, and still remained within the borders of the motherland. A larger part of him was worrying about the lack of a K-loader, for it was he who'd transmitted the requests to Vice-Admiral Avdoshin at the Russian MoD to have one present.

With the promise of salvation in the imminent arrival of the American team, Holloway began trying to think ahead to the next phase. He tracked down the senior Russian officer and arranged to take an advance party down to the ship to which they'd been assigned. He took Pete Nuttall and Marcus Cave, leaving the rest of the team milling about the plane, waiting.

Pete Nuttall stepped into the Russian saloon car to join Captain Holloway and Marcus Cave to head down to the port just as the long twilight was settling in. At 53 degrees North in August, there would be only four hours of darkness. The vehicle was rusting and its upholstery threadbare.

It took a little while for the tinny-sounding car to pick up speed. Every seam in the airstrip concrete made the car judder thanks to its knackered suspension, but Nuttall was just relieved to be leaving the plane and to get moving. He wanted to get his teeth into a part of the operation where he could actually do something. How Scorpio was going to be unloaded was not his problem. He needed to make sure that Scorpio could do the job when they got out to site.

The vehicle rolled noisily towards the gate, passing some gloomy hangars. He'd seen some situations in his career, but this one already felt like a surreal Cold War movie. Then the car passed in front of the imposing silhouettes of several MIG fighter jets. Further off the main apron, shrouded by the mist and hidden by bushes, giant Tupolev and Beriev bombers lurked.

The rain and the long, fading northern twilight made Nuttall feel at home. Although the military angle was new, the strangeness of being on Russian soil didn't faze him. He'd crewed on ships all over the world, including Nigeria, China, and Japan. He'd worked off Russian ships that had been chartered to offshore engineering companies, and admired the Russians as people. They might look pretty dour and serious, but they had a good sense of humour and they liked to party.

An engineer by training, Nuttall also appreciated that the Russians had designed equipment that was unlike anything seen in the West. The separate evolution had spawned everything from enormous hovercrafts and helicopters to completely different ways to lift heavy loads – such as a submersible – over the sides of ships. On Western ships, an A-frame is usually swung out over the water, but Russian vessels often used a system of twelve pulleys all mounted at different angles with a spider's web of ropes to control the deployment. It was complicated, but it allowed cargo to be landed anywhere on the deck without a big, expensive crane.

Although strange and exotic locations were a given in the offshore business, some things always remained the same no matter where you went. Since the boom in offshore oil exploitation in the 1950s and 1960s, the ingredients for successful underwater operations had been all but standardised. When new technologies appeared and were proven, they were taken up by all serious players. One of these was Dynamic Positioning. Guided by satellite, individual thrusters on each corner of a vessel allowed it to hold not only its position but also its orientation. Other kit made work easier or safer. Saturation diving bells were launched from moon-pools located in the very centre of the vessel, and cranes were fitted with compensators that could cancel out the movement of the swell beneath. Underwater tracking systems could monitor the location of any vehicle or diver in three dimensions on screens in the control room. But in the end these were niceties. Give Nuttall power and a stable platform, and he was confident he could get the job done.

Outside the airfield, the drab, military style of the architecture continued through the outskirts of town. The wide, potholed roads had been patched so many times it was hard to make out the original tarmac. Occasional wrecked cars studded the scenery. Ragtag groups of people stood around bleak concrete bus shelters whose walls screamed with indecipherable graffiti. Every now and then a bus or a lorry rumbled past, leaving the air laced with sulphurous smoke. A few of the vehicles were home-grown, boxy Ladas, but being so far east there were more cheap Japanese imports than anything else.

Lost in thought and anticipation, the three rescuers watched in silence as this strange and remote world rolled past them.

As they reached the edge of town, Captain Holloway turned and said a few words to the driver, who nodded. A few minutes later, the car pulled off the main road and stopped beside a bleak-looking shop.

'Right, what sort of chocolates do you like?' asked Holloway.

Nuttall and Cave looked at one another. 'Er, we're in a bit of a hurry, mate. Can we get going?' Nuttall replied.

Holloway knew better. He'd been on Russian Navy ships before. At his insistence the two men shrugged and came inside to help him pick out a bag full of chocolate bars – Curly-Wurlys, Mars Bars, Snickers, Picnics, Twix – and biscuits. Russia might lack a lot of things, thought Nuttall, but some stuff you could get anywhere.

The minibus lurched back on to the road and left the town behind. About an hour after they'd left Elizovo airport, they pulled off the main road and crunched to a halt in front of a security gate. A rusting sign indicated to Holloway that this was Petropavlovsk's civilian port. At the sight of the approaching vehicle, two guards with pistols on their hips stepped out into the road from their hut. Although it was not a military facility, according to official guidelines, permission to gain access to it would require a 45-day notice period. Holloway was praying that the two-track system would work here as it had at Moscow airport, but there was a chance that it would not. Thankfully, after only a ten-minute delay, the guards swung open the gates and pointed them in the direction of their designated vessel.

The team squinted through the windshield as they approached the jetty. Around a dozen ships were lined up alongside the crumbling concrete, one behind the other. In the darkness it looked to Nuttall much like other remote dockyards, dominated by looming hulls and cranes. Holloway, too, was used to the sight of Russian dockyards and reasoned that though the vessels might look rusty and decrepit, their designs were simple and rugged enough to withstand the decades of neglect. At least none of them were sinking, he thought. They finally stopped in front of one, the anchor-handling and buoy-laying Sura-class tug *KIL-27*. She seemed the best of the lot, her squat shape giving her an air of sturdiness, if not speed.

As they stepped out of the car a uniformed officer strode up to meet them. His aloof bearing, together with the thin red stripe nestled between the officer's stripes on his epaulette, marked him out as a member of the Naval Infantry or a staff officer, but his bearing and behaviour suggested he was from the feared Main Intelligence Directorate, the GRU. He announced that he was there to see to their needs, Holloway immediately recognised he would be watching their every move.

Led on board by this escort, the advance party stepped on to the rusting deck on which they were going to install their rescue system. While the ship's master was talking to Captain Holloway, Nuttall and Cave began plotting where they were going to install the gear. They would need clean deck space to weld down their control container, the deployment crane and the winch for the spool of umbilical cable, and there had to be a clear exit to swing Scorpio over the side. The master nodded, gesturing for them to look around and pick their spot. A welder would be despatched to help them immediately.

'We're also going to need a three-phase power feed, between 380 and 480 volts. And what's your hertz? A screen from the positioning system would be nice too,' Nuttall said.

The master frowned as he listened to Holloway's translation. 'There's no Dynamic Positioning on the vessel,' came the reply through Holloway. 'He says it's thirty-five years old.'

Nuttall caught his breath. How were they going to pull this off if they couldn't hold position over the site? But he didn't object. There was more than one way to skin a cat. Besides, there was nothing he could do right now – he had to work with what he'd been given. He and Cave began walking the deck to work out where their equipment should be sited. In the end there was only one place it could go: slap in the middle of the ship. But even then there wasn't a big enough gap for the crane to be installed and still leave room to swing Scorpio overboard. Workshops had been installed around the perimeter of the whole ship. The best solution would be to put the crane on top of one of them. They started to investigate.

'Jesus,' said Cave. 'Look at this.' He was kneeling on top of the workshop they'd identified as the only place to site the deployment crane. It wasn't ideal, since the crane would have to be at full stretch to reach over the side, but it was all they had. But Cave was holding up a large flake of rust, poking at more loose fragments that lay beneath. The whole roof was peeling away. It didn't look as if it was going to be able to take anything like the loads they were about to exert on it, and there was no way for them to check. Every other vessel they'd used on exercise had been taken through rigorous strength testing. Now, just when the stakes were at their highest, they were going to have to weld their crane on to not much more than rust.

Saturday, 6 August
SS + 51 h 40 mins
08.10 UK – 11.10 Moscow – *20.10 Kamchatka*
Elizovo Airport, Petropavlovsk-Kamchatsky

At 20.10 there was a roar from the darkening skies above the Elizovo airfield. The noise grew and grew until suddenly the enormous belly of the US Air Force's C5 dropped out of the low cloud. Its drooping wings were reaching towards the ground, which it touched down only seconds later. The aircraft didn't appear to be slowing down at all, its inertia carrying it further and further down the runway until it had all but disappeared. Riches was about to arrange a lift over to them when someone noticed it had begun taxiing back towards the UK team. At last, some good news, he thought. They were going to direct the C5 to park nearby, allowing easy coordination. But the huge American plane rumbled past, crossing the taxiway on which the C17 stood and on, eventually disappearing behind some trees and bushes. They were not allowed to stop until they'd got in front of the airport's commercial terminal buildings, two miles away.

Riches turned to the Russian escorts and asked them to take him over there in one of their vehicles. He was anxious to go and see them immediately to present his case to their senior officer, to try to persuade him to loan their K-loader when it arrived. Commander Kent Van Horn, the Commanding Officer of the US Navy Deep Submergence Unit, should be on board. The two men knew each other from the recent NATO exercise in the Mediterranean, so there was a chance he'd listen. But the Russians just shook their heads.

'*Niet.*'

Until the C5 had cleared customs, there would be absolutely no contact with the American crews, Riches was told. Worse still, there was some talk that he would not be allowed to see them at all. He tried everything. He talked calmly to the guards, reasoning that this delay could be costing the lives of their countrymen. He demanded to see superior officers. He tried veiled threats of future repercussions.

Every time the same reply came back: 'Just wait.'

Commander Kent Van Horn sprang to his feet as soon as the C5 stopped, and was waiting by the hatch when the crewmen broke the seals and swung it open. He was poised to leap out into the waiting fleet of transport vehicles that would rush his men down to the port and on to the vessel to which they'd been assigned. But his square jaw fell open when he saw what awaited him on the tarmac. There was not a vehicle in sight. Instead, walking up to the unfolding aircraft's steps was a scrappy group of around eight people, some in uniform, some not. And rather than looking glad to see them, the expressions of the military men were sour as he made his way down the stairs and across Russian soil to meet them.

Van Horn must have appeared as the archetypal American to the Russian welcoming party – 6 foot 3 inches tall, broad, with a prize-fighter's jaw and gleaming white teeth. He was still in his trainers from the flight, and shook hands with the man who appeared to be the senior Russian officer. He was greeted by a few gruff-sounding words in Russian, accompanied by gestures towards the aircraft. At his side, an attractive girl in her twenties in civilian dress translated into thickly accented English.

'You need to get back on the plane,' she said.

Van Horn protested, but was told that until the correct checks had been made, no one on the plane was allowed to get off the aircraft. Realising there was nothing he could do but cooperate, he walked back up the stairs and into the C5, followed by a handful of the Russians.

'We need to see your passports,' the translator said, following another burst of harsh-sounding language from the Russian officer when they'd got back inside. Van Horn was incredulous. This was the last thing he had expected.

'Not everyone has them,' he replied. 'We have military IDs instead.'

The Russian accepted this, and one by one the American crew filed past to present their IDs. With each of the 36 men on board, the Russian compared the photo with the face, then wrote down the name on a clipboard. Van Horn was itching with impatience – the whole procedure struck him as a monumental waste of time, given the situation. They'd flown direct from the US across the entire Pacific, refuelling the aircraft twice mid-air in order to shave off every possible minute, and now this.

Then the Russian officer demanded the same as he had of the UK team – a complete list of all equipment and its value. The request had caused enough problems with one C17 load of gear – for Van Horn to do the same thing with the contents of a C5 was a huge task. In many cases ascribing a value was also practically impossible – much of the kit that they carried was custom-made in the Navy workshops, or at least customised to such an extent that its worth was very difficult to gauge. Once more van Horn had to swallow his frustration and agree. He took one of the loading manifests and snatched figures out of the air to reach a wild estimate of the total. Once again, the customs man made him sign to guarantee that he would take it all out of the country when they were finished.

Behind him in the plane, frantic calls were being made to try to speed things along. The US Naval Attaché in Moscow eventually got through to Vice-Admiral Avdoshin, and finally, at 22.10, the C5 was cleared.

Saturday, 6 August
SS + 53 h 40 mins
10.10 UK – 13.10 Moscow – *22.10 Kamchatka*
Petropavlovsk-Kamchatsky

Now the waiting was eating away at everyone. The lack of urgency from the Russians seemed doubly acidic given that seven of their fellow servicemen were enduring a slow, frozen suffocation. The looming crisis seemed to be making them slower and more bureaucratic. The central government was apparently taking this seriously – a few hours earlier the team had heard that Putin had despatched the Defence Minister, Sergei Ivanov, to Kamchatka – but progress on site was still glacial.

All of the team's hard-won speed reaching Petropavlovsk had been wasted. It remained to be seen if the entire mission would be wasted too. The thought of facing the television cameras with that news made Riches' stomach tighten. Beyond that, he could only have imagined how such a failure might feel. He could rationalise it all he liked, deflecting the blame onto others, but deep down he'd feel it had been his responsibility. The only thought that loosened the knot in his belly was that the advance party was down at the ship making preparations there.

The state of the vessel didn't sound encouraging, but at least they were moving ahead where they could, planning and preparing the decks. All that was needed now was some equipment to put on them.

The team had congregated beneath the wings of the C17, and were drinking cups of tea and coffee to pass the time. Gold had instinctively turned on his phone when he arrived, and to his surprise found that it had picked up a signal. He called Susan and shared his frustration. They were in Russia, but paralysed. He'd been elated at the thought that the UK team was going to be first in line to pull off this rescue, but now their lead had evaporated.

After he'd hung up and was back kicking his heels under the wing, he noticed some activity around one of the flatbed trucks. He went over to have a look, only to find several soldiers wrestling to change a flat tyre. Gold could hardly believe the state of the truck. The wooden deck of the flatbed was totally rotten with holes everywhere.

Half an hour later, while still waiting for the USAF C5 to clear customs, the clouds opened once more to reveal another transporter. This time it was a C17 like the RAF's, looking like a toy compared to the bulk of the C5. The British team all watched with interest where it would be directed to park. It ended up on the same taxiway, but about a mile closer to the terminal buildings. The thinking was baffling. The aircraft was nearer to the British aircraft than their US counterparts in the C5.

It was a full two hours after the C5 had landed that Riches finally managed to persuade the Russian officers guarding them to take him to the American aircraft. With the northern sun finally set and darkness fallen, he walked up the stairs to the cavernous belly of the C5. He'd been preparing his arguments carefully, but after all this waiting he was sure that the US team would be reluctant to allow another delay to their own operation. To his relief the first person he met was Van Horn, but he'd forgotten how huge the American was. He felt like a Jack Russell facing a bull mastiff.

Riches tried to smile casually as Van Horn's shook his hand in a bone-crushing grip. He launched straight in. 'Kent, we've got a problem,' he said. 'The Russians promised us they'd have a K-loader here for us. They don't, and we're stuck. We've already prepped our VOO [Vessel of Opportunity] and we're all clear to go, but we just need to get our gear off. We've only got our single Scorpio and its kit, that's it – your stuff will take twice as long to unload.'

Riches reminded himself to slow down. His words were coming out in a torrent, having been bottled up for two hours.

'I need to borrow your K-loader. Half an hour is all I need. The C17 with your K-loader is parked closer to us than you. It can make the trip up towards us and be back with you in no time. We'll get out to the incident site a few hours ahead. As you know, that might be the difference between life and death. What do you think?'

Van Horn's eyes narrowed as he thought about it. He'd brought along almost 40 people, partly in order to allow him to split his team into three sections who could all work on separate tasks at the same time. But his carefully choreographed plan was already stumbling over Russian inefficiencies and lack of equipment. There weren't enough trucks to be able to transport their kit down to the docks in parallel with the British – everything had to be done in serial fashion, one after another. The Brits were well ahead with preparing their ship, and it was certainly true that the UK's single Scorpio was going to be quicker to shift. Besides, he hadn't even seen his ship yet.

But there was an important factor that was missing.

'How are weather conditions on site, Ian?'

'All our reports are that they are holding. It's looking as good as it gets right now,' Riches replied.

'And projections for the next twenty-four hours?'

'We're still working on that,' he said. The low pressure system that had hung over the airport was intensifying, but as yet there was no evidence that things would change out in the bay.

Van Horn nodded. Part of the reason that the US system was so much bulkier than the UK's was that they had come with a much more heavyweight deployment system. The single Effer crane that the UK had brought to lift Scorpio in and out of the water would quickly be overwhelmed by bad weather. When recovering the ROV in a strong swell, the one-and-a-quarter tonne machine would be supported by a wave one second and left hanging in the air the next. The resulting 'snatching' created huge dynamic loads that had the potential to tear the lightweight crane apart and leave them without a way to bring the machine back on board.

The US Deep Submergence Unit had brought along a purpose-built mini-A-frame that was strong enough to deploy their larger Super-Scorpios (at 3.5 tonnes more than twice the weight of Scorpio) in conditions up to Sea State 4, with swells of up to two metres. If bad weather was going to be a factor then this could make the crucial difference, allowing them to launch successfully.

A few seconds later Van Horn nodded. 'Okay,' he said. 'If the sea's looking good the right answer is that you take the K-loader first. But listen, we've got to run this past the Commodore first.'

Riches' heart sank. They'd brought along a Commodore. This was presumably to have sufficient authority to match any high-ranking Russian officers – a Commodore was equivalent to a senior Russian Captain or even a junior Admiral. Like a game of chess, if a diplomatic situation arose you needed to be able to match powerful pieces with powerful pieces. The military hierarchy is persistent, and even if two nations are at war the relative superiority of ranks are mostly respected. But if the US had brought a Commodore without a detailed knowledge of submarine rescue he might not realise the benefits of letting the UK use the K-loader first, or even put political interests ahead of practical importance.

Their fears were unfounded, and Commodore Mike McLaughlin of the San Diego Submarine Squadron immediately agreed. Riches breathed a sigh of relief. The UK team had cheered in the aircraft when they had heard they would land ahead of the US team, but that competitive spirit had now evaporated. They knew very well from exercises that cooperation was the key element in submarine rescue, but real-life operations could sometimes play out differently. Now it was clear to Riches that this was not a race between the various submarine rescue services, but a race against time. And, so far, it was time that had the edge.

Fifteen minutes later, a low rumbling grew from the darkness in the direction of the terminal buildings. The noise got louder and louder, until finally the American K-loader appeared with a forklift trundling along by its side.

Just forty minutes later, all the UK equipment had been rolled out of the back of the C17, on to the K-loader and then loaded on to the waiting flatbed trucks with the Russian crane. While some of the trucks had the standard twistlocks to secure shipping containers at their corners, most of the gear had to be lashed down with ropes and chains.

Riches stared in disbelief when he saw a couple of police cars pull up. The last thing they needed was another level of authority to hold them up now that they were finally ready to get the equipment down to the docks. But he was mistaken: this was their escort. As soon as two of the team had hopped into one of the truck's cabs, the whole convoy began to roll.

Gold was watching the convoy as it disappeared into the distance, looking unhappy. Not for the first time, Riches wondered if Gold's partner at home ever felt jealous of his devotion to that machine. Little did he know then just how prescient Gold's concern would turn out to be.

It wasn't long before a drab, military grey minibus arrived to pick up the rest of the team as well. Finally things were moving, Riches thought. But once he'd slammed the door the driver set off in the wrong direction. They weren't headed for the gate at all, but back towards the terminal. The driver explained – through the translator – that they had to go and pick up the American team, who had just been given permission to go and inspect their vessel. Riches shook his head in the darkness. Surely the Russians could have allocated more vehicles for an incident that had evidently become a national concern?

It was close to midnight when they finally escaped Elizovo airport. The night was pitch black as they made their way out of the gate and down the wide, smashed roads. The minibus's suspension was shot, giving the passengers a precise feeling for the state of the road surface beneath them. In contrast, the heating worked extremely well. Within minutes they wished it didn't, as it was stuck on full blast and everyone was slowly roasting.

The streets of Petropavlovsk were dimly lit by irregular street-lights that caught looming shapes of concrete buildings, sections of huge pipework and occasional wisps of escaping steam. Cavernous potholes forced the bus to a near standstill at traffic lights. No one was on the streets, and there was hardly a car in sight. There was silence in the bus as everyone peered into the darkness, all lost in their own thoughts. It had begun to rain again.

At the edge of town the bus slowed, and turned on to a dirt track. As it headed into absolute blackness the atmosphere on the bus changed. This couldn't be the main road to a military port, Riches thought. The Russian officers on board – one of whom had delighted in revealing that he worked in Intelligence – were talking between themselves in low voices, and even the interpreters were starting to look uncomfortable. The thought crossed Riches' mind that they were being taken to a dark corner of the city to be despatched, as if they were in some John le Carré spy story.

Then a glow appeared ahead, against it the silhouettes of defunct-looking cranes and crumbling storage facilities. Soon they could make out the side of a rusting ship lit by yellowing spotlights. An officer announced that this was the *Georgy Kozmin*, *AS-28*'s mothership, that had returned from the site in order to host the American rescue team. Only her stern was tied against the dock; her bow was held out in the bay by two anchors. It was a strange way to be moored as it made loading difficult. It was common in crowded Mediterranean marinas, but there was no other ship close to the *Kozmin*. Then again the dock didn't look like anything Riches had ever seen before: it was more muddy field than concrete jetty. The Americans were in for a tough time, he thought. Just getting the vehicles down here with all their equip-ment was going to be bad enough; transferring it on board was going to be a nightmare.

There was no time to commiserate. The US advance party was dropped off and the bus turned straight around, threading its way back up the dirt track to the main road and then onwards to the port. Finally it pulled up to the gate, rain streaming down in front of the floodlights and rattling the roof. The tension in Riches' chest released a fraction when he saw the entrance. They'd arrived. Finally they were going to be able to do what they'd come all this way to do.

Then the guard stepped from his hut. His body language was wrong. Kalashnikov at the ready, he marched up to the window and began barking questions at the driver. The Russian officers stepped out into the rain and began explaining who the party were, but the guard was having none of it. Riches had been told of Captain Holloway's delay at the gate, but assumed that now everything had been explained their admission would be a short formality. At last the guard agreed to call his superior and after ten long minutes another official approached the inside of the gate, hunched against the rain. He demanded all of the team's passports, then disappeared.

More minutes rolled by. Riches asked the Russian translators what was going on, but they shrugged their shoulders. He asked them to find out, but they shrugged again. He called Captain Holloway, but got no answer. Then he got out of the bus and hailed through the fence to the guard.

'Hello! We are here at the request of the Ministry of Defence, on an urgent mission. You have to let us in!' he called.

The guard ignored him.

'Guard! Time is running out! Come here and explain the delay!' Riches shouted, hardly able to control the frustration in his voice. He was standing in the drenching rain, yelling and waving his arms, but the guard would not even look his way.

Riches climbed back in the bus, slammed the door and swore. He took a deep breath. This delay was not a major problem, he told himself. Holloway and the others were already inside and they'd be let in eventually. It didn't help. Maybe he was still tired from the flight, but black thoughts were returning. If they'd had this much trouble just getting to the ship, what was waiting for them when they headed out to sea?

Saturday, 6 August
SS + 54 h 35 mins
11.05 UK – 14.05 Moscow – _23.05 Kamchatka_
_**AS-28**_**, 210 metres beneath Berezovya Bay**

Captain Lepetyukha's one good lung was labouring hard from the increased carbon dioxide level, and the cold had now penetrated into his body's core. He was trying to focus on keeping the crew under control, but it took him minutes on end to recover after speaking even a short sentence. He could see the others struggling too, and having to rest after every movement.

Popov and Ivanov, two of the younger Warrant Officers, had begun vomiting, a sign of oxygen deprivation. Lepetyukha was stretching the endurance of the V-64 canisters too far. He relented, and ordered a new one to be opened.

Everybody was drowsy, numbed with cold and crazed with thirst, but order had to be maintained. Lepetyukha commanded Milachevsky to keep making the hourly report. All through that long night he sent them, telling the world above that pressure on board _AS-28_ was normal, and the temperature stable at 4°C in the front compartment, 8°C in the aft.

In tough times Russian men often resort to a rousing song to keep up their morale, but Lepetyukha had banned all singing in the interests of conserving air. Not that anyone in the cramped, dripping compartment would have the energy.

Sergei Belozerov, the 34-year-old electromechanic, was still working to keep the spirits of his fellow sailors from sinking too far. Whenever his watch showed it was time for breakfast, lunch or dinner aboard the mothership, Belozerov hauled himself up from the huddle and passed out the crackers with great ceremony.

The dry fragments of cracker stayed sharp on their tongues for what seemed like hours afterwards. Worried by the tiny reserve of water remaining, Bolonin had cut their water ration to only two mouthfuls of water each per day. Lifting the mug took such an effort that they needed to rest for 15 minutes afterwards, but the sailors looked up gratefully at Bolonin as he passed it around.

With Captain Lepetyukha all but incapacitated on the floor, the experienced submariner and civilian engineer had become the one to whom they were all looking for guidance and hope. Although respectful, they could be more familiar with him than with their captain. As Milachevsky relinquished the water mug, he looked up at Gennady Vasiliyevich Bolonin and with a grim smile said, 'Well, Vasiliyevich, you have not quite made it to your sixtieth birthday.'

Bolonin nodded. 'Perhaps. But you will make it to yours. I know this British system of rescue very well. You will see,' he said with as much confidence in his voice as he could muster. He did know all about the international rescue community, and knew that with their involvement their chances of escape were indeed growing. But he also knew how much still stood between them and the fresh, warm air above.

Saturday, 6 August
SS + 54 h 45 mins
11.15 UK – 14.15 Moscow – *23.15 Kamchatka*
On board *KIL-27*, Petropavlosk-Kamchatsky docks

The naval architect Marcus Cave had grave reservations about the strength of the roofing where they needed to weld the 6-tonne Effer crane. Not only was the upper surface rusting away, but so too were the supports beneath it. That didn't bode well for the steel in between. Like everyone on the team, he was suffering waking nightmares of his being the weakest link that spelled the end for the Russian submariners. Given the condition of the deck he could just see it – an 11-hour flight, a traumatic offload, the hard work of installing everything while time was racing by, the sprint out to the accident site and then, as Scorpio was lifted over the side, the sickening scream of tearing metal as the crane – and operator Charlie Sillet – disappeared over the side.

'This deck won't hold,' Cave said to Captain Holloway. 'We're going to have to strengthen it before installing the crane. Can you ask these guys where the welders we requested are?'

Holloway nodded. He'd asked for three or four welders to be at the ship to meet them in order to speed up their mobilisation, but so far had seen no sign of them. He approached the Ship's Master, but a huge black dog suddenly appeared on the flying bridge above him, snarling and barking. He tried to ignore it and began talking, but almost immediately another wolf-like animal appeared behind the Master, also barking fiercely. Finally he raised his voice, and explained to the master that the deck needed strengthening to take the crane.

The Master laughed, and after the din had been calmed somewhat, relayed Holloway's words to his Deck Officer with a smile. The man shook his head, and delivered his reply with upturned palms and a shrug.

Holloway frowned, and turned back to Cave. 'He says not to worry. Apparently they carried much bigger, heavier equipment than our crane on that bit of deck just last week.'

Cave nodded. Considering the state of the ship that just made his fears worse. 'We're going to have to strengthen it anyway,' he said. 'We need those welders. I'm going to go and find some suitable steel.'

Holloway turned back to the Master and tried to explain what they needed in order to start work, but suddenly realised he had not got a clue how to say 'welder' in Russian. His language training had been tailored to the demands of high diplomacy and cogs of bureaucracy, not to dockyard operations. On deck in his Royal Naval uniform, he began as dignified a mime of a welder as he could muster.

Thankfully it didn't take long to get the message across,

and a bearded Russian soon appeared from a deck store with a weathered-looking oxy-acetylene torch. '*Da*,' said Holloway, and added that they needed four such sets.

The Master shook his head. State regulations only permitted one welder to be working at any one time, he explained. Holloway took a deep breath. He should be used to this by now, but somehow he'd hoped it would be different in an urgent rescue situation. Protocol in Russia was a powerful force indeed. Holloway insisted and eventually the Master pulled out his mobile phone and called the port authorities, but it was soon clear how the conversation was going. The port was run by civilians who were remote from the Navy's problems. They felt no urgency to break the law. Holloway's attempts at eroding their stance came to nothing, and they were left with just one welder to strengthen the deck and secure their equipment.

Once Pete Nuttall had finished pacing out deck areas to plan the placement of the various pieces of equipment that were now on their way, he joined Cave in the half-lit darkness on the pierside, and together they began picking their way through the scrap that lay around in the weeds, looking for suitable pieces of steel to use as reinforcement.

Saturday, 6 August
SS + 55 h
11.30 UK – 14.30 Moscow – *23.30 Kamchatka*
Petropavlovsk-Kamchatsky

Nothing was shifting at the security checkpoint. The rain still beat down. The guard was still in his hut, the door closed. Only the minute hand on Riches' watch was moving, steadily creeping around the face. The frustration was making his skin crawl.

After 30 long minutes, the official reappeared on the other side of the gate. The guard spoke with him for a second, then walked over and handed over the passports without a word. The gate swung open and the bus was waved through. Later it transpired that when a new shift had come on duty they had not been told anything about a foreign military team arriving in the dead of night. Riches suddenly felt a little guilty about his outburst at the gate. In the guard's position he'd have been just as suspicious.

The bus followed the road onwards into the port, winding round jagged piles of discarded marker buoys, rusting anchors, chains and old boats. Finally it turned a corner and the jetty appeared. Cranes were offloading Scorpio and the rest of the equipment from the lorries. Riches glanced up at the ship that was moored up alongside. Holloway had warned that the Sura-class buoy tender *KIL-27* was a little rough, but Riches hadn't been expecting quite such agricultural technology. She looked as though she'd been abandoned for months, even years.

Just as he was starting to get that sinking feeling again, he saw a familiar figure in Russian uniform at the bottom of the gangplank. The shock of white-blond hair was unmistakeable. Gold was leaning forward in his seat. He'd noticed the same man.

'Would you look at that!' said Gold. 'It's Dmitriy!'

They spilled out of the van and on to the dockside, and Dmitriy Podkapayev came striding over, a big grin on his face, and enveloped both Gold and Riches in bear hugs. Just two months before they'd been with him in the Gulf of Taranto. Russia hadn't participated in the NATO exercise, but had sent along a handful of observers, and Podkapayev had been one of them. He'd come aboard the UK's mothership more than once and seemed to have taken a shine to the British way of doing things.

Podkapayev – and his loud, frequent laugh – had been a big presence on the exercise. Having him in Petropavlovsk was a relief for the team as not only would they have an ally but also someone who understood and trusted the way that they worked. Though he spoke no English, it was obvious that he was eager to get things moving as fast as possible. Worry lined his expressive face.

* * *

Captain Holloway was waiting at the top of the gangplank to introduce Riches to the Master, who immediately began a welcome speech. The mariner looked as though he was in his mid-fifties, with nicotine-stained hands and teeth and wearing a woollen sweater that was unravelling in several places. As the words kept coming, Riches began to try to cut him off, but a look from Holloway stopped him. The Naval Attaché patiently translated the Master's words, as he described how proud he was that his ship had been selected to assist the British rescue effort.

Dogs were barking, apparently from every part of the ship. The sailors who passed by were all dressed in jeans and black-and-white striped T-shirts, their faces unshaven. Riches felt like he'd walked into a rusting, steel-clad gypsy camp. Although the ship was owned by the Russian Federal Navy, the crew were evidently civilians – a similar set-up to the buoy-laying vessels the Royal Navy sometimes contracted to conduct submarine rescue exercises. It turned out that they were devoted to their ship: they'd recently fought and won a battle to save her from the scrapyard. They hadn't found any more money for upkeep though – *KIL-27* looked like she'd had no maintenance during 40 tough years of service.

When the Master finally wound up his speech, Riches thanked him and told him how honoured the team were to be on board and that they were keen to get their gear loaded and secured as soon as possible. The Russian took this as encouragement, and began a tour of the vessel's essentials. Riches tried to look interested and impressed as they ducked inside the first hatchway and wound their way down a filthy, dimly lit passageway and into the Mess. It was cramped, bare and grimy. If an army marches on its stomach, this one wasn't going very far, he thought. After looking in on the cabins, they finally began walking aft towards the door that he hoped would get him back out on deck. At the last minute the Master stopped, took his arm and led him back to a scuffed, oil-smeared door just forward of the outer hatchway. With a toothy grin he swung it open.

Riches almost gagged at the aggressive stench of excrement. The room was bare except for a stack of torn pieces of newspaper hanging on a string and there was a hole in the deck through which he could make out a ragged circle of sea. The Russians were using the 18th-century version of the ship's lavatory, and were missing their target regularly. They'd better get this rescue done quickly, he thought.

The crane driver revved his engine to get more power and a black plume of diesel smoke drifted across the floodlights. He swung the arm over to the waiting trucks with impressive speed, and soon the hook was flying down towards Scorpio's control container. Just before impact there was a loud metallic clunk from the crane's gearbox, and the hook jarred to a halt.

Steel wires were fixed to the corners of the container and slipped over the hook, and the crane started to lift. Everything was holding. But when the crane's arm swung back towards the ship it did so at the same high speed. Alarmed, Riches asked Captain Holloway to remind them that the rescue equipment was fragile and had to be treated gently. The answer came back that the operator would do his best to be gentle, but that the crane had only two speeds. Watching its progress, he could now see this was true: uncontrollably fast, or stopped.

The disintegrating infrastructure in Russian ports was notorious. The cranes in the Naval dockyards had all been built in Odessa when the Ukraine was still joined to Russia as part of the Soviet Union. The last maintenance contracts were awarded in 1998, but since then there had been none. As a result, only three of the 14 100-ton cranes operated by the Russian Federation Navy still worked, and of the 63 40-ton cranes, only 17 were operational. In 1999, the Commander-in-Chief, Admiral Vladimir Kuroyedov, had formally requested new funding, declaring that Naval ships couldn't offload their weapons for critical inspections because the cranes were a safety hazard. Kuroyedov eventually won a $17m contract for new cranes and essential maintenance but, despite the Deputy Prime Minister saying he would personally supervise the budget, in early 2000 the funds were diverted into building a new submarine instead.

Only months later the *Kursk* exploded, and investigations revealed that the huge and temperamental Shkval 'Fat Girl' torpedo that caused the initial blast had landed hard on the dock-side during loading nine days before the accident. The jerky movements of the long-neglected crane had caused the chains and strops that were holding the missile to slip and, in order not to lose it completely, the driver had been forced to get it to the ground, fast.

Two months before that, in June 2000, a crane accident in the Pacific Fleet had caused a missile to release some of its toxic fuel, killing one sailor and injuring another 11. Loading live weapons with decrepit equipment was so dangerous that once shipped on to the submarines that carried them, they were often not offloaded either for maintenance or for exercises. If they had been, the devastating secondary explosion that ripped through the *Kursk* would not have happened.

Scorpio's control centre – housed within its converted 20-foot shipping container – was landed safety thanks to a skilful piece of braking by the crane operator just before it hit the deck. Nuttall, his long hair matted on his back from the rain, didn't look concerned. He said he'd seen plenty of dockyards whose cranes were a bit rough and ready. They were designed for loading and unloading bulk cargoes, he reasoned, but the operators were usually used to their quirks and got pretty good at their job.

Scorpio itself was next. The crane driver had been told several times how fragile the equipment was, so all they could now do was hope. Tense concern reappeared on Gold's face as his precious machine was jerked off the flatbed truck and swung over the midships section of *KIL-27*. Scorpio hung there for a second, then the crane driver let the cable spool out. It was hell-raisingly fast, apparently uncontrollable. The driver stopped its fall halfway with a jerk, and allowed Scorpio to settle again before releasing it once more. Twice more the cautious driver stopped it, getting the robot to within a metre or so of the deck before trying one last spool-out. Scorpio crashed to the deck, even bouncing slightly before settling. Nothing fell off, but it was as hard an impact as he'd ever seen it take.

Saturday, 6 August/Sunday, 7 August
SS + 57 h 30 mins
14.00 UK – 17.00 Moscow – *02.00 Kamchatka*
Petropavlosk-Kamchatsky

Back in a bleak, grey apartment block in Petropavlosk, Yelena Milachevskaya lay in her sister's bed looking at the phone. She was still unable to eat. At least Artyom was looking after the girls, taking them out for walks and giving them food. What would she have done without him? Following Guzel Latypova's lead, other journalists had filmed interviews with her, and now her sobbing face had become a staple on the news reports about the ongoing drama.

Marina Belozerov, wife of Warrant Officer Sergei Belozerov, whose café was doing such brisk business on the stricken submersible, could not bear to remain inactive any longer. She had hardly slept at all since first hearing about the accident almost 60 hours ago, and had not let her phone out of her hand in case she missed some news. When she heard that the British rescuers were about to head out on a ship, she gathered up her daughter and made her way to the Naval headquarters. She had to get on board and get closer to her Sergei. If he died, she wanted to be as near as possible. If he escaped, she wanted to be the first to see his smiling face.

They were turned away at headquarters. There was no room on board, they were told, and their presence might hamper the efforts to rescue the men. Reluctantly, Marina led her daughter away and back into the night.

Tatiana Lepetyukha was not so easily deterred, as befits the wife of the captain. The quiet, insistent voice inside her head that had guided her since her father's death had returned at the church service she'd organised the previous day. It told her that all was not lost, and that a bad ending was not yet a certainty. Deep within herself she had a growing feeling that all was going to end well. The voices – for there were now several of them – didn't end there. They told her that she had to be on the rescue vessel, as close as possible to her husband.

Leaving her 13-year-old son at home to look after the dog, she made her way to the Naval headquarters. First the guards, then the officers tried to assure her that things would be smoother and easier without her there, but she didn't listen. She would not take no for an answer. It was an impulsive decision, but was no less firm because of it. A part of her was watching her insistence as if from outside, cringing at the thought she was making so much trouble for Valery's beloved Navy at a time like this. But the inner voices won, and she persevered.

Eventually, the Master decided to let her come on board. When a woman is in such a state of mind, he thought, it would be very difficult to stop her. *KIL-27* was a civilian ship after all, and there was already a woman on board, working in the galley. He weighed up the danger of her breaking down in hysteria or with a panic attack and decided to bring a doctor along from the hospital just in case. She was ushered on board quietly, without informing the British rescuers, and told that under no circumstances must she interfere.

Saturday, 6 August/Sunday, 7 August
SS + 57 h 50 mins
14.20 UK – 17.20 Moscow – *02.20 Kamchatka*
Petropavlovsk docks

It was almost half past two in the morning before the UK team had a chance to sit down with Dmitriy Podkapayev and get a full briefing on what awaited them beneath the surface. While the rest of the crew continued to shift, unpack and prepare equipment, Stuart Gold, Captain Holloway and Comander Riches followed Podkapayev's white-blond head down a peeling passageway and into the officers' mess.

They filed in, finding places to sit on disintegrating chairs. Beneath the harsh lights of the cabin, Podkapayev looked haggard; his shoulders rigid, his eyes dull and tired. Despite Russia's enormous geography, the members of the Priz fleet of rescue submersibles were relatively few and he'd trained with three of the trapped men from time to time. He didn't know the younger sailors, but he was worried for them too – they were little older than his own son. More than anyone he was concerned about his good friend Gennady Vasiliyevich Bolonin. He'd spent many long evenings with the civilian engineer, the esteemed co-designer of the Priz class, back in Nizhny Novgorod. And Podkapayev knew that though Bolonin's mind was bright, his 60-year-old body was not as robust as it once had been. How would he be dealing with the freezing temperatures, his lungs heaving ever harder to feed from the thinning air?

Podkapayev began talking in bursts, waiting with barely restrained impatience for Captain Holloway to translate before continuing.

'I'm not sure what reports you've heard, so I'll start from the beginning,' he said. 'The *AS-28* is stuck at 210 metres, trapped in cables. The depth of water is about 230 metres. The accident happened when they were inspecting an underwater antenna. We have seven men on board, and their air is already very limited. They have been down there since Thursday – almost three days. At our most optimistic estimates, they have between twenty and twenty-four hours of life remaining. I have reports from the bathyscaphe's commander, as well as some photos and video taken with our Tiger ROV.'

In the cramped and salt-sticky cabin Podkapayev pulled out a modern, state-of-the-art laptop from his bag. He fed it a DVD. The grainy pictures showed swirling sediment, and each of the team strained forward to see what was there. A white band moved across the screen. At first they thought it was interference on the camera, but Podkapayev jabbed at it with his finger. Sure enough, in a few moments it resolved into the striped paintwork of the submarine's hull.

The picture got no better. For 15 minutes the British rescuers peered into the jumping, distorted images. Any clues they could glean from the recording would give them a head start and maybe even prompt them to make adjustments to Scorpio before she went down. But for all their eagerness to make sense of it, they couldn't see enough to draw any firm conclusions about how the vessel was trapped.

'Can you explain to us what's going on? Maybe you got a better idea while watching it live,' Gold said, and Holloway relayed the question.

Podkapayev nodded. From a file he pulled out a simple line drawing showing two long tubes – the floatation tanks – and up at the far end of the upper one, the submersible with a cluster of lines wrapped around the fin. From the picture it looked as though the craft could just reverse to free itself, so something was obviously missing. Various dimensions were scrawled on the drawing, the numerals jumping out from the Cyrillic characters. The tubes were huge – 102 metres long. They floated 8.5 metres above the bottom on chains anchored to large concrete blocks on the seabed. *AS-28* was ensnared towards the top of the array some 25 metres above the seabed. That meant working mid-water, without the ability to stabilise Scorpio by resting her skids on the seabed.

Seeing the diagram, Gold brightened. It was a clear representation of the situation at last, even if it was incomplete. He began asking questions, starting with what the lines were made of. This was of vital importance. Scorpio could cut wire cable up to 20mm with ease, but they had also brought LR5's cutter, which could be fitted to Scorpio. It was more unwieldy, but it could cut up to 70mm. So far all he'd heard was that none of the lines were larger than 18 mm, but nothing could be taken for granted. All Podkapayev could do was shrug.

'We've tried to estimate from the pictures. I can only show you what I saw,' he said. He turned back to his laptop and pulled up some colour images. Their quality was better than the video, but despite lots of discussion and theorising no one could say for sure what the lines were made of. If they were rope then that was one thing, if they were wire it was quite another.

'Okay,' said Gold. 'We've got a picture of how things look down there now. Now we need to work out how things are going to look up top. Since this ship does not have Dynamic Positioning, what kind of an anchor web are you thinking of?'

Gold was long in the tooth enough to have worked off ships and platforms that had no DP and were held in place by an altogether more rudimentary system: anchors. With one – or sometimes two – stretching from each corner on long cables, a work barge could be accurately positioned by reeling in or slackening off the cables. It was slow, cumbersome and affected by changing tides, but at least it was safe; trying to operate an ROV from an unsecured vessel without Dynamic Positioning was a sure way to lose the vehicle. Currents and wind would push the ship around, tugging at the umbilical. Sooner or later the ROV would hit something or get tangled up with something on the seabed. If the ship was being carried away the all-important umbilical might be stretched, kinked or snapped. But pay out too much slack to try to avoid this and you risked a loose loop of umbilical drifting into the path of the ship's propellers, which would be equally disastrous.

Holloway relayed the question.

'The water there is too deep for *KIL-27* to anchor. We don't have enough cable,' Podkapayev replied.

Gold looked over at Riches, alarmed. Podkapayev caught his expression and began explaining in fast Russian, taking a salt shaker from the table and motioning with his hands across the cracked lino table. Seeing blank looks on their faces, he called out of the corridor and a minute later a sailor appeared with a whiteboard and a marker.

He drew a triangle to represent *KIL-27*, then two other triangles at either end. 'These are ships that are able to be moored on site. They have enough anchor cable. They will be positioned at either end of the hydrophone array. When we arrive, we will attach lines to them from our bow and stern, and they will hold us in position.'

Gold was staring at the whiteboard, his eyes flicking between various parts of Podkapayev's diagram. He was calculating the stresses and strains, testing the idea in his head, trying to work out how the complicated set-up would react to different winds, currents and swells. He'd never heard of anyone using such a system, and neither had the others. Podkapayev was adamant that it would work, but if it didn't Scorpio could end up being lost – together with the men they were there to rescue.

'I'm not sure it can be done. There's any number of things that could go wrong with it,' said Gold. He knew only too well that, given time, the sea would find the weakness in their system as surely as it would find cracks in a hull. 'But it sounds like it's our only option. All we can do is give it a try.'

Much would depend on the weather. Remembering his assurances to the USN Commander, Kent Van Horn, about the condition of the elements, Riches asked Podkapayev what the latest forecast was.

Podkapayev nodded. 'For the moment it is good – calm and with only small waves. But there is a front coming in from the southeast. We don't know when it will hit.' With that he looked around the table at each of the three men. The question in his eyes was unmistakeable. This would be the main problem then. Without heavy winds or swells pushing them around they had a good chance of remaining securely moored between the two ships. But if conditions worsened then the complex chain of connections between the anchors and their vessel could amplify the movements, giving them real trouble. They'd have to be on their toes; if the weather came in fast from the wrong direction, Scorpio could end up getting trapped with its umbilical acting as a further noose around *AS-28* and the men inside it.

Saturday, 6 August/Sunday, 7 August
SS + 58 h 40 mins
15.10 UK – 18.10 Moscow – *03.10 Kamchatka*
Petropavlovsk docks

It was past three o'clock in the morning and still there was work to do to ensure everything was secured on deck. The single welder did his job methodically, the glowing beads of molten metal creeping with agonising slowness across the joints. Once the half-deck where the crane would sit had been strengthened, Marcus Cave and Charlie Sillet set the welder on to attaching the crane itself. Its arm would be at full stretch when lifting Scorpio, putting a lot of strain on both the deck and the welds. If something gave out, it wasn't just the ROV and the crane that would go crashing into the sea. Given Sillet's seat on the front of the crane, he'd most likely follow them down.

As long as the weather didn't turn nasty, there wouldn't be nearly as much strain on Scorpio's control cabin. Instead of wasting valuable time waiting for the welder, the crew of the ship were sent to find chains and shackles with which the cabin could be lashed down. With that done, Riches went with Captain Holloway to inform the ship's Master that they were ready to go. Riches told him he was confident nothing was going to fall off the ship if they started moving and that, in this weather, the welder could finish the job as they made their way to the rescue site. It had stopped raining, the wind was light and the sea looked calm.

The Master listened, nodded and agreed the ship was ready to depart. But nothing happened. No orders were given, and on the dockside there was no sign of imminent departure; no-one was standing by near the mooring ropes or preparing to stow the gangplank.

As they waited, Kent Van Horn called and asked if the British had any divers on their team. The answer was no. Low on space, they'd brought only a stripped-down squad to operate Scorpio. Van Horn was worried about what might happen if the trapped submersible was freed and came to the surface in an uncontrolled manner. If *AS-28* hit one of the surface vessels, it might become ensnared once again, or worse, damage a buoyancy tank and sink back to the seabed. Divers might well be needed to investigate such problems, or at the very least act as surface swimmers to remove debris from the submarine when it appeared on the surface. He'd brought some elite Navy divers – and a Navy doctor well versed in decompression sickness – and, since the UK team would be reaching the site first, it would make sense if they joined the UK's vessel of opportunity rather than stay on theirs.

It was a good idea. Riches had established that *KIL-27* had no divers and no medical facilities, despite the fact that they were a standard requirement on any rescue vessel. Beyond treating the effects of prolonged exposure, dehydration and foul air, the atmosphere inside a damaged submarine often slowly becomes more pressurised as water seeps in, exposing the men inside to decompression problems once rescued. Whether there were any medics on any of the other Russian vessels was unclear, but it was far better to have a spare doctor than end up with none.

Riches put the idea to Podkapayev, expecting an enthusiastic response. Instead he shifted uncomfortably and looked down at his feet as he replied that there was really no need, and that the Pacific fleet had both divers and doctors on hand. Riches nodded, but pressed his case. These were some of the best divers and medics in the business – having them on board could help and would certainly not hurt. The problem was evidently political, but thankfully Podkapayev had witnessed the efficiency of having backup teams during the NATO exercises and – after interminable checking with his superiors over the radio – agreed that the divers could be taken on board.

Saturday, 6 August/Sunday, 7 August
SS + 58 h 50 mins
15.20 UK – 18.20 Moscow – *03.20 Kamchatka*
The Elizovo–Petropavlovsk road

With the offload of the C5 at last complete, Kent Van Horn had finally managed to leave the airbase and was heading for the dockyards. He had with him his ship-preparation team together with the three divers and the Medical Officer. Van Horn was feeling strangely dislocated, not just as a result of the unfamiliar geography, but also of the strange atmosphere. He found the marked lack of alacrity surreal, as if nothing was really the matter. All the training he'd been through with his team had been about doing everything they could to shave vital minutes off the response time. Yet here he was, sandwiched between two Russian military personnel, bumping through a pitch-black night in drizzling rain, about to do a school bus-style drop-off at different vessels because the Russians couldn't spare enough vehicles to give each team a separate ride. Twenty-four hours ago he'd been in bed with his wife, looking forward to the weekend, and now he was somewhere – he wasn't quite sure where – in the Russian darkness.

The bus passed through the dockyard gates with minimal delay, and lurched up alongside a rusting ship. Van Horn twisted in his seat, readying himself to jump out, but the Russians gestured to him to stay put. Instead they stepped out of the bus, shut the doors and walked over to the ship. There was a short conversation and the Russians walked back, got back inside, and explained that this was the US ship, not the UK one where the divers were to be dropped. Orders were given to the driver who took off again, bumping down the potholed dirt roads of the dockyard, taking a tortuously circuitous route through the rusting machinery. Ten long minutes later, the bus pulled up alongside another rusting ship. Again the Americans were kept inside while the Russians talked with the sailors on the dockside. Once again they returned and got back into the bus. There had been a mistake, they said. The first ship had in fact been the British ship – *this* was the one that had been assigned to the Americans. Van Horn and the other members of his advance party were not allowed to get out, however. All of them had to go all the way back to the first ship to drop the divers on the British ship before returning to prepare their own.

At 03.40 the minibus finally arrived back at *KIL-27*, and the four American divers jumped out and hotfooted it up the gangplank with their gear. After being introduced to the Master they were shown to their quarters by one of the Russian crewmen. They returned two minutes later, their noses still wrinkled. Whether it was an intentional message or not, lying in the middle of their allotted cabin was a huge, fresh pile of dogshit. Carefully avoiding the mess, they put down their kit bags, together with a box of ration packs, and made their way back out on to deck.

The ship's engines had been running since the team had boarded in order to get power to their equipment and to the welder, and their throbbing had blended into the background of the busy thrum of activity on deck. The US divers and doctor had been on board for around ten minutes when Riches felt the deck shift beneath him. He looked up from what he was doing to see the docks sliding past. A dockworker – having evidently just let go of the ship's lines – was scrambling backwards, fast. With a terrible screeching noise, *KIL-27* scraped down the concrete jetty and sheared huge chunks of concrete off the pier.

Normally in a ship this size, if you couldn't get tugs to pull you from your berth you prised the stern from the jetty by pushing forward against mooring ropes attached to the bow, then reversed away. It didn't take long. Instead, *KIL-27*'s captain had decided to steam out ahead under her own power, and lots of it. The rudder was hard over to starboard and the ship was wreaking havoc both with the pier and with her own hull. None of the crew seemed to bat an eyelid. Having more than one welder in an emergency was out of the question, but destroying the harbour on departure was evidently fine.

Worried about power fluctuations caused by the welder, Gold had not yet allowed Scorpio's control container to be connected to the ship's power supply. He needed a constant supply of anywhere between 380 and 460 volts, but sudden peaks and troughs could cause havoc. Now, with everything in place and the welder's torch just reinforcing the spot welds holding down the control container and the umbilical cable winch, Gold asked for a pause in the welding work, took a deep breath and engaged the main circuit breaker, linking Scorpio's electrical systems to the Russian vessel's for the first time. Several gauges in the control van sprang into life, but the needles settled on 360 volts. Gold paused, took a breath, then double-checked the main connections. Still the three-phase power coming to him was short. Although Scorpio was supposed to function at anything from 380 volts, he'd never made do with less than 400 before.

Gold called out to Holloway to alert the ship's electrician. Ten minutes later, Holloway returned, having asked the Master to shut down all non-essential electrical power to the ship. All electrical capacity available on the ship was now being routed towards Scorpio's control cabin, he said. Gold flicked the switch again and the voltage needle jumped up and settled. Gold groaned: 375 volts.

'We'll just have to wing it,' he said. He'd passed on the vehicle's electrical requirements to the Russians via Holloway in the initial flurry of communications, but this was evidently the best they'd get. There would be damage in the long run and the thrusters might be sluggish, but for now all systems should operate just about normally, he reckoned.

Inside the 20-foot-long control room, a converted shipping container, Gold went through his standard system checks. The basics seemed fine. He double-checked Scorpio's umbilical cable connection to the control cabin's external port. He knew that Forrester and Nuttall would already have done this, but years of experience with the unforgiving sea had taught him the value of triple-checking. He'd yet to fire it up, but when he did the umbilical cable would carry all the vehicle's power (stepped up to 11,000 volts to reduce losses in the 1,500 metres of cable), low-voltage connections for running the guidance systems and coaxial cable to carry video from Scorpio's cameras. A shield of steel fibres twisted around them, while around that a yellow rubbery coating ensured that the whole thing was almost buoyant in the water and so wouldn't pull the vehicle either up or down.

Gold ran his eye from the connection down the cable, on to the winch and on to the vehicle. It was always possible that it could have got snagged on something sharp or had something dropped on it during loading, and with such high voltages it was vital to spot a possible short-circuit in the cable before putting power through it. But all seemed normal.

So, the moment of truth. Through long experience with ROVs, Gold had been trained to expect things to go wrong with them. The mix of seawater and electronics was never a good one, and a major part of being an ROV pilot was knowing how to fix them when they went wrong. Thankfully, Scorpios were different. They were the most reliable models available, and with Gold as its continuous and faithful guardian, this particular Scorpio had never had more than the usual small niggles here and there. Powering her up ahead of the launch was merely a matter of habit, a final check to make sure he'd be able to deploy as soon as the ship had a stable position above *AS-28*.

'Okay for vehicle power?' shouted Nuttall from the control cabin.

'Yep, everybody clear,' Gold replied from the deck.

'Okay, firing her up!' came back Nuttall's voice.

There was silence for a few moments while Gold waited for the telltale flash of Scorpio's main lights. Nuttall would then flick each of them on for a second – no longer, or the hot bulbs would burn themselves out without the cooling effect of seawater around them. He'd test the electrics – the cameras, lights, sonars – then run through the hydraulics. Each of the thrusters would whirr only briefly, designed to run for longer only with the resistance of water around them. Last of all the manipulators would take a stretch and the cutter would snap shut a couple of times.

But the seconds stretched out, and nothing was happening. Gold looked back towards the cabin. Silence.

Inside the control cabin, Nuttall could feel a frown spreading across his forehead. Two of the cameras had flickered into life, but the other two were completely dead. So was the sonar. Something was wrong. It wasn't even worth flicking through the thrusters and lights if this wasn't working. Without sonar, Scorpio would be completely blind. There was no point in diving at all without it – they'd never get close enough to the submersible to use the cameras, even if they could do the job on the two that were working.

Gold's face appeared in the door. 'What's going on?' he said. Nuttall shook his head.

In ten years of looking after Scorpio, Gold had never switched it on and got such a strange combination of faults. He closed his eyes for a second, as though gathering his thoughts, but inside he was trying to loosen the sudden grip around his heart. It was like a nightmare. All this way, and now sailing towards the site of a genuine accident, where men's lives were at stake, and for the first time ever the bloody system doesn't work. He'd been training for this very situation, existing for this very rescue, for what seemed like most of his life. And now this.

The two men wasted no time chasing the voltages down through the system. Gold quickly ascertained that the problem was within Scorpio itself. There was no power at all getting to the starboard pod. He drained the main termination box of the oil that protected it from both pressure and water, then opened it up and began testing the connections inside. Meanwhile, Nuttall was stripping out all the connectors between the two long watertight containers that held the electronics. The connections between the pods were common areas to find faults, and it was easier to replace them rather than check them.

With all main connections changed and the earth connection to the main termination box tightened, Gold turned on the power once more. Scorpio stirred. Another camera twitched, but nothing more. This was unlike anything he'd ever seen. Was the low voltage causing the problem? He pulled out the manuals and started to check the voltages all the way through the system. It seemed to get more and more confusing; nothing was making sense. Ordinarily, finding a fault was like a detective story, slowly narrowing the options until you'd got the culprit cornered. But now every time he opened up and inspected a new component there seemed to be more faults and things got more complicated, not less. It was as though the system he knew so well was suddenly speaking a different language.

Knee-deep in manuals and circuit diagrams, Gold was starting to sweat. Not only did he need to solve this for his own self-respect, but he could also feel the eyes of the Russian sailors on him. The US Navy divers were pulling out their Iridium phones to tell their people that they'd better get a move on because it looked like the British team had tanked after all.

Gold was trying to reassure himself that he knew Scorpio, that it was just a machine and a reliable one at that. There were always causes, and there were always solutions. He'd get to the bottom of it, no problem. Whether or not it was fixable was another matter, but that's why it was important to have redundancy. With the Americans close behind them and the Australian oil exploration vessel steaming up from the south, at least the sting would be taken out of a failure by the British team.

Saturday, 6 August/Sunday, 7 August
SS + 60 h 40 mins
17.10 UK – 20.10 Moscow – *05.10 Kamchatka*
***Georgy Kozmin* mooring**

Just past five o'clock in the morning, more than an hour after *KIL-27* had left the dockside, the trucks carrying the US Super-Scorpios finally arrived at the dockside. Commander Kent Van Horn looked longingly at the crane and wished it would immediately swing into action, but instead was drawn into protracted discussions with the ship's Master, Captain Novikov.

One of the pack of journalists that had been sniffing outside the gates of the port, Oleg Kashin, had managed to slip inside and got talking to Andrev Yuryevich, the second assistant to Captain Novikov. Yuryevich was dismissive of the US Navy's efficiency. 'The Americans were late, they were,' he said. But when he realised that Kashin was a journalist, he changed his tune. 'No help can be unnecessary,' he oiled. 'It is indeed a military fraternity . . .'

Meanwhile, the dark shape of a new ship, bristling with antennae, had appeared in the harbour. Fraternity or not, the presence of the Americans was evidently still suspicious enough to warrant a dedicated surveillance vessel.

With two C17s and the enormous C5 on the ground, Van Horn was becoming increasingly suspicious that the Russians were trying to obstruct them. Forty minutes ago – at 04.30 local time –

an order had been received from a Russian Admiral to stop offload-ing the ADS suits. Van Horn wasn't too worried about the bulky atmospheric diving suits: the helicopters needed to transport them to the ships on station had not materialised, making them useless. In any case, it now seemed that none of the vessels had enough clear deckspace to take a helicopter delivery.

But it did bother him that his Super-Scorpios had been halted at the same time. The trucks had rolled up to the airport gates only to be told that they should go back to their aircraft and wait. The British team were already on their way to the accident site, the official had said, and American assistance would not be required.

Other than continuing to talk and calling their superiors to complain about the obstructions, there was nothing Van Horn or his team could do. Half an hour later, they'd been given permission to continue, only to run into more delays in getting the vehicles to the dockside. In their rescue projections they'd estimated a Time To First Rescue of 07.10, but after an hour's discussion with Captain Novikov it was close to 06.30 and they hadn't even started loading the ship yet, let alone found themselves steaming towards the incident site.

Now that he was at the dockside, it was obvious that loading was not going to be straightforward. With the vessel moored with her stern to the jetty and no crane available on the bank, they would be relying on the floating crane that had been provided. While up against the shore the crane's arm could reach their equipment but was unable to reach the deck where it was to be installed. To get their gear in the right place, they would first have to lift it on to the platform carrying the crane, move the barge that the crane was mounted on further towards the ship's stern, then lift the gear on board. It would at least double the time it should have taken them to load.

When the sequence of lifts and set-downs had finally been estab-lished, the crane started moving – just. Like the crane serving the UK's ship, the floating crane serving the US ship had two speeds, but in this case they were slow and excruciatingly slow. It would eventually take the team between three and four hours to load their equipment on to the crane's apron, another hour to move the crane into its new position, and another three to four hours to load it on to the ship. And while some of the port crew seemed to be anxious to move things faster, the majority seemed completely unconcerned by the slow pace of their progress.

Other elements of the large-scale American effort were also falling away. Another C17 containing a Deep Drone ROV system was supposed to land at Elizovo at 06.55 local time, but was stuck on weather-hold at Anchorage, Alaska, instead. With the ILS at Elizovo airport down, they had to wait for the weather to clear enough to ensure a safe landing. The bad weather and low cloud that had threatened to repulse the British rescue effort had finally arrived, closing the airfield to landings. The RAF C17 had squeezed in just in time.

During the glacial loading of their equipment, the US team on board the *Georgy Kozmin* soon came across the British-built Venom ROV that Captain Novikov had initially deployed to try to free *AS-28*. As part of his team, Commander Van Horn had brought two specialist ROV technicians from the civilian marine technology firm, Oceaneering. They inspected the stricken robot and found the umbilical cable had been badly mangled – apparently by its own thrusters – but otherwise the unit was pretty new and in good shape. They had all their tools and reported that they could swiftly effect a professional repair job; since there was nothing else for them to be doing, they would have been glad of the occupation. Their offer was sharply declined.

Van Horn was now fuming. It was nonsensical. This was an emergency situation. If the technicians had managed to get a fix with the Venom ROV, he had pilots able to operate it. The *Kozmin* could have sailed with that, rather than waiting at least seven hours for the ancient crane to load the Super-Scorpios. The Australian ship from Shell Exploration had reported that it would not reach the site until 08.00 on Monday morning, and given the problems the British were reporting, backup was now vital. But for all his efforts, Van Horn's explanations, demands and pleas fell on deaf ears. He was beginning to appreciate just how deeply Russian culture had excised original thinking. There was no reward for coming up with solutions or thinking outside the box, just punishment for not doing exactly what you had been told.

Commander Bill Hamblett had been passing the time on the ship watching the Russian officers. He'd noticed that Captain Novikov was often accompanied by senior Russian Naval staff. He didn't look happy, and from the scraps of conversation that he'd managed to overhear it seemed the commander of the *Georgy Kozmin* was already being dressed down for his part in the accident – for deploying *AS-28* without means to rescue her if there was a problem, and for allowing a non-qualified person to use the Venom ROV and destroy it in the process. Hamblett got the distinct impression that the officers were there to relieve Novikov of his command once the Americans had left the ship. He was also getting a strong feeling that the Russian officers didn't want the Americans involved in the rescue, nor for Novikov to have any chance of playing a part in a successful outcome.

Saturday, 6 August/Sunday, 7 August
SS + 63 h 30 mins
20.00 UK – 23.00 Moscow – *08.00 Kamchatka*
***KIL-27*, Berezovya Bay, 52°18′N, 158°43′E**

After five hours of steaming, an hour ahead of the Master's esti-mate, a flotilla of grey, military vessels and shambolic-looking civilian ships and tugs appeared on the horizon ahead of *KIL-27*, marking the vessel's arrival above the huge hydrophone array and the submersible it had ensnared.

Gold glanced up to see the assembled fleet. Scorpio lay in pieces in front of him, both pods stripped out, and his team were still running through the mazes of connections and circuit boards with manuals propped open in front of them. They were closing in on the rescue site, and still they didn't have a functional rescue vehicle. Time was running out.

The dogs weren't making anything easier, either. Every time anyone moved about on deck, the huge black Rottweiler half-breed on the bridge deck above would give a blood-curdling series of barks. The German Shepherd guarding the main deck would respond fiercely, while guarding the one patch of deck that the team needed to get to. When not actively defending its territory it was marking it out, relieving itself on Scorpio and the control cab. Trying to shoo it away was treated as an attack. Eventually, it was led away by one of the crew, leaving only a spaniel wandering the aft deck.

By 09.00, all the circuit boards inside both of Scorpio's pods had been re-seated, connectors had been changed and everything that could be re-secured with duct tape had been. Before re-sealing the pods, Gold took a deep breath and went back to the control cabin to try powering up the vehicle again. If Scorpio didn't work this time, he didn't know what he was going to do. He'd tried everything.

He flicked the switch. For a second everything seemed to freeze, and then all four camera screens burst into life with images of rusting deck. Gold's eyes flicked from gauge to gauge, checking power levels and sensor functions. He turned a dial on the sonar and felt his stomach unclench as its familiar wedge of orange static sprang on to the screen.

He didn't cheer, not yet. He walked to the container door and looked out at Nuttall, and nodded quietly. Moving back indoors, he flicked through the lights one by one.

'Front main check good, rear check good,' came the call. This was more like it. He switched on the hydraulic pump, and moved the joystick forward. He could hear the comforting whirr of the thrusters before Nuttall confirmed it.

'Dive thruster check good,' Nuttall shouted. Gold move the stick to the left, then the right. 'Lateral one check good, two check good,' he heard.

They were in business. The only thing that seemed strange was that the main front camera was showing a picture in black and white, not colour. He'd never seen that before, but Gold put it down to the low voltage, which was still hovering around the 375-volt mark. He sat down heavily in the pilot's chair and let the relief flood through him. Nuttall walked in with a lopsided grin. 'Whisky?' he said.

'That'd do the trick, aye,' said Gold. 'But not yet.'

Nuttall usually brought some whisky along – his father had shares in the Arran distillery, shares that paid out in different vintages of malt rather than in cheques. But they were a long way from being able to celebrate anything. They still needed to get the casings back on the pods; sealing them up properly was vital. It was all too easy to rush putting things back together, and at the pressures which Scorpio would soon be experiencing, a small mistake would mean a flood of water and a dead vehicle.

First the seats of the O-ring seal were carefully cleaned to make sure they were free of any grit, then the rubber O-rings themselves were inspected and greased with a thin film to help them slide around and seal any minute gaps. With the lid carefully placed, the hex bolts around the casing were screwed in on alternate sides, ensuring an even application of pressure. Although each member of the team had done it hundreds of times before, none of them were any less cautious. Mistakes here were easy and this time they would be expensive, not just in electronics but in terms of human life.

Just as *KIL-27*'s engines began to slow, indicating that they'd reached the site, Scorpio was back together again. At last, holding a steaming cup of coffee, Gold looked across the deck and out over the western Pacific. While the ship's crews sorted out the unorthodox mooring arrangement, he'd have a little time to gather his thoughts for the next phase of the rescue. Seeing calm sea and its unruffled surface, he could hardly believe their luck. More than anything, good weather could be a lifesaver. It didn't matter where in the world you were – you could be right off the Scottish coast, surrounded by the best underwater intervention technology available, and if the sea was in a bad mood then there was nothing that could be done until the storm had cleared.

Saturday, 6 August/Sunday, 7 August
SS + 64 h 50 mins
00.20 UK – 03.20 Moscow – *09.20 Kamchatka*
Rescue fleet, Berezovya Bay

The time was 09.20, and *KIL-27* was wallowing in the limp sea. Tugs were pushing the *Alagez*, a large submarine salvage and rescue vessel that was acting as the command ship, and the *KIL-168*, a Kashtan-class rescue and crane ship, into position with excruciating slowness. Huge black clouds burst from the tugs' funnels and water churned from their sterns, but progress was slow. Podkapayev's plan was that together the two big vessels would hold *KIL-27* in position, with the *Alagez* across the bow with three anchors out and *KIL-168* tethered astern with a single anchor stretching from her bow. The several large and small tugs would help with the precision control.

A light wind was blowing from the south-west, accompanied by a slight rolling swell, but essentially the weather was perfect. Wires were attached to both *KIL-27*'s bow and stern, and stretched towards the *Alagez* and the *KIL-168*, but manoeuvring was not easy. There were two little tugs bumping and boring into the starboard side, trying to shove the ship laterally into position.

The Submarine Rescue Service's initial estimate – made just hours after they'd heard of the accident – had been that they'd make contact with the trapped submersible within 36 hours and now, despite the countless delays, they'd at least made it to the accident site in that time. Commander Riches pulled out one of the three laptop-sized satellite phones they'd brought with them and began to set it up on the deck outside the Scorpio control cabin; he wanted to report the good news to the MOD command centre in Northwood. He twisted the antenna towards the equator, then realised there was an enormous iron derrick in his way. Holding the bulky equipment in front of him he shuffled towards the bow, looking for a spot with a clear view of the sky that wasn't guarded by the dogs. That's when he spotted one of the American divers, apparently delivering a report to his CO on an Iridium satellite phone no bigger than an early mobile phone. He felt a flash of envy. Then he remembered where he was. If he was feeling resentful at technology five years ahead of his, how must the Russians feel about being surrounded by gear that was 30 years ahead of theirs?

Gold had asked Podkapayev to put their ship in a position where the trapped submersible would be between 150 and 250 metres off their port beam. They needed their ship to be far enough away to be clear of the Russian submersible if they managed to free it and it came shooting to the surface, but not so far that Scorpio became uncontrollable. The umbilical cable that joined Scorpio to the ship was slightly heavier than water, and if there was too much off the reel it would start to drag the vehicle backwards.

On a vessel with Dynamic Positioning, getting themselves in the right spot, and facing the right direction to deploy Scorpio over the port side, would have been a matter of clicking on the desired spot on a digital map and setting the orientation of the ship. Thrusters would hold the ship on those exact coordinates until they – or the weather – decided it was time to move her off. Dynamic Positioning was like being strapped in one position despite the shifting surface of the sea. Their current, makeshift system of being strung between two ships was more like working from a kite blowing in the wind. If things started to go wrong, they'd go wrong very quickly.

Attaching lines to the two other ships had been accomplished fast, but getting the whole assemblage into the correct position was a different matter. Their tenders were not designed for pulling other vessels, and the resistance from *KIL-27*'s hull to being dragged sideways through the water was evidently immense.

Just as the ships began to make finer adjustments, an Anoushka-class fast missile boat roared up alongside the *Alagez*, its distinctive white radar dome and triple torpedo tubes stabbing either side of the bow beaming menace. The Russian top brass had arrived to supervise the situation, including the Defence Minister, Sergei Ivanov. There was now quite a fleet clustered on the surface, though it was nothing compared to the *Kursk*. Then, 12 combat ships, 21 rescue vessels, two diving ships and five search planes had been scouring the sea, first for the submarine, then for sounds of life, and, finally, for clues as to what had happened.

At 11.15, Podkapayev finally turned up at the Scorpio control cabin and gave the nod. They were in position. The ROV team gathered together around Scorpio while everyone else hung back. In a calm, quiet voice, Gold began to run them through the plan.

'Let's all take it nice and easy. We've been blessed by the weather, so let's make use of it as long as it holds. As you all know, our platform is hardly stable. We're trying something that we've no experience of, and we're still not sure if it can be done. I'm sure you've all heard what happened to the Venom that the Russians tried to deploy – they got it all tangled up and now it's a nasty mess. If we're not very careful the same thing could happen to us. That's got to be a major worry, so everyone let's stay focused on that umbilical the whole time. Will, you've got to be on that winch every second, paying out and taking up slack as we shift about – and believe me, we're going to be shifting about. This time if we get tangled it's not just embarrassing or expensive, it could mean guys dying. So nice and slow. Yes, we're in a hurry, but taking an extra minute now is better than screwing it all up for ever.'

With that everyone moved to their stations. Gold stayed beside Scorpio, his hand resting proprietorially on the starboard floatation tank, while Nuttall walked into the control cab, sat down in the pilot's chair and began a second series of pre-flight checks, running through the lights, camera and thruster functions one by one. Everything was working fine, except for that rogue main camera that was still giving only a black-and-white picture. Will Forrester took his position at the winch's control panel with the enormous spool of umbilical poised for deployment in front of him, the apparent simplicity of the direction lever and power switch belying the importance of his job. Charlie Sillet stepped up to the half-deck above and slipped into the crane-driver's seat.

'You got your extra lifejacket on there, Charlie?' shouted Nigel Pyne, standing beside Will Forrester. Sillet laughed, an edge of nervousness in his voice. When a crane is installed on a UK ship – even if temporarily for an exercise – after all its hydraulic pipes have been inspected it will be subjected to a full load test. Out here all they'd been able to do was put a bit of weight on the crane and stand underneath the deck to see if there was any flexing. Cave had added as much extra metal as possible, but to get Scorpio over the side the crane would be at full extension, putting maximum strain on the fresh welds that held the crane to the rusting deck. He was in position on the deck below, watching for any signs of trouble, but Sillet knew that if something went wrong it would in all likelihood happen too fast for him to get free.

'Okay, let's do it,' said Gold. Riches was about to give a nod, when he turned to Podkapayev. They were guests on a foreign vessel and needed to be sure everybody knew what they were doing.

'Okay to launch, Dmitriy?' Riches said and Holloway translated.

Podkapayev gave a half-nod, but held up his hand to say hold it there. He lifted his radio and fired off a quick burst of Russian.

'He's asking for permission to launch,' said Holloway. They waited. Holloway and Podkapayev conversed for a second, then

Holloway turned back to Riches. 'He's asked the Master for permission to launch, and the Master is now clearing it with the command ship,' he said, nodding towards the *Alagez*.

Nuttall appeared at the door of the control cab with a question on his face, but a look from Gold sent him back inside.

Five long minutes later, Podkapayev's radio crackled and he nodded to Riches.

Riches passed the nod to Gold, and added, 'Good luck.'

Gold motioned to Sillet with a circling motion of his finger, indicating to start lifting Scorpio. Gently the crane took the load, and everybody's ears braced for the telltale shriek of tearing metal. Nothing. The welds were holding. Gold's hand rested on one of the vehicle's yellow floats to stop it from swinging as David Burke and Alan Hislop cleared the deck of the wooden blocks Scorpio had been sat on. Gold gave Scorpio a little pat. Ten years together and now this was their chance to prove themselves.

Sillet began to dip the boom over the water, and a dull *bong* sounded through the deck as a piece of metal flexed. Riches' heart was in his throat, but Cave's voice came up from the deck beneath saying everything was holding.

With Scorpio clear of the deck, Gold gave the thumbs-down.

'Okay, Charlie, down on the wire,' Gold said, and Sillet started spooling out. At 11.30, 28 hours after they'd set out from Glasgow's Prestwick airport, Scorpio's frame hit the water, and soon seawater was washing over its bright yellow floats.

'In water, Pete, power on,' he said. When the current started flowing, each of the lights flashed on and one by one the thrusters whirred into life before spinning to a halt once more. When everything checked out, he lifted the switch mechanism he held in his other hand. 'Releasing the block,' he said, and pushed a button. A signal travelled down the crane's thick armoured flex and on to the coupling that held Scorpio, and with a heavy clunk the vehicle dropped free into the water.

'Bit of starboard lateral,' Gold said, as the vehicle swung slightly to port. The yellow umbilical was snaking loosely up on to the deck and into Pyne's hands, and was now the ROV's only connection to the ship. Connection was not the issue at this stage, however. Scorpio was dangerously close to the ship's hull. Gold needed to guide it out of danger as soon as possible, and kept feeding instructions to Nuttall until the yellow floats were 50 metres away.

'Okay, Pete, clear to dive. Go and get it,' Gold said into his boom mike. Most of their time with Scorpio together had been on simulated mine-recovery exercises for the Navy, and the terminology had stuck.

With a chopping snarl, the sea between Scorpio's two floats erupted into a distant fountain of white water and the yellow flash of Scorpio faded into the gloom.

'Diving,' came back Nuttall's voice from the control cabin. 'Fifteen feet now. Sixteen. Seventeen.' Like the C17 they'd flown in on, Scorpio was of American manufacture, so everything was in imperial units.

'Okay, out of sight of surface,' said Gold and he began walking over to the control cab. With Scorpio launched, he would now leave deck operations to Pyne and Forrester.

Inside, Nuttall was sitting at the control desk. Mounted in front of him were the four screens and a series of other coloured displays showing sonar readouts and battery levels. On the flat area were his flight controls, all centred around the joystick. Gold came in and stood behind Nuttall, while Podkapayev and Riches stood alongside, flanked by one of the interpreters. Even with only five inside it was already crowded. It was almost midday, and there was not a hint of breeze to dissipate the sun's heat.

The four cameras showed a blizzard of sediment caught in the lights streaming upwards, against a backdrop of darkening blackness. There was silence in the cab but for Nuttall's voice reading off the depths. As he went past 100 feet, the screens were showing fewer snowflakes and a pitch-black background. Riches could almost feel the pressures starting to crush in on Scorpio, and the fingers of cold probing around all the recently opened seals.

'Shifting past 345 degrees, a bit of port lateral on auto,' muttered Gold. He was keeping an eye on the electronic compass, keeping Scorpio pointed towards where the Russians said *AS-28* was stranded.

Nuttall frowned. Scorpio's nose was dipping. He leaned forward to a microphone on the panel. 'A little more speed on the winch there, Will.'

'Roger, more speed on the winch,' came the confirmation from Forrester. Scorpio settled back to its correct trim, the umbilical no longer lifting the stern.

The team were using an open microphone system, meaning there was no need to press a button to transmit. That allowed all hands to stay on the job at all times, be it piloting the ROV or operating the crane or tending the umbilical. It also meant that they could all listen in on what was going on inside the cab. Every one of them knew that their presence in the cab could be a costly distraction to the two ROV pilots. By listening in they could at least keep track of how the rescue was going.

As Scorpio passed 500 feet, Gold reached forward and started tuning the Ametech sonar mounted in the centre of the control panel. When the volume was turned up, a metallic throbbing sound filled the cab. The sound – like an idling circular saw – was the signature noise of an active sonar. Together with the pulsing signal on the screen it made part of Riches settle back into his submariner's skin. Like all of those in that room, Riches now felt as though he was on board the robot.

'Six hundred feet,' said Gold. 'Bottom is only about one hundred below –' Before he could finish his sentence, the pie-slice wedge that showed the sonic image of the water ahead of Scorpio suddenly filled with a hard-edged orange block, and the circular saw now sounded as though it were off-centre, scraping itself with every revolution. 'Holy moley. What the hell is that?'

'Antenna,' said Podkapayev. Even in Russian his meaning was clear. Gold and Nuttall looked at one another. That was a bigger sonar reading than either of them had ever seen before in the open sea. This thing was huge. It looked like a harbour wall, thought Gold.

There was a reason why the hydrophone was so enormous. Long wavelengths travel furthest, either through land or sea, so to listen out for far-away events an early-warning system needs to be able to pick them up. To do that, a microphone needs to be at least as large as that wavelength – in this case over 100 metres long, and 17 metres high. This unit was part of a network of similar arrays stretching a thousand miles up the entire Russian east coast, listening for rumbles from across the entire Pacific Ocean basin. Their exact locations were a closely guarded secret, but in this region they were reputed to be located seaward from the Schipunskiy Cape, from Anglichankai, as well as from Berezovya Bay.

The fact that the array was installed just below 200 metres was no accident. It had been suspended in the upper reaches of what is known as the Deep Sound Channel, a natural conduit that funnels sound far greater distances than at other depths. In the same way that the mirrored inner surfaces of a fibre-optic cable can transmit pulses of light round corners and over thousands of miles by continually reflecting the light, different densities of water above and below the Deep Sound Channel make them reflective. The upper boundary – at around 200 metres – is relatively warm and salty while the lower boundary – deeper than around 1,000 metres – is very dense and cold. Sounds produced in between them will tend to travel great distances, bending around the curvature of the Earth.

Russia was not the only nation to install listening posts in the Deep Sound Channel. The first SOSUS (Sound Surveillance System) network installed by the USA and UK became operational in the early 1960s, tracking Russian nuclear submarines as they passed through narrow channels between Greenland, Iceland and the UK. Other than passing through the dangerously shallow North Sea and English Channel, this was the only route that Russian submarines of the Northern Fleet could take when leaving their bases on the Kola Peninsula in the Barents Sea for the Atlantic or the Mediterranean. By picking up their acoustic signatures there Russian submarines could be tracked, either remotely via arrays, or physically with UK or US submarines. After it had proved its worth, the system was then extended to cover other areas in the Atlantic and the Pacific. In August 2000, the NATO arrays had picked up a strange noise – a noise that turned out to be the death-throes of the *Kursk*.

It took skilled operators to disentangle the sounds, but it could be done. In 2008, the UK's underwater listening post in Gibraltar was able to pick out the propellers of the *QE2* as she pulled out of New York. But while the metallic thrashing of a civilian pro-peller might be easy to detect, when cloaked with military sound insulation and muffled by distance, the signals become harder to read. For all humanity's attempts to scrape it clear of life, the sea is not a silent place. Snapping shrimp are infamous among sonar operators for the din they create, a marine equivalent of a field of screeching crickets. And whales also use the Deep Sound Chan-nel to communicate with astounding acuity. Some scientists believe that the blue whale – the biggest creature ever to have lived on this planet – is able to distinguish between individuals across the entire Pacific. Other sounds are more mysterious still. In the 1970s, sub-sea snoops were blasted with a noise that has remained unidentified to this day. It was loud enough to have been an underwater land-slide or earthquake, yet its waveform appeared to be biological in origin. If it was, then whatever produced it would have had to be bigger than a blue whale.

Approaching the array, Gold felt like he was looking at such a monster on the sonar. His role in the exercises that he'd taken part in over the years was always to find the submarines that were play-ing dead. Although such diesel-electric and nuclear craft can be huge, their hulls are usually coated in rubbery tiles. Aside from providing valuable heat insulation, they are specifically designed to muffle the probing pings of active sonar. A 100-metre submarine could have a sonar paint that was easy to miss. But not this hydro-phone array.

* * *

'Okay, let's hold this depth and get over there,' muttered Gold.

'Start feeding out there, Will, slow and steady,' Nuttall said into the deck radio, and started pushing Scorpio through the water towards the looming shape on the sonar.

The room was getting hotter, and Nuttall was aware that beneath his long mop of hair his shirt was already starting to stink. He'd not had a chance to change since leaving Barrow-in-Furness. He put it out of his mind and concentrated on keeping his eye on the direction indicator, the sonar and the depth pressure gauge while continually scanning the instruments and warning lights for any sign of trouble. So far, so good.

Less than five minutes later, he slowed the forward thrust. The sonar reflection was menacingly close, but still he couldn't see anything in the unfamiliar black and white of the front camera display. Then something began to appear. A huge, curving wall of barnacle-coated metal filled the screen.

The video, stills and drawing they'd seen showed the *AS-28* up at the end of one of the cylinders with the structure on its starboard side, so Gold told Nuttall to head to port.

Twisting the joystick, Nuttall turned the vehicle in that direction and started heading along the side of the array, keeping the looming, sealife-encrusted metal on the right of the screen. The visibility was excellent compared to what he was used to. In the North Sea you'd often be lucky to see a metre, but here he could see more than ten. Scorpio pushed onwards through the light snow of sediment, but all that appeared from the darkness was more featureless metal until the enormous tube suddenly ended.

There was no submersible. Podkapayev began talking excitedly, and the interpreter explained that they must go around to the other side of the array and continue to the other end. Gold and Nuttall looked at one another. That meant having to loop the umbilical over the top of the array. In the rush to deploy Scorpio, *KIL-27* had been moored with the array between the ship and *AS-28*. Either that, or their improvised mooring system was moving a whole lot further than it should have been. Neither thought was particularly reassuring.

'We should reposition,' said Gold. 'If the umbilical gets stuck we're not going to be helping anyone.'

But moving over to the other side of the array could take hours, given how long it had taken to get into this position in the first place. After a short discussion, Gold nodded to Nuttall, who spun Scorpio around and began flying back along the top of the array, keeping it slightly to his right. With the vehicle travelling as fast as it would go – about two knots, or walking pace – the tubing passed beneath like an outsize pipeline, reminding both men of the endless oil and gas pipeline surveys they'd done in their offshore existences.

The array was now occupying the whole of the right-hand side of the long-range Ametech sonar display. Gold began twisting a knob on a second console, the high-frequency array. Pinging at 675 megahertz as opposed to the 100 MHz on the long-range, the colour Tritech was much more twitchy, but much more sensitive. Tune it right, and you could pick up the echo of a 5-litre paint pot sitting on a sandy bottom. The colour gave a sense of how hard the objects up ahead were, ranging from blue for non-existent, through hues that got warmer as the obstacles became harder until they became white for solid metal. With both sonars now groping forward beyond visual range, Gold suddenly cleared his throat.

'All right, what's this little beastie now?' he said. A white lump had appeared on the high-frequency array. 'Slow up a little there, Pete.'

Sunday, 7 August
SS + 67 h 32 mins
00.02 UK – 03.02 Moscow – *12.02 Kamchatka*
***AS-28*, 210 metres below Berezovya Bay**

When word came from the surface that the British rescue submarine was on its way, Gennady Bolonin flicked on the outside
navigation lights of *AS-28*. It might use up valuable battery supplies, but looking at the state of the crew anything that would bring
help faster was worth it.

Back in the aft compartment, huddled on the floor, the men's
faces were frozen masks. Their eyes were dull compared to the
glistening of the weeping submarine walls in the red emergency
light. If there was hope here, it was deeply hidden, thought Bolonin.
Then there was a murmur from the huddle. It was Milachevsky.
He'd heard something.

There was a visible straining of ears, and then Bolonin heard it
too, the almost unbelievable murmur of the foreign machine. It had
an electrifying effect. Milachevsky hauled himself up and through
the hatch to the forward compartment to the periscope. It was a
Herculean effort that left him panting and grasping on the handles
as he scanned the water around them. He couldn't see anything.

The murmur seemed to be coming down straight on top of
them. How had the British managed to locate them so precisely? It
seemed miraculous.

Standing at the periscope, Milachevsky's body tensed. 'It's
here,' he said, his voice a hoarse whisper. 'I can see the lights.
It's here.'

Sunday, 7 August
SS + 67 h 35 mins
00.05 UK – 03.05 Moscow – *12.05 Kamchatka*
Rescue fleet, Berezovya Bay

The flow of barnacles beneath Scorpio's runners slowed, and all eyes in the control van were boring into the grainy blackness of the front camera. Suddenly out of the gloom appeared a white stripe. For a second no one could be sure, and then there she was, solid and real, with '28' painted on her fin.

Looking at the squat, foreign shape of the Russian submersible's hull, Riches felt another surge of adrenaline tingle through his veins. He was now acutely aware that this was not an exercise, that there were men inside this steel container and that if his team didn't do their job properly they would not live.

Each of them was staring intently at the screens and control panel. Nuttall was focused completely on keeping Scorpio exactly where he wanted it, his eyes flicking between the camera displays, sonars and instrument sensors, trying to sense the conditions in the water around the robot and gauge any dangers to his mission. With the immediate piloting being dealt with by Nuttall, Gold was trying to plan the best way of reaching the visible lines that were trapping *AS-28*, mapping the shifting matrix of ships, anchors, umbilical cables and array structures at the same time as taking Scorpio's temperature from the various dials in front of him. Podkapayev's face was hard to read, as though buffeted simultaneously by both hope and fear.

'Take it easy there, Pete,' said Gold. 'Let's take a good look around before getting too close.'

Nuttall didn't need reminding. At the forefront of his mind for the last 30 hours had been the fear of blundering in too fast and getting Scorpio stuck.

Holding Scorpio still in the water, he began using the front camera's pan and tilt to take a look what was holding *AS-28* tight against the array. It seemed broadly similar to the diagram that the Russian survey had produced. Most of the cables were bunched towards the front of the fin. They had evidently been there for some time, for they had accumulated a crust of marine growth. From the propeller guard protruded what looked like a tuft of fishing net.

'Okay, let's go say hello,' said Gold. Nuttall nodded, and increased the power until the submersible's vertical stripes filled the camera and the solid cutting arm that protruded like an insect's proboscis struck the foreign machine's hull. Riches' mind was so fully inside the robotic vehicle below that he fully expected a loud 'bong' as metal struck metal. But there were no microphones on Scorpio. The silence that filled the room instead seemed chilling.

It was standard practice to tap a distressed submarine on first arrival, and Gold had done so on every exercise he'd joined. Even though the Russians said they had communications with the men inside, he wanted to create a bond between his team and the shivering, half-suffocated men inside. Given his experience of misinformation from the Russian authorities on the *Kursk*, he had no idea what condition they were really in. Morale might be the only thing that got them through these few final, critical hours.

In most submarine rescue scenarios, raising spirits was one of Scorpio's main functions. Aside from locating the site and testing the surrounding currents, checking hull integrity, conducting a radiation survey of a disabled nuclear submarine, and clearing any debris from around the escape hatches, Scorpio would carry down canisters of supplies to drop into specially designed hatches on the deck of UK and other NATO submarines. If the rescuers were in contact with the sailors, they could pack whatever was required inside the pods. If not, they would try and anticipate what would be wanted. Among the practical items like water and food were stashed whisky and pornographic magazines – anything to stir their resolve to live to see the surface again.

★ ★ ★

On the other side of the thick steel walls of *AS-28*, the effect of Scorpio's handshake was like having woken from a nightmare, and all the crew stirred, some managing to pass weak smiles.

'I told you they would be here, did I not,' heaved Lepetyukha. 'Now calm down. Conserve your energy. We're not free yet.'

Sunday, 7 August
SS + 67 h 50 mins
00.20 UK – 03.20 Moscow – *12.20 Kamchatka*
***KIL-27*, Berezovya Bay**

As Nuttall guided Scorpio back away from the hull, he squinted into the small monitor that displayed the rear-facing camera, checking no nets had drifted into his path. *AS-28* looked like a coffin, lying inert and lashed to the side of the huge cylinder of the array. Although it had none of the barnacles that coated the huge listening device, the Russian submersible didn't look exactly pristine, with rust-brown scars evident on many of the welds. He nudged Scorpio towards the stern to inspect her propeller. The tufts of fibre he'd noticed early on resolved into what they'd all feared – fishing net. Somehow, either while going into the trap or trying to reverse out of it, *AS-28* had fouled its propeller as well.

Apart from the net in the propeller, there was nothing obviously wrapped around *AS-28*'s stern, so Nuttall slowly span Scorpio to face towards the bow. Sliding along close to the hull, he could see what *AS-28*'s crew evidently had not – a spider's web of lines that now strapped her firmly to the buoyancy tank of the array. There were at least five of them converging on the angle between the Russian bathyscaphe's fin – or conning tower – and the forward hull.

Before starting to try to cut the lines, they needed to know what they were made of. The first Russian reports had all spoken of steel cables, but the closer the team got with Scorpio's high-definition lens the more wisps of filament they saw waving in the current. The lines were starting to look more like tightly bunched fishing net than steel. But one of them was different. It was thicker and apparently coated in some kind of rubber.

Keeping a few metres from the port side of the submarine, Scorpio rose above the bunched cables and around the bow. Something didn't seem quite right. The submersible was held close up against the array and had jammed itself into the nets so tightly that they'd been mistaken them for steel cable, so why had it not recoiled? Was it just friction from the encrustations that was holding it there? Or had other cables snagged it somewhere out of sight? From above they weren't able to get a good enough angle to peer between the submarine and the steel cylinder. Looking up from below would be their only option, but that's where Gold drew the line. That was the one place they wouldn't be checking, he said.

'If we were positioned on the other side of the array, then maybe,' he said. 'But like this we'd have to loop our umbilical over the top of the submarine and put ourselves beneath it. If anything shifted we'd be in trouble, and it's not worth it.'

With no other rescue service within range in the crew's estimated survival period, getting Scorpio trapped would be disastrous. What's more, Scorpio's thick umbilical cable would have joined the web ensnaring *AS-28*.

Positioning problems aside, the jury-rigged, Russian-style positioning system did not seem to be affecting Scorpio too badly, despite the building swell. Nuttall and Forrester were working well together, making sure the umbilical was paid out and heaved in to compensate for the long, slow sway of *KIL-27* in the gentle waves. Combined with the water clarity, the conditions were better than on any training scenarios they'd been through. After all the dramas of the journey, it seemed as though everything was going to work out OK. All being well, the cutting operation shouldn't take more than half an hour, an hour at most, and Podkapayev assured them that the sailors inside *AS-28* were still conscious.

They were ready. Gold cleared his throat. 'Right, let's get this thing done,' he said, as Nuttall began repositioning Scorpio alongside the fin, with the vehicle in line with the bunched cables.

Just as Nuttall started moving forward, Podkapayev began talking into his radio to the command ship *Alagez*, waving his hand signalling Nuttall to stop. The team all looked at him. The interpreter explained that Podkapayev wanted confirmation that they could start cutting. Riches was about to object that now was not the time for time-wasting protocol, when the translator explained that Podkapayev was uncertain as to how buoyant the submarine was.

AS-28 had previously blown their ballast tanks in an effort to get free. If they were still full of air, the submarine would be straining at those cables and when she broke free she might do so at a dangerous angle, only to come crashing back down again. No one seemed to know how long it had been since they were blown, but to Riches' eyes it seemed it had all seeped out. She didn't look as though she was tugging upwards, and neither did it look as though she wanted to sink. Every indication was that she was neutrally buoyant.

Gold turned to Riches. 'We're wasting time here,' he said. 'You can tell that thing's not going to go anywhere. Look how she's lying. There's nothing holding her down at the stern, but she's not going to sink suddenly or shoot upwards upside down. Maybe she's slightly positively buoyant, but nothing that's going to cause a problem.'

Riches nodded, but waited. He was acutely aware of the need not to crash through Russian protocol. Holloway had warned just how fast the curtain could fall on the collaborative operation if they were judged to be out of control. He could feel his jaw clenched tight trying to contain himself while they waited for a reply from the *Alagez*, who were themselves waiting for a reply from the frozen, half-suffocated sailors. Riches looked at the panel of their own through-water communications system in front of him. Needless to say, NATO and Russia operated on different frequencies, leaving them unable to talk directly to the submersible.

At last Podkapayev's handheld radio crackled, and he turned to the others and began talking, pointing at the screen.

'The Priz is not positively buoyant,' he announced through the interpreter. 'You must begin by cutting this cable here, and you have permission to begin.'

Gold looked at Riches again, his eyes full of warning. This wasn't going to last.

The fixed aluminium head of the cutter was slowly nearing the first line, its movements swaying loosely against the backdrop of *AS-28*'s hull. Nuttall was keeping the thrust joystick pushed forward just an inch, but Scorpio was slowing, twisting sideways.

'Give me another half a wrap there, Will,' he said. The instruction was picked up by the open microphone and relayed out to Forrester on the umbilical winch. After just a couple of seconds Nuttall felt the resistance ease, and Scorpio moved forward again. As the cable got closer and Nuttall started trying to move it towards the mouth of the cutter, the lack of anything solid in their set-up started to become obvious. The jaws and their target were loosely swaying close together one second then a foot or more apart the next. Scorpio was suspended in mid-water, its umbilical stretched across 250 metres of open sea with a current running, attached to a rolling ship that was being held in position only by a precarious balance of opposing forces. Given that, it was a miracle that the cutter and the cable were only moving around by such a small amount.

Even so, trying to catch the rope in the cutter's jaws was not going to be easy. The depth perception from binocular vision is removed when using a television monitor, making it difficult to judge whether an object is too close or too far. Some expensive stereoscopic camera systems had been developed and fitted to ROVs to try to combat this problem, but all had an apparently unavoidable drawback: after a few hours at most, the artificial 3-D display gave operators a splitting headache. For a job that often meant sitting in front of screens for up to 12 hours a day, it was a critical fault. Besides, like other long-time ROV pilots, Nuttall's brain had begun to rewire itself with the sensors available to it. Scorpio had two forward-facing cameras and, although not linked up to function in unison, after spending so many hours using them he'd unconsciously started to interpret their signals as one, giving him rudimentary three-dimensional vision.

But Nuttall's sixth sense could not counter the foot or so of loose movement. Every time the cutter's mouth rose up towards the cable and a snatch looked certain, everyone in the cabin leaned forward at the screen, willing it in like fanatical – but mute – football supporters whose team were close to a goal. But each time something would shift, and the cable would somehow slip to the side of the cutter's jaws. Nuttall was having to use a lot of power to move, yet he was sure he'd got enough slack on the winch. Maybe it was the low voltage cutting the power available to his thrusters, he thought.

Watching Nuttall struggling to manoeuvre the entire ROV to get the cable into the cutter's jaws, Gold had an idea. He pushed backwards past Podkapayev and settled himself against the back wall where the manipulator control was mounted. Everyone bunched up towards the door to give him more room.

With his back against the wall, Gold reached up to a robotic arm that protruded from the wall above his shoulder. Taking the hand grip in his left hand, he adjusted and aligned the various joints to match the orientation of the manipulator arm on Scorpio, 200 metres beneath them.

'OK, Pete, unfreeze me,' he said.

Nuttall flicked a switch in front of him that would link Gold's master arm to the slave below. On the screen in front of them, Scorpio's arm twitched. Trying to control four joints of the manipulator with levers, buttons or even joysticks made for time-consuming, clumsy work. It was more intuitive to use a master arm whose every motion was replicated by that of the 'slave' below on the ROV.

With an easy, practised swing, Gold twisted his fingers and smoothly pulled his arm downwards, and the camera showed Scorpio's manipulator releasing its grip on a rail and faithfully follow Gold's movement downwards until it was poised dead ahead of the vehicle.

Gold now extended his arm outwards and opened his fingers, and on the screen the manipulator's metal claw opened and began reaching out to grab the cable. Able to move independently of Scorpio's bulk, it was quickly able to capture it. Once in the manipulator's grasp, Gold could easily pull the cable towards the cutting arm that was fixed to Scorpio's frame. The ROV was now attached to the cable, giving a little bit of stability.

Nuttall was so focused on controlling the ROV that he was oblivious to all the movement and anxious commentary around him. He was trying not to think of the men trapped inside the steel coffin in front of him, instead concentrating on his task. At last the cable slipped in between the guides and into the jaws – only then did his ears open to the tense murmur of encouragement.

'We're in. Cutting now,' he said and flicked a switch to his right. The cutter arm juddered as the hydraulic blade rotated across the gape of the jaws, and specks of sediment rose like slow-motion dust from the rope, then suddenly the two ends could be seen drifting apart. A big cheer filled the cabin. The time was 12.20 local.

Riches stepped outside for a second. The sea was oily calm, and the scene on the hot, rusting deck was strangely dreamlike. Men were clustered around the crew members who had headphones on, staring in different directions as though imagining the events happening in the darkness somewhere below them.

Stepping back into the control cab, Riches hit a wall of heat and the smell of sweaty men mixed with the stale nicotine coming off Podkapayev and the interpreter. The room was dark to help the operators see the screens, and the aircon had been turned off to preserve the precious voltage. The atmosphere inside was tense again, and looking at the screen Riches could see why. They were already close to catching the second, rubbery line. Gold's back was up against the wall, his arm protruding into the middle of the cabin beneath the robotic control, snatching as though trying to grab something from mid-air in slow motion.

At last the claws closed around the tube and Gold slowly drew his hand closer to him and across to his right. Deep beneath them Scorpio's manipulator mirrored the motion and swung across to the jaws of the cutter arm. There were a couple of missed attempts at fitting it inside, then the line was in the jaws.

Nuttall flicked the switch. The cutter arm juddered once more as the hydraulic blade slid forward in its housing, and then suddenly there was a burst of gas and a cloud of bubbles exploded from the cutter and fled for the surface.

Everyone exchanged glances, except for Podkapayev, who remained intently focused on the screen. That was no cable. That was a gas hose of some sort, and not an old one either. Under that kind of pressure the gas – whatever it was – would have found some way to escape if it had been there for any length of time. It seemed to Riches that the Russians had not just been inspecting the hydrophone array as they'd claimed. Perhaps they had been working on it, topping it up with air to keep it buoyant and the antennae taut.

No wonder that Podkapayev was looking uncomfortable. Everyone knew how dangerous it was to use a rescue craft for maintenance work. Their whole design was for short interventions, and they contained no provision for getting in trouble themselves. To operate one without backup was asking for trouble.

Gold and Nuttall remained totally focused on their task, and were already lining up for the third rope. Just over an hour after the very first cut, the third rope was severed. They were working with methodical efficiency, and Riches began projecting forward. At this rate, they should be done within another hour.

Sunday, 7 August
SS + 68 h 15 mins
00.45 UK – 03.45 Moscow – *12.45 Kamchatka*
***AS-28*, 210 metres beneath Berezovya Bay**

Huddled in the damp, frozen chamber of the submersible, Gennady Bolonin was having to fight hard to prevent his body from starting to shiver uncontrollably. Once started it would be difficult to stop and might spread to others. Given that they didn't know how much longer they'd be down there, an outbreak of shivering could be lethal; it would use up their remaining oxygen three times faster.

Bolonin could see the writing on the wall. The glistening eyes of contained terror had long ago been replaced by dull, blank stares. When the vomiting had started, he'd looked over at Lepetyukha. The captain might have been dead, but suddenly his chest began a heaving, hollow-bellied cough as his damaged lungs tried to find fresh air.

There was none. The acrid smell of vomit was now overlaid with a fug of urine. They were using sealable bottles for their liquid waste, but the weaker the men got, the more frequently they missed or spilled them. The used cans of V-64 could only be imperfectly sealed, and nauseating, acrid tendrils of excrement stink were filling both their nostrils and their subconscious.

At last Lepetyukha glanced back at Bolonin for long enough for the engineer to nod. The significance was not lost on the Captain.

They had used seven of the V-64 emergency air regeneration canisters they'd had on board. They'd eked the chemical out for as long as they possibly could. Now only one remained. Once this was opened, the psychological crutch of having an unopened canister in reserve would be gone. Once the chemicals in this canister were spent, they were on a slow march down the road to death. As the carbon dioxide level rose, the headaches and nausea they were already suffering from would worsen and they would then lapse into unconsciousness followed quickly and unknowingly by the end. But there was no choice. If it wasn't opened now the crew would start dying anyway, and Lepetyukha's nod affirmed he saw that too. They hadn't changed a cylinder for 18 hours – already a Navy record.

Lepetyukha's rheumy, bloodshot eyes swivelled slowly, trying to find Milachevsky. He grunted the young pilot's name. Huddled against the horror in mind as well as body, Milachevsky didn't respond until his name was spoken a second time.

Lepetyukha didn't lift a finger, but swivelled his eyes slowly over to the remaining canister. Milachevsky understood, and began plotting his movements to pull himself within reach of the cylinder. Every lift of his arm felt as demanding as climbing one of the volcanoes that surrounded Petropavlovsk, and contemplating a sequence of such movements was daunting. But he set his jaw and began. When he at last reached the canister he squatted against the curved steel, closed his hand over the valve and twisted. The grip slid past his skin without shifting. He couldn't summon enough strength to hold it tight enough to crack the seal.

Taking both hands, Milachevsky tried once again. Focusing all his attention on his hands, he managed to break the valve's bond with the canister. Slumped against the wall, Milachevsky placed the V-64 carefully on the deck, and began to gather the energy for his return journey. Through his throbbing headache, he imagined he could feel the ache in his head lessen as the chemicals in the canister drew carbon dioxide from the air. The pain lifted slowly, but alongside the relief came realisation. His mind was becoming capable of thought once more, not just deadened reactions, and that thought brought dread. Once this canister was finished there would be no others to open. This time the slow suffocation would be final.

Sunday, 7 August
SS + 68 h 45 mins
01.15 UK – 04.15 Moscow – *13.15 Kamchatka*
KIL-27

With continual communication between the control cabin and the deck crew, taking up umbilical slack and spooling out a little more, the movement caused by the swell and *KIL-27*'s wandering was all but cancelled out. Nuttall and Gold were in a zone of total concentration, barely having to talk to each other as they worked together to move in on the dwindling number of cables.

Podkapayev was nodding enthusiastically as Scorpio neared the fourth cable. Nuttall jockeyed the stick forward, compensating heavily for what he was presuming to be the strange effects of the low voltage, when something caught his attention from the corner of his eye. On the panel to the right of the joystick, a red light had started flashing on and off. Gold had also seen it in the same moment.

'Oil level alarm,' said Gold loudly, but to himself. This was exactly what he'd dreaded – something going wrong at this critical stage. The alarm indicated that the main termination box compensator was losing oil. There was no way of knowing how fast. The box – where the umbilical met the ROV itself – was filled with oil to keep seawater away from the electrical connections. Gold was running through the possible causes of a leak. Was the oil being forced up the umbilical, as it might if Scorpio hadn't dived deep for a while? Was one of the bolts not tightened properly during their frantic efforts to get everything up and running again? Did something get trapped in the seal? Or was it just a false alarm caused by a fault in the circuit, one that could mean the difference between life and death if he chose to take it seriously. There was no way of telling without inspecting Scorpio.

Gold's mind was running through the system, combining all the various factors and scenarios. The alarm circuit was rigged to warn that the oil reservoir for the main termination box was running low, yet he himself had made sure it was topped up when the vehicle left the surface. Scorpio had already been down for an hour and a half. There hadn't been any hard impacts on the machine while it had been submerged, so he couldn't imagine it was down to recent trauma. Assuming it was a constant loss and not a recent breach, that meant it was losing oil at a fairly slow rate. If so, it would be another hour before enough oil had leaked away to allow the first drops of seawater inside. There was always the chance that something else was wrong – especially given his experiences in the last eight hours on the ship – but Gold decided to trust the instincts that had evolved over 12 years' working with the vehicle.

'Ignore it for the moment, Pete. Let's keep cutting.' Gold's voice was pure Scottish calm, but inside his stomach was turning knots.

With the red light pulsing like an opened artery, Nuttall and Gold moved in on the fourth rope and at 13.25 they made the cut. Two more lines remained, though neither was as accessible as those that had gone before.

Sunday, 7 August
SS + 69 h
01.30 UK – 04.30 Moscow – *13.30 Kamchatka*
***Georgy Kozmin*, Berezovya Bay**

The last pieces of Commander Kent Van Horn's gear were finally completing the tortuous two-stage loading process on to the American ship of opportunity, the *Georgy Kozmin*. Once they'd all been loaded, he expected that the *Kozmin* would cast off and leave in short order. But nothing happened. When he approached Captain Novikov with the attaché alongside him, he was informed that they were still 'waiting for permission'.

Five hours before, the Americans had got personal confirmation from Vice-Admiral Avdoshin of the Russian main Navy staff that the *Kozmin* was cleared to leave as soon as loading was complete, but for at least half an hour they waited on the dockside. Van Horn was sitting in one of the staterooms of the *Kozmin* discussing technical issues with the Russian officers and obliquely trying to break the deadlock that was preventing them from leaving. The impression of those on board that the authorities were trying to restrain Novikov seemed increasingly likely; it wouldn't be until 15.00 local time that the ship was finally allowed to cast off from the dockside. With the site at least four hours away, the chances that they would reach the trapped sailors while they were still alive were fading.

Sunday, 7 August
SS + 69 h
01.30 UK – 04.30 Moscow – *13.30 Kamchatka*
***KIL-27*, Berezovya Bay**

Standing on the bridge of *KIL-27* with her beige raincoat wrapped tightly around her against the cold breeze, Tatiana Lepetyukha scanned the scene on the stern deck for clues as to what was happening. With her blonde hair and city clothes, she felt out of place, suddenly self-conscious about forcing herself on to the rescue ship. She'd been true to her word about not interfering, although she had not been able to restrain herself from putting a hand on one of the British sailors' shoulders to say thank you for his work. He might not have been able to understand her, but that didn't matter. She just needed to say it.

It was hard to tell what was happening from the postures of the foreigners as they crowded around the yellow cable that led to their machine, or from the faces of those going in and out of the control cabin. She badly wanted to get the latest news of the situation, but didn't want to make more trouble by asking. The translator inside the robot's control container was a friend of hers, but there was no way he could come out and give her a report at a time like this.

More transparent than the hard-to-read faces of the outsiders were those of the Russian Oxygen Rescue Team. They were preparing to treat her husband and the other sailors when – Tatiana's inner voice promised her that it was when, not if – they were brought back to the surface. But the expressions of these medics were painful to watch, for every minute that passed they changed. It was just nerves, Tatiana told herself. The official Navy estimates of the remaining air supply were the ones that should be regarded, not the expressions of mere doctors.

Sunday, 7 August
SS + 69 h 15 mins
01.45 UK – 04.45 Moscow – *13.45 Kamchatka*
Scorpio control cabin, *KIL-27*, Berezovya Bay

Nuttall was trying hard to work Scorpio into a position where he could get to the second-last line, but the filaments always somehow evaded the cutter's jaws. Both remaining lines were pressed between *AS-28* and the buoyancy chamber of the array, making them much harder to get at. They didn't seem to be holding her too tightly, yet the submersible wasn't moving. The air that had been blown into her ballast tanks in an effort to break free from the fishing nets before they had arrived had clearly leaked away.

With another attempt failed, Gold, Nuttall and Riches discussed their options. None of them liked the look of the ropes still apparently holding her, but there was insufficient room to manoeuvre Scorpio to get at them properly. With the oil level light still blinking insistently, Gold suggested that they should take a look around the stern of the submarine to try to get a better idea of what was still holding her.

Nuttall backed away from *AS-28*, and gently span Scorpio towards the stern.

'Something's definitely up with the thrusters, Stuart,' he said. 'It's feeling very sloppy. Just not sure it's the voltage.' By now he was familiar with how the tugging of the umbilical from their loose platform felt, and it wasn't that. He was getting a bad feeling about this.

As Scorpio drew level with the propeller housing, Nuttall applied some differential thrust to rotate back around to face towards the fin. Just at that moment, *KIL-27* heaved on a passing swell and tugged Scorpio's umbilical. Nuttall jammed on full opposite power, but it wasn't enough, and the vehicle was tugged in towards the array. The submersible's solid steel rudder frame had been clear by a good few feet, but they were suddenly careering towards it. The cutter arm, protruding from the front of the robot, took the impact. The image on the screen jolted, hard.

'Oh shit,' said Nuttall, still holding on the power to try to get some distance between Scorpio and the submersible. 'Deck give me a full turn of slack!'

Gold disengaged the manipulator master arm and sprang forward to take a close look at the monitor. The V-shaped guide that protruded above the cutter's jaw was made of two wide, flat pieces of aluminium. The one closest to the camera had bent forwards and now ran parallel with the other, rather than at ninety degrees. The cutter's gape into which the cables had to be fed was now more like a tight-lipped grimace.

'Not looking good, Pete,' said Gold. 'It's bent right over. Not sure we'll get anything in there now.' He paused for a second, looking at the screen. Then he turned to Riches.

'We're going to have to recover Scorpio and sort this out. We're useless otherwise. It's a simple job to fix that, and it means we can take a look at the oil problem too. But it means we're going to have to get ourselves back on deck. I reckon we can be back on site in about thirty minutes.'

Riches turned to Podkapayev and relayed the news. He didn't like it. Riches tried to explain that there was no other option, but Podkapayev was shaking his head vigorously before he'd finished. He began jabbering in Russian and chopping with his hands. The interpreter reported that he was saying that under no circumstances could Scorpio be recovered now and that it had to stay down to finish the job.

Gold, Nuttall and the deck crew were doing their job with calm professionalism. Riches felt the need to give them the space to continue. Podkapayev was evidently caught in a tricky position, with the nation's Defence Minister only a few dozen metres away from him expecting him to control the situation. But there was too much at stake here – the time it would take for the Minister to rubber-stamp the recovery of the ROV could be the difference between the mission's success or failure, between life and death.

There was one more thing they could do before bringing her up. 'Stuart, we've cut four lines now,' Riches said. 'Why don't we give her a nudge and see if there's anything still holding her?'

Gold shrugged. 'Right you are, Commander,' he said. 'Get yourself off the starboard side of that prop housing there, Pete, give her a shove.'

Nuttall nodded, and carefully approached the stern of *AS-28* until Scorpio's skids were rubbing against the submarine's casing. Then, applying a burst of full power, he tried to push the trapped vehicle away from the array. To his surprise the submarine began to shift, swinging away from the steel float. But after only a metre or so it stopped, and swung back in, pivoting on the bow. One or more of those lines were still holding her in place.

Gold, Nuttall and Riches looked at one another. It was clear what was needed.

'It's no good, Dmitriy,' Gold said. 'We are going to have to recover.'

Once more Podkapayev began protesting, but after only the

briefest of confirmatory glances between Gold and Riches, Nuttall was already pulling up and away from *AS-28* and instructing the deck crew to take in a wrap of umbilical and prepare for recovery. Podkapayev frantically started calling on his radio to the command ship, his face reddening.

Outside on deck, Captain Jonathan Holloway sensed the change in mood before he heard what had happened. When he saw the winch begin to start reeling in the umbilical, he began to notice movements among the Russian crew members on board both *KIL-27* and the nearby *Alagez*. The lady he'd seen watching the proceedings from the bridge had buried her face in her hands. It never occurred to him that this might be the wife of one of the stricken crew, let alone the Captain's.

Once he'd heard the cause of the disturbance, Holloway's knowledge of the Russian mindset began to burrow into his thoughts. If the repair took too long, it was possible that they would lose confidence in the foreign equipment, and suddenly decide to try something else instead. That would not only be a disaster for the UK team, but also possibly for the seven men stuck 200 metres below them.

Meanwhile the American divers and doctor were agitating for a role. They were feeling as disconnected as Holloway, only they had the tools and training to be feeling the need for practical involvement. They changed from their camouflage slacks and big dark jackets into diving dry-suits. The depth of the submersible was too great for them to reach without special gas mixes and a decompression chamber at the very least, but they wanted to be in the rescue launch and be ready to get in the water as soon as it surfaced. Holloway relayed the messages, but with predictable results. The Russians said they had their own divers. Reading between the lines, they weren't keen to have another piece of the rescue taken from their hands, and especially not by the Americans. With the Defence Minister, Ivanov, watching their every move, the more they could do themselves, the better.

A subtle mistiness in the air was beginning to solidify into a distant fog, and the sea was starting to stir. The long, low swell had grown imperceptibly and the previously oily surface was now ruffled with occasional flecks of white. The low-pressure system that had been forecast looked like it was finally arriving.

Sunday, 7 August
SS + 69 h 30 mins
02.00 UK – 05.00 Moscow – *14.00 Kamchatka*
***AS-28*, 210 metres beneath Berezovya Bay**

When the news came through the underwater telephone that the British robot was damaged, a cold feeling took root in Sergei Belozerov's stomach. The controller's voice said that the estimated repair time was only 30 minutes, but his long experience of working with machinery and the sea told him different. If it was such a simple thing, why didn't they just continue and fix it afterwards. There wasn't much that could be fixed in 30 minutes. And, anyway, the same controller had told them that the Venom ROV had only had a small problem and yet it never came back. There was no reason to believe that this would be any different.

All of them were now slipping in and out of consciousness. Sleep was welcome when it came for it brought relief from the sodden grip of the cold, but muffled alarms rang in their minds. Their fuzzy thoughts could hardly remember the warnings about the seductive lure of slipping into the deadly, silken arms of carbon dioxide. All they knew is that it was better than the choking, carbon monoxide-laced smoke that would accompany fire in the compartments.

It was not just the crew of the *Kursk* that had suffered this agony. Back in 1989, the *Komsomolets* – an experimental submarine with a titanium hull strong enough to take her to a depth of 1,500 metres – was hit by an electrical fire after a short-circuit in the aft compartment. The submarine surfaced during the battle to contain the blaze, and its reactor scrammed and shut down. Fifty-nine men managed to abandon ship, but many of these drowned because there were too few lifeboats to take them all. The Commanding Officer and four others were still on board when the submarine slipped back beneath the surface and began plummeting to the seabed 1,680 metres below. The five men climbed inside an escape pod mounted in the fin and ejected, but the pod had already filled with toxic gases from the fire, and all but one died inside.

Gasping for air – but thankfully not choking on it – Milachevesky raised the spanner and slowly tapped three times against the hull, signalling that they'd received the message that the robot was leaving them. Although they were still receiving communications on the underwater telephone, they'd stopped using it for replies. Transmitting used too much power, and they had little to report that couldn't be answered with a yes or a no. Hammering on the hull was exhausting, but it was better than draining the batteries.

Before the last clang had finished reverberating through the hull, the comforting murmur of the foreign robot had already begun to recede. The sailors were left in silence again, more conscious than ever of the clock that was ticking, entirely beyond their control.

Sunday, 7 August
SS + 69 h 30 mins
02.00 UK – 05.00 Moscow – *14.00 Kamchatka*
Petropavlovsk-Kamchatsky

Guzel Latypova was exhausted. She'd been up all night following the arrival of the international rescue teams, standing in the rain with her camera crew waiting for the aircraft to unload, then again down on the docks as the Americans were methodically loading their gear. Now everything had gone quiet, but it wasn't an easy calm. The key drama of this whole story was being played out, but she wasn't there to witness it. Despite all her efforts, only a television crew from the federal TV news agency had been allowed to join the fleet at the accident site.

She couldn't sit still, so she decided to go over to see Yelena Milachevskaya again. The pilot's wife was getting regular updates on the situation from headquarters over the phone. It was such a good information conduit that Latypova had been using it to inform her half-hourly updates to Interfax and her own newsroom at STS-Kamchatka.

Latypova found Yelena sitting in a chair, her hand resting on the telephone receiver. She was drowsy from her drugged sleep, but Latypova could still feel the panic that gripped the woman. The phone had been silent for too long, Yelena fretted. Something had happened that they didn't want to tell her. Already she could feel Slava was close to the end, she said. The journalist put a hand on her shoulder and tried to calm her. They're probably just busy, she said. After all, there was no reason to think anything had gone wrong.

Sunday, 7 August
SS + 69 h 35 mins
02.05 UK – 05.05 Moscow – *14.05 Kamchatka*
***KIL-27*, Berezovya Bay**

Gold stood on deck, patiently waiting to usher Scorpio back on to the ship. Nuttall had retreated the robot a safe distance from the array then brought it back to the surface, and now was relying on Gold to guide him back in towards the lifting point.

Charlie Sillet was getting himself prepared on the crane, ensuring the boom was perfectly positioned with the catcher unit ready to be lowered. Will Forrester, the umbilical drum operator, was gradually taking in the slack on the winch. He didn't want it snagging, but he didn't want to drag the vehicle by its tail either. Damage to the umbilical was the last thing they needed right now. Problems in the 900-metre cable were tough to find at the best of times and even tougher to fix, especially in a hurry.

Nigel Pyne had disappeared into the workshop, housed in the other half of the control cabin container, on a hunt for some aluminium plate that could be used to replace the bent cutter guide. He and Alan Hislop had soon set out the tools and materials and cleared a workspace, and now stood out of the way. They all waited like mechanics in a Formula One pitstop. Each of the six engineers would tackle a different task: Pyne and Forrester would take the bent cutter guide, Sillet and Hislop would be on the oil problem, and Nuttall would give the vehicle a quick once over looking for other potential problems. Gold would be there, overseeing as the pit boss, while Dave Burke stood by ready to help if anything else came up.

Watching Scorpio close in on the ship to the accompaniment of the umbilical winch's groan, Gold prayed that there were no unpleasant surprises waiting for him. He guided the robot in beneath the catcher unit, which engaged with a clunk, and Sillet began to lift it clear of the water.

Nuttall cut the power and scrambled out of the control cabin. The Alsatian appeared in front of him, jolting his mind back to the fact that he was on a Russian vessel above a top-secret military installation. He could feel the eyes of the foreign crew on him as he strode over to Scorpio, adding to the pressure.

Sillet lifted Scorpio across to the workspace, and as it swung over the deck six pairs of arms reached out to steady it. Gold was already peering inside at the oil termination box, while the others were shooting glances at the cutter guide, confirming their tasks.

When Scorpio finally hit the rope-padded deck, all six engineers sprang into action. Pyne began unbolting the bent cutter guide. Replacing it was the only option – bending it back would weaken the aluminium, increasing the risk of it deforming a second time. He'd already cut the replacement plate to size; all that remained was to use the bent one as a template to drill the mounting holes, and it could be refitted.

Sillet released the pressure seal cap of the oil reserve. It was almost at the bottom. He and Hislop began carefully tracing back down the lines, looking for telltale traces of oil. When he got to the main termination box he ran a finger around the edge, his fingertip expertly gauging the gap and feeling for any bulging of the rubber O-ring that sealed it.

Nuttall was checking the thrusters. Although it was probably the low voltage and the motion of the ship causing the bad handling he'd been experiencing, he wanted to rule out any other causes. When he got to the port lateral thruster, he did what he'd done to all the others and took the blades in his palm and tried to spin the propeller, checking for the usual resistance in the hydraulic system. There was none – it span freely. The shear pin had gone. It was that simple. He could pull the propeller straight off. That was lucky, he thought. They could easily have lost it, or, worse, it could have jammed in place. He jogged back to the workshop and fished out a new shear pin. Five minutes later he had slid it into position and crimped it, binding the propeller to its shaft once more. He checked all the thrusters again, and confirmed that propulsion was good to go.

Sillet had found no major leak. The pressure on the seabed – more than 20 tons per square metre – must have forced some of the oil back up the umbilical. It was a fairly common problem, especially if the vehicle hadn't been deep for a while. He powered the hydraulics up to full pressure and could see no sign of a drip. There would have to be a major leak to empty the newly filled reservoir in the few hours they'd need to remain on the site, so he stepped back from Scorpio, his fix also finished.

Twenty minutes had passed, and Pyne and Forrester were making the final twists to the bolts holding the new cutter guide on to the cutter arm. At 14.30 they too stepped away from Scorpio and Nuttall turned on the power once more, flashed the lights and spun the thrusters. Everything worked. Sillet lifted the vehicle back up off the deck and at 14.35 it was back in the water, heading back to the array and to the seven men still trapped against it.

The Russians were smiling again. Unbeknown to the UK rescue team, someone aboard the command ship took Scorpio's return to the water as evidence that the rescue was now certain, for the *Georgy Kozmin* carrying the American team and their Super-Scorpios was turned back to port. The online ISMERLO forum of submarine rescue experts erupted in horror, for the safety net of the backup system had just been removed. Admiral Roughead put in an urgent call to Vice-Admiral Avdoshin, but all his calls for the American team to be allowed to continue to the site were refused.

On *KIL-27,* the team knew only too well that the rescue was not over yet. Scorpio might be back in the water, but they still had a job to finish.

Nuttall was more comfortable approaching *AS-28* second time around. The bulk of the array on the sonar didn't unsettle him, but beckoned him instead. He felt refreshed after the break from the screen, ready to finish the cutting. But as Scorpio crested the array and looped over to examine the remaining bonds keeping *AS-28* lashed to the apparatus, his heart started to sink. He couldn't see anything substantial holding the submersible there, yet it was still there, unmoving. Why hadn't the submersible tried to shift? He was getting a bad feeling about this. Looking at the remaining cables, he wasn't sure how many more he was going to be able to cut.

He manoeuvred Scorpio in close to the striped hull. The front-camera monitor was now flashing into colour every so often, showing the stripes to be a deep red. The upper surfaces of the craft were now littered with the debris of barnacles scraped off the floatation chamber of the array by Scorpio's movements.

'Another turn of slack there, Will,' he said into the mike. 'Getting tugged around a bit. That swell picking up out there?'

'More slack coming. Will keep an eye on it,' came Forrester's reply.

The most exposed part of the fifth cable was between the fin of the submarine and the array, but the gap was too small for Scorpio to reach it properly. Nuttall was trying to approach at a skewed angle to get in tighter, but it was difficult piloting. Gold was still against the wall, his left arm held out in front of him gripping the manipulator master arm. He was intently focused on the screen over Nuttall's shoulder, face screwed up with the strain and his arm hunching and lunging as he tried to grab at the line in the water. Holding it in such an awkward position was making his muscles burn. He could feel beads of sweat starting to trickle down his spine.

At last he snapped the claws shut. An agonising fraction of a second later he saw the jaws respond, the rope caught in their grip. Slowly he fed it across into the newly replaced guide. Nuttall reached across and flicked the switch for the cutter, jabbing it forward to engage it before snapping it back. Nothing seemed to move until a few strands sprang back from the cut. But the main body of the rope remained taut. The line was still intact. It hadn't been deep enough into the cutter's mouth to be fully severed.

Gold tried jiggling the arm to push the cable in deeper.

'Try that,' he said.

Nuttall flicked the switch once more, but still the blade couldn't reach the meat of the rope. Something was preventing him for getting any closer.

'I can't get in there. I think the skids are getting in the way,' said Nuttall.

'Try changing the angle a little? If we can just get around a little . . .' said Gold.

But nothing was working. Gold's frustration was mounting as he adjusted the position of his arm to try to get the cable into the cutter, but the space was just too tight.

Eventually, at about 15.30, they gave up. They had to try something else. With Scorpio retreated from the close quarters at which she'd been for the last 20 minutes or more, they could see *AS-28* was swaying in the current. She had to be loose, they told each other. It seemed obvious.

'She's got to blow her tanks,' said Gold. 'It's the only way.'

By releasing high-pressure air into her ballast tanks from her air reserves the submersible would become positively buoyant. The motion should pull her free from the few remaining bonds, as long as they weren't substantial enough to keep her there. They had to risk it. The downside was that they knew she had already blown her tanks at least once to no avail. This blow would probably be her final chance of reaching the surface.

Podkapayev would have none of it when Riches explained their thoughts. He was shaking his head violently before the translator was even halfway through explaining. He demanded that Scorpio be driven underneath *AS-28* and up her starboard side as far as it could go to make sure the submersible was entirely clear.

'I can't do that,' said Gold. 'Taking a look underneath that submersible means our umbilical will be looped right round her. If anything happens and we get stuck, then those guys are trapped down there much more securely than they were by those nets.'

Riches agreed. But Podkapayev was looking very uncomfortable. Was there something he wasn't telling them? As far as the UK team knew the ballast air was separate from the main supply, but their knowledge of the detailed workings of the Russian submersible was limited. It was perfectly possible that the ballast air also supplied the main crew chambers. In that case, blowing the tanks would substantially reduce the life expectancy of those on board.

'We can't do it Dmitriy,' Riches said. 'It's too dangerous to go underneath. We know how quickly things can go wrong, and if they do then we're suddenly back to square one, but this time without any time to solve it.'

'We cannot blow the tanks. You must cut all lines,' came the stubborn reply.

'She's loose. You can see it,' urged Gold.

'If she is not free when she blows she can lose her balance and go on her side. We cannot,' said Dmitriy. Depending on where on the *AS-28* the cable was still attached, it could tip the craft at a dangerous angle. Such a sudden change could easily cause something unexpected.

'That's a risk we're going to have to take,' said Gold. 'We've run out of time, and out of options.'

Eventually, Podkapayev left the cabin to discuss the situation with his commanders on the *Alagez* over the radio. Agonising minutes passed before he returned, declaring that the Russians wanted an alternative plan. Gold and Riches had already discussed the possibility of using one of the lifting eyes they'd seen on *AS-28*'s hull. On training operations Scorpio was often sent to retrieve dummy mines for the Navy by dropping lines on to them so they could be hauled up on deck. There was plenty of steel cable available on the ship; *AS-28* could be pulled free using one or two of the small tugs. If *AS-28*'s ballast tanks were full of air, her positive buoyancy would cause her rise to the surface. If not, the cable could be reeled in to bring her up. It wasn't ideal because the craft might come up at an awkward angle, with all the problems that entailed, but at least it would get them to the surface.

With any luck this backup plan would not be needed. If *AS-28* could get enough positive buoyancy, she should have a good chance of breaking free and coming straight up.

For 40 minutes the arguments had gone back and forth between the UK team and Podkapayev, and between him and the command ship. All that while, *AS-28* hung in the monitor of the control cab in front of the team. Her silent bulk was swaying slightly in the current while a gentle snow of sediment drifted downwards around her. She looked like a tomb.

At last word came that the backup plan had been accepted. The order to blow the tanks would be given, and if *AS-28* failed to rise on her own, then Scorpio would come back for a towline. Until then they needed to monitor what happened. After a few minutes of discussion with Gold and Nuttall, they decided to pull Scorpio back around the end of the array, just within visual range of *AS-28*'s striped hull, but not close enough to get tangled in any lines should she move. A minute later Scorpio was in position, the umbilical out of the way, with Nuttall holding her in mid-water.

Gold nodded to Riches.

'OK, we're in position. Tell them to blow the ballast,' Riches said to the interpreter.

Podkapayev knew what was coming and already had the radio up by his mouth. As he relayed the order to the command ship, his eyes were glued to the screen. If the bathyscaphe didn't move now it was a very bad sign. The seconds ticked by. Nothing happened. Word came over the radio that the command had been delivered, but that no response had been received. Up until now, all orders and requests had been answered. Now there was silence. *AS-28* just hung there. There was no other movement, just a funereal silence. As the seconds passed with no sign of life from the submersible, their hearts began to sink. They were too late.

Sunday, 7 August
SS + 71 h 45 mins
04.15 UK – 07.15 Moscow – *16.15 Kamchatka*
***AS-28*, 210 metres beneath Berezovya Bay**

Captain Lepetyukha was up off the floor, propped against the wall of the aft compartment. All of them were breathing heavily, lungs trying to fill with oxygen and flush carbon dioxide but only managing to flood their senses with the rancid mix of vomit, urine and excrement. Gennady Bolonin relayed to him the order given by the surface commander that they should blow their ballast tanks and surface, and saw the Captain stir. Bolonin urged caution. He knew exactly how unstable the submersible he'd helped design was. They didn't know for sure that all lines had been cut. If one remained snagged on their hull, hidden from the British ROV by the bulk of the array's floatation tank, it could easily tip them off balance with disastrous results.

'We must secure everything absolutely,' said Bolonin. 'Only when this is done can we start to blow, and even then we must use great caution.'

Moving with numbed slowness, the men began trying to lash down anything that might move. Before long the buzz of the underwater telephone sounded through from the forward chamber. The watchman answered, and a few moments later his voice came through the hatch. 'Surface want to know what is happening. They say they have given us a command and yet we do not surface.'

Bolonin could see the Captain reacting, his military training urging him to follow orders, blow the tanks immediately and break for the surface. Bolonin looked Lepetyukha in the eye.

'We must not rush this,' he said.

If the submersible was still caught, they could end up like a balloon on a string, held upside down while heavy equipment crashed down on top of them amid a rain of battery acid.

With everything as secure as they could make it, Bolonin positioned himself in the front compartment. He nodded to Belozerov, who started slowly turning a valve. An initial hiss turned into a deafening roar as air blasted from high-pressure bottles into the ballast tanks. Magnified by the cylindrical hull, the noise was like an explosion.

Sunday, 7 August
SS + 71 h 47 mins
04.17 UK – 07.17 Moscow – *16.17 Kamchatka*
Surface rescue fleet, Berezovya Bay

All eyes were boring into the main screen showing the view from Scorpio's front camera. Podkapayev, Nuttall, Gold and Riches were leaning forward, peering into the murky image. Scorpio was as far away as possible while still being within visual range of *AS-28*'s striped hull. The gentle swaying of the submarine and the continual adjustments that Nuttall was making to keep Scorpio steady were hypnotic. Gold felt like they'd been waiting for more than 30 minutes already, even though it had only been two. Riches was staring so hard he could feel his eyes drying up, and he had to force himself to blink.

Something seemed to be shifting on the screen. It was hard to tell if it was the striped hull moving upwards or the camera moving downwards, but suddenly they realised that the faint white stripe had disappeared. Riches erupted at the same time as Podkapayev, shouting and pointing at the screen.

'She's gone!' Riches shouted, but Podkapayev had already bolted, pushing past behind him and on to the deck.

'Vzblivayet! Vzblivayet!' he was yelling. 'It's coming up!'

Peering into the swirling murk of the screen, the grey-brown bulk of the end of the array was discernible, but there was no longer a submersible attached to it. They burst out after Podkapayev and on to the deck. The whole crew surged towards the port side and began scouring the featureless surface of the sea. This was the moment they'd all been waiting for. Holloway pulled out his camera to catch the momentous moment when the stricken craft broke the surface.

The burst of excitement was immediately followed by silence. Not a calm, soft silence, but a tense, sharp expectation that sliced through the background throb of the ship's engines. The wind had died away, leaving the day supernaturally calm, sunlight slipping from the low, rolling waves in great slabs. The scattered armada of rusting civilian and naval vessels swayed like giant, irregular metronomes. Around the fleet every person knew the order had been passed and the submersible should be on its way up.

Tatiana Lepetyukha stood on the flying bridge of the *Alagez*, having been transferred there from *KIL-27* during Scorpio's repair. She was scarcely able to breathe as she squinted out over the placid surface. She clutched at her faith as though it were the only thing keeping her alive. Alongside her, the Defence Minister, Sergei Ivanov, also stared out across the blank water, his face a mask. The political nightmare of the *Kursk* backlash cannot have been far from his mind. And although this was only seven sailors and not 118, Ivanov had no doubt that if he failed here the cost would be high.

Nothing moved on *KIL-27*. The dogs, sensing the change in the atmosphere, had stopped barking. Russian sailors gathered with British and American rescuers at vantage points on the port deck, wherever equipment allowed a clear view of the sea. Heads slowly rotated as each scanned the surface with increasing incredulity. With every passing minute, the clarity of the day got more oppressive. Where was *AS-28*?

Sixty miles away in Petropavlosk, Yelena Milachevskaya held her twin daughters close. She knew that the rescue robot had gone back down to the seabed, and the operator had told her that there only remained a single cable to cut. A blanket of silence seemed to cover her house too, muffling the insistent sound of the television news and its coverage of the unfolding events. In the next room, Slava's father sat bolt upright at the kitchen table, staring at the screen.

Connected to the situation through a shifting network of satellite communications and lightning-fast pulses travelling across ocean floors through fibre-optic cables, Trond Jurvik sat hunched at his laptop in Norfolk, Virginia, monitoring the ISMERLO website for the latest news. Despite Scorpio's return to the water he was worried. Despite the best efforts of nations around the world, there was now no backup plan, thanks to the American team having been turned back.

Roger Chapman sat in a puddle of light in an otherwise darkened house, a cup of tea getting cold by his side, as he too watched ISMERLO for updates. His wife was asleep in bed upstairs – it was four in the morning, after all. Although there was nothing that Chapman could do from so far away, there was no way he could sleep knowing that those men, frozen and suffocated, were so close to being saved by the techniques and equipment that he'd helped develop and had championed for so long. Every blink of the cursor seemed to take an age. It was unbearable. Messages relaying the top-level scrabble to get the US ship turned back around were popping up, but there were no updates from the British team. The last that mentioned them was from a US Navy Executive Officer from the Deep Submergence Unit:

> 02:36:24 US VOO has returned to port upon Russian direction. Commodore is still requesting to get underway. British ROV is currently in the water, status unknown of cuts.

The team on deck paced the rails nervously, listening for any hint of information over the open mike from the van. It was quiet.

Gold and Nuttall had stayed where they were inside the van. They knew the fact that *AS-28* had shifted was not necessarily the end of the story. Nuttall pitched Scorpio's nose upwards by about 20 degrees to angle the wide, flat beam of the sonar up through the water column. On the orange wedge-like display of the sonar the shape of the array's floatation tube slipped away. Nuttall swept the beam up through the water above. Nothing. He adjusted the frequency, and swept down and up again, careful to keep Scorpio's nose pointing in a direct vertical line from where *AS-28* had last been seen. Still nothing.

'Seems to be clear down here,' Nuttall said into the open mike. 'Any sign up there?'

'Nothing,' came back the reply from Forrester, standing on deck with the umbilical in hand.

Sunday, 7 August
SS + 71 h 47 mins
04.17 UK – 07.17 Moscow – *16.17 Kamchatka*
***AS-28*, 210 metres beneath Berezovya Bay**

'STOP!' shouted Bolonin as loud as he could. His weakened voice was drowned out by the roaring of the air filling the ballast tanks, but Belozerov reacted as fast as he could with his frozen fingers and weakened grip, eventually managing to twist the half-open valve to a fully closed position. Suddenly everyone on board felt what Bolonin had sensed moments earlier. The submersible was moving. They were rising through the water. But looking at the dial on the depth gauge, they were going too fast.

Bolonin knew he had to dump some air from the ballast tanks to slow them down, but the high-pressure bottles outside the hull must be running short of gas. If he dumped the air, there might not be enough to lift them to the surface afterwards. He was frozen, watching the depth gauge with eyes wide. 210 metres. 200. 190.

They were almost 30 metres clear of the array. Had they made it after all? Were they free? With every passing mark on the gauge the tension in Bolonin's throat eased. They weren't safe yet – lurking above were the sharp hulls of the assembled rescue fleet, any one of which could end the submersible's uncontrolled ascent with a disastrous crash.

The submersible hurtled up through the black water towards the surface. As the depth gauge hit 180 metres *AS-28* suddenly gave a sickening lurch to starboard as a previously unseen cable caught on the side of the submersible snapped tight.

For an agonising moment it seemed as if it was going to be overturned, when with a shudder the final tentacle from the deep gave way and released the submersible for good.

Sunday, 7 August
SS + 71 h 50 mins
04.20 UK – 07.20 Moscow – *16.20 Kamchatka*
Surface rescue fleet, Berezovya Bay

Podkapayev's white-haired explosion on to the deck had sent an electric shock through the waiting fleet. All eyes were looking to the west over *KIL-27*'s port side. Riches was trying to calculate in his head how long *AS-28* should take to surface. A lot depended on how much ballast water she'd been able to blow, but she should have tried to flush it all in order to break free, and that would have meant a rapid ascent, say 70 metres a minute. From 210 metres, that was three minutes. In the excitement of having seen her disappear from the screen, he hadn't checked his watch to see the exact time, but already it felt as though far more than three minutes had passed, and there was still no sign.

A shout went up from behind the crowd staring over the port rail. As one they whirled around and there, bobbing amid still-roiling water off the other side of the ship were the bright red and white stripes of *AS-28*. Everyone ran over to the starboard rail, shouting. There was cheering coming from all of the ships. Podkapayev was yelling into his walkie-talkie.

AS-28's red and white stripes were bright against the sea as she bobbed on the surface, still reeling with the energy of her ascent. Just a few metres beyond her was the massive, sharp bow of the *Alagez*.

A huge roar of joy went up from all around. Arms were flung high and every face was beaming, but there was an added element to the expressions on the members of the UK team. Although overjoyed to see the submersible on the surface, everyone could see how close they'd come to seeing secondary disaster. For *AS-28* to surface on their starboard meant she'd either been caught in strong currents that carried her over 200 metres towards them during her ascent, or their mobile mooring system had drifted that far in the direction of the array. They should have been 100 metres away or more, but at some point they would have been directly over her. If she'd come up directly underneath the *Alagez* or *KIL-27* she could easily have damaged herself badly enough to plummet straight back down to the seabed, this time with freezing cold water flooding in to replace the foul air.

A moment later, Riches found himself enveloped in Podkapayev's arms as he gave the Royal Naval officer an enormous Russian bear-hug and covered his cheeks in wet kisses. Out of the corner of his eye, Riches saw a burst of white water erupt from the side of *AS-28*. A grin spread across his face. At least one person was still alive and was together enough to remember to blow their tanks again – a standard submariner's procedure to get as high as possible in the water before opening the hatch.

Inside the control cabin the speaker erupted in distorted yelling as the volume maxed out the circuits. Nuttall instinctively turned it down, before turning to Gold. They allowed each other a half-hug, an extended British pat on the back, before turning back to the screen. They still had to get Scorpio back on board safely, after all. Then the door was flung open and Podkapayev burst in. He yelled a huge cheer and flung his arms around the seated pilot, and Nuttall had to let go of the joystick for fear of sending Scorpio crashing into the antenna. Gold then got the same treatment.

Out on deck all of the team were now clustered around the starboard railing, desperate to catch a glimpse of the men when they emerged. Within a minute of them seeing the submersible surface a 30-foot launch had arrived with seven men on board. Five of them clambered on to the submersible's exposed hull, but they didn't rush to open the hatch to allow fresh air inside. Instead, the first thing that they did was attach a line to the bow and start towing it around to the far side of *Alagez*, out of sight. The American divers, who had eventually managed to talk their way on to a boat, were being kept back on the other side of the Russian command ship. Suddenly Riches' elation was tinged with fear. Why were they towing it away? Was this routine Russian secrecy still permeating everything, even in such an urgent situation? Or did they know something about the state of the men inside that he didn't, something that they wished to hide?

Sunday, 7 August
SS + 71 h 56 mins
04.26 UK – 07.26 Moscow – *16.26 Kamchatka*
Surface rescue fleet, Berezovya Bay

Tatiana Lepetyukha gripped the railing hard as she watched the launch tow the red-and-white striped hull of her husband's submarine around the bow of the *Alagez*. The special support squad of naval doctors were on board the launch, together with the Oxygen Rescue Team. Tatiana watched them wrestling with the valves on top of the submersible's hatch. They seemed to be having difficulty opening it. One of them took aim with a hammer and started banging it. Tatiana's heart clenched. Her husband's men usually opened the hatch themselves, she knew. Why were the surface team now doing it for them? Was it too late, after all that?

Suddenly she heard a metallic clang that didn't match a strike by the sailor who stood above the hatch. It had come from inside the submersible. Someone was alive inside! She later learned that it was her husband's crew trying to tell those on the surface that they were turning the handle the wrong way, and to let them open it themselves.

Confusion over a simple matter such as which way to turn a hatch had caused disaster before. In 1961, the Soviet submarine *S-80* disappeared without trace in the Barents Sea. She was eventually found after a seven-year search effort, and investigations revealed that the boat had been lost simply because a crewman manning one of the hatches had been trying to close it by turning the wheel in the wrong direction. The threads had been badly damaged by his desperate attempts, his conviction caused by the fact that he had recently transferred from another submarine whose hatches closed by turning the wheel in the opposite direction.

Forty years on, the matter was still causing confusion. When saturation divers had at last been allowed to approach the silent hull of the *Kursk*, they'd been directed to open the hatch anticlockwise by the advisors from the Russian Navy, but it was apparently jammed. The divers were prevented from trying to open it clockwise by the Russian Naval officers in the room, who feared damaging the thread as had happened on *S-80*. Only when the Russians were out of the control room did the supervisors tell the divers to try turning it in the other direction, and found it opened freely.

The crew of *AS-28* had managed to make themselves understood, however, and the frantic efforts of the surface crew to open the hatch with a hammer were prevented. The wheel began to turn in the opposite direction and, after a few seconds, the hatch at last swung open.

Tatiana could see hands, a head. It was too far away for her to make out if it was her husband, even when squinting and shielding her eyes from the sun. The sailor slowly clambered on to the deck where he immediately stooped to light a cigarette. Another head appeared, and the sailor emerged and lit up. Finally she saw a uniform she thought she recognised. She wasn't sure until she saw the way the figure lit his cigarette. Then she knew for sure. Her husband was alive.

Sunday, 7 August
SS + 72 hours
04.30 UK – 07.30 Moscow – *16.30 Kamchatka*
Petropavlovsk-Kamchatsky

Yelena Milachevskaya was at her sister's house when the call came from headquarters with the good news. 'My feelings were dancing,' she later said. She ran out to the market to buy a bottle of wine, shouting to everyone she encountered that all the men had been saved. Everyone cheered, buoying Yelena's mood still further.

Back at the house, Guzel Latypova was still there, playing with the twins. She too was swept up in the tide of emotion. Just as the news broke, the sun emerged over Zavoyko, casting a rare golden light over the district. Tapping out her latest update to Interfax, she found herself unable to stick to the pithy facts required for the datafeed as she described a bright and cheerful sunbeam that had burst over the scene.

When Yelena Milachevskaya whirled back into the house they drank the wine together in celebration, but even after the last drops had been finished, Yelena said didn't feel like she'd drunk a thing.

Sunday, 7 August
SS + 72 hours
04.30 UK – 07.30 Moscow – *16.30 Kamchatka*
Surface rescue fleet, Berezovaya Bay

On board *KIL-27* the news that all the sailors were alive sparked another surge of elation to cascade through the ships, spread via hugs and back slaps. Even Dmitriy's immediate superior, who until now had remained on the bridge of *KIL-27* along with the ship's Master, came down to thank the rescue crew.

Amid the chaos of celebration, the Scorpio team were still at work. As Gold emerged from the control cabin on to the deck. Riches shook his hand in a brief moment of congratulation. Gold was smiling, but still intent and focused. Scorpio was still in the water, and he wouldn't relax until his machine was safely back on deck. At last the umbilical winch began to slow and a yellow shimmer appeared in the water off the port beam, and a cheer went up as it broke surface. Gold guided Nuttall to position the robot beneath the catcher unit, which clicked into place, securing it to the crane. Marcus Cave took position beneath the half-deck supporting the crane to make sure their operation did not end with Scorpio, the crane and Charlie Sillet being dragged down to the seabed from where they'd just recovered *AS-28*.

As Scorpio began to lift out of the water, Gold gave his last command to Nuttall over the radio. 'OK, shut her down, Pete,' he said. Brimful of pride, he watched his robot emerge, seawater sluicing down through the machine's convoluted innards. They'd done it. Dozens of pairs of hands reached out to Scorpio's dripping frame to steady its return to the deck, like fans receiving a stage-diving rock star. They guided Scorpio down, and finally it was resting back on the rusting deck. Its job was done.

Nuttall pulled out a bottle of ten-year-old malt whisky that had been left hidden away in the control cabin after the last mine-recovery exercise. He said he'd never been so glad to see a bottle of the old Arran single malt, as he poured a generous measure into each of their coffee-stained mugs and handed them out. 'Good job, boys,' he said as they all raised their mugs.

Gold separated himself from the mob and walked over to where Scorpio sat, puddles of seawater still on the deck around it. He put a hand on its frame, then leaned forward and planted a kiss on Scorpio's still-salty yellow floatation blocks.

He later called his partner Susan on the satellite phone. When he heard her pick up he said hello, but at the sound of her voice he suddenly choked up. He couldn't speak. All the tension of the last 72 hours, kept tightly under control and focused on getting the job done, suddenly came bubbling up. Hearing nothing but silence, she assumed something was wrong and that the mission had failed. At last he managed to speak, and told her that they'd pulled it off, and that the Russian sailors were safe.

ISMERLO was being flooded by well-wishing congratulatory messages from the submarine rescue community around the world. Among them was a message from Roger Chapman:

03:40:37Z Fantastic news. Well done to all nations, Russia, US and UK and all members of the s/m rescue community for this joint effort. Congratulations Ian, Stuart and the Scorpio 45 team and supporting personnel from James Fisher Defence and for all the support we received from the US on mobilisation. Best wishes from the LR5 team to the Scorpio Boys. We hope the crew of Priz are safe and well with no ill effects.

Chapman's own ordeal back in 1972 had lasted 84-and-a-half hours. For him the clutching cold, the rancid smells and the killer headache were only too clear a memory. At the moment of his own rescue, when the submersible *Pisces* had finally begun to be lifted to the surface, he recalled that his mind had been so addled by the carbon dioxide that he'd been irritated at the disturbance.

As the team were securing Scorpio and her systems for the voyage back to Petropavlovsk, Podkapayev arrived and asked them to join him in the officers' mess. They agreed to join him once they'd finished the lashings – they didn't want to lose any of their equipment now, especially with Riches' favourite customs officer doubtless waiting for them at Elizovo airport, checklist in hand.

Up in the officers' mess the Ship's Master had pulled out all the stops. A huge spread of cheese, meat and pickles had been arrayed across the wardroom table, along with five or six different brands of vodka, evidently rounded up from various crewmen's cabins. The remains of Nuttall's single-malt whisky were added to the lineup. With the entire British team, the Americans and the Russian escorts and translators and some of *KIL-27*'s officers crammed into the small space, the waiting shot glasses were filled with vodka and handed around. When everybody had one, the Master raised his vodka and gave a long, rambling toast, looking each of the UK team in the eye as he did so. Holloway translated his words; they were a formal tribute to the professionalism of the British team.

When he was done, everyone tipped back the warm vodka. Their throats were still burning when the bottles were sent around to refill the glasses. This time it was Podkapayev who made the toast, praising in his booming voice the friendship that had stretched from the Gulf of Taranto to Petropavlovsk. He then announced that thanks to Submarine Rescue Service the crew of *AS-28* had a new birthday now: 7 August. Finally he raised his glass above his head.

'*Za náshoo dróozhboo.*'

'To our friendship,' the team cheered back.

Then Captain Holloway was invited to propose the third toast. It was a special honour to be given the third toast, Holloway explained, and a reflection on their achievement as a team. There could be no choice other than the Russian Navy's traditional third toast, which had a particular poignancy on this occasion. He cleared his throat to quieten the room, and raised his glass, freshly topped off with vodka once more. 'To those at sea,' he said, catching the eyes of all the British team. He then repeated it in Russian, collecting the gazes of all the Russians in the mess, uniting everyone in the room in the memory of both the living and the lost. Sometimes this was a sad toast, commemorating those who had died and whose bodies lay in the deep, but this time it was the exact opposite.

'To those at sea,' everyone repeated.

With that third vodka, a sudden wave of tiredness washed over Riches, followed by a surge of emotion. They'd done it. They'd pulled it off.

Conversations were already sparking up around the mess, the vodka helping the three nations to communicate without the help of a translator. Podkapayev – who had morphed back into the jovial character who'd visited the Mediterranean earlier in the summer – announced that he'd always known the men would be rescued on the Sunday. It was the 7th, there were seven men on board, and it was his lucky number. It made perfect sense, he said.

A Russian officer sidled up to Dave Burke, the ex-Navy officer on the UK team, and leaned in close.

'I know what you do,' he said.

'I'm sorry? What do you mean?' replied Burke, confused.

'I know you. You watch. You spy like me. You watch people.'

'I'm not! I'm not a spy!' protested Burke, but the Russian just gave him a conspiratorial smile and slipped away.

When the other vodka bottles were all empty, the party turned to the last, chilli-flavoured bottle. Soon everyone was getting emotional. Pete Nuttall recounted his recent traumatic experience of having been too late with the lifeboat to save a father and son trapped by the tide. With this rescue now behind him, the previous experience overflowed in a sudden flood of tears. The celebration wouldn't finish for another six hours.

Sunday, 7 August
08.00 UK – 11.00 Moscow – *20.00 Kamchatka*
Petropavlovsk Naval Base

The Defence Minister, Sergei Ivanov, was keen to smooth the dents to national pride when he stepped ashore for his news conference. 'I would like to congratulate all Russians,' Ivanov began, his hands behind his back, before talking through an outline of the rescue. 'The guidance for the work was carried out by a Russian Underwater Vehicle called Tiger,' he said, before blaming the thickest of the cables on a poacher's fishing net. As Guzel Latypova and other local journalists were quick to point out, the Tiger was in fact a British-made machine, bought in the wake of the *Kursk* five years before. What's more, the thickest cable on the site was assuredly not from one of the fishing nets, but was the air-filled hose that appeared to Riches as being used to service the underwater array.

'It is symbolic that as soon as we lifted the vehicle the sun appeared in the sky and when we started to leave, killer whales swam alongside,' the minister concluded, saying the crew would soon be arriving at the harbour of the Bogorodskoye Lake in Petropavlovsk-Kamchatsky.

Later that evening, the Nanutchka-class missile attack boat *Moroz* pulled up to a dockside thronging with reporters and television cameramen desperate for a glimpse of the crew of *AS-28*. Captain Valery Lepetyukha was not on board, having transferred aboard the command ship *Alagez* to see his wife and talk to the Defence Minister. As a result, it was Slava Milachevsky – wearing a dry set of overalls, a jacket and his naval cap with its gleaming gold centre-piece directly above his eyes – who led the still stunned-looking group of crew members ashore. As he approached the gangplank at the stern, Milachevsky saw the assembled press pack. With the pictures being transmitted on live television, he stumbled to a halt and pulled an uncertain salute. Bolonin, walking behind him, almost crashed into him.

With a half-smile fixed on his face, Milachevsky then continued, walking down the gangplank first. In Lepetyukha's absence he was introduced as the senior officer, sparking a furious reaction in the Russian press over putting such a young man in charge.

Guzel Latypova was at the very front of the pack with her microphone ready and got the first question in.

'How do you feel?' she asked.

'I'm fine,' he replied. No one was allowed to ask any other questions, and the crew were quickly herded away to a waiting military ambulance.

During the hustle another sailor, his bloodshot eyes matching his reddish hair, also repeated the mantra. 'I'm fine,' he said. 'At least now I'm fine. It was cold, very cold. I can't even describe it.'

Once all six men were inside the ambulance, its dark green doors were slammed shut and the van tore off towards the hospital.

The relatives of the sailors had not been allowed on the dockside, presumably to prevent tearful reunions being broadcast across the nation, but many were clustered at the gates of the base. The ambulance slowed but did not stop, leaving wives and mothers to cry out and clutch at the windows in vain.

Yelena Milachevskaya was at home, glued to the television along with her sister and her children, and when they saw their Slava walking down the gangplank they all leapt up and started bouncing around the room. The footage of Slava was being played over and over again on the news, and all his loved ones yelled each time, laughing hysterically at his blue nose, calling him 'Grandfather Frost'.

Yelena needed to see Slava in person, not just on television. She decided to go to the hospital where he was going to be taken for examination. She knew they would try to turn her away, but she'd find a way in. When she'd been pregnant in hospital, Slava climbed up the fire escape to the third floor and broken into the ward to see her. She'd do anything, including disguising herself with doctor's whites and a moustache if need be, but she was going to get in there.

In the end the bluff wasn't necessary. Once the submariners had passed an initial checkup and been put into wards, their relatives were allowed in. When Yelena first saw Slava he was stooping, emaciated and depressed, his nose and eyes still red. She ran up and wrapped herself around him. She held him tight, both of them weeping with emotion, speechless.

Wrapped in his wife's arms, Slava Milachevsky confided that in that steel coffin he'd lost all hope of rescue. He'd kept his farewell note, he said, because he wanted his children, when they'd grown up, to know the trauma he'd been through.

The couple were left for just five minutes before a doctor arrived and told her to let him go. He said she might cause more damage than he'd already suffered, crushing him like that, he said. Slava was led away, to be kept in the hospital for the standard 21 days of medical surveillance.

Having become a media figurehead for the sailors' families during the drama, Yelena was repeatedly asked for her reactions to the safe return of her husband. She was effusive in her praise for his rescuers, saying if she had a chance to meet them that she'd kiss them and carry them in her arms for the rest of her life if need be.

Such sentiments would do nothing to cheer up Slava. He was fiercely patriotic to the point of racism, according to his wife. He had respect only for Russians. Now not only had the craft that he'd been piloting become trapped – something he would surely be blamed for and which would for ever be a stain on his career record – but he'd had to suffer the ignominy of being rescued by foreigners.

Monday, 8 August 2005
Sunday evening, Kamchatka
Georgy Kozmin, Petropavlovsk docks

When the *Georgy Kozmin* had eventually returned to the Petropavlovsk docks after its aborted mission to reach the action, Kent Van Horn put in a request with the Russian Liaison Officer to organise a hotel or some other accommodation for his men before they began the tortuous two-stage offload process. He didn't want them making mistakes through their tiredness, and the urgency was now over. The Liaison Officer checked, then came back with the order that all American equipment had to be offloaded from the ship immediately, as soon as they docked. *Kozmin* needed to get underway again as fast as possible, he was told.

Van Horn was taken aback, but tried to remain professional. If they needed the ship, they needed the ship. He decided to compromise. His men would help offload *Kozmin*, but the equipment would stay on the dockside while they went and got some sleep.

He would still be needing a hotel to put them up. It didn't need to be fancy. It could even be some barracks, he didn't care. Just some racks to rest his men.

The Russian officers didn't seem to like the idea. They conferred, and decided that *Kozmin* didn't need to leave quite so urgently after all. Once the equipment was loaded on to the dockside, the men were all found bunks on board the vessel.

Monday, 8 August 2005
02.05 Kamchatka
Petropavlovsk docks

Just past two in the morning, *KIL-27* pulled up at the quay with a little more grace and a little less damage than she'd inflicted when departing some 23 hours earlier. Journalists had started calling Riches as soon as the ship was back within range of the mobile phone network, and soon he was slipping into easily repeated phrases describing how the rescue had been accomplished. Only when he eventually spoke properly to his wife Aileen did it sink in quite what a roller-coaster it had been. It hardly seemed possible that just three days ago he was looking forward to a quiet weekend at home.

A Russian television crew were waiting on the dockside when they arrived. After they'd done an interview, Gold, Nuttall, Holloway and Riches were taken to one hotel, the rest of the team to another. Although exhausted, Holloway and Riches headed straight to the bar.

When Gold got into his hotel room, the first thing he did was call his son's mobile number. Allan knew Scorpio well – he'd worked on the mine recoveries sometimes, and would know immediately the significance of what they'd achieved.

The ringtone ended and was replaced with a blast of noise. Gold winced and held the phone away from his ear.

'What's all the din? Where are you?' Gold yelled into the phone.

'In the pub, Dad. Riley's in Haymarket. How did you do?' said Allan.

'No, first things first. You tell me. What was the score?'

'We beat 'em! 4-1!' came the reply. A big grin spread across Gold's face. His team had won. Hearts had beaten the Hibernian football club, their main rivals in Edinburgh. Now this really was turning into the perfect weekend.

Monday, 8 August 2005
09.00 Kamchatka
Petropavlovsk

As the rest of the UK's response team caught their first sleep since their catnaps on the outward flight and began a round of official thanksgiving ceremonies, Squadron Leader Hewitt at the airbase noticed that the Americans had already packed up much of their kit. Because they'd been forced to take all their equipment off their ship the previous night, they were a step ahead of the UK's team. That could be problematic, he realised. If the Americans left with their K-loader before the UK team had a chance to pack, he might end up getting stuck in Kamchatka. He immediately sent word to MOD Northwood, warning them that if the Americans took off before he'd loaded his C17, the aircraft could be here when the winter darkness and ice closed in.

Not that the thought of being stuck in Petropavolvsk for the winter felt as terrible as it would have only 24 hours ago. They were heroes now, after all. Hewitt had been out at a restaurant in Petropavlovsk as a guest of a Russian Lieutenant-Commander from the airbase – an ex-submarine man himself – when news of the Scorpio team's early successes began to come in. Hewitt had felt the full brunt of the Russian emotion over the story. The place had been transfixed by the television reports, transmitted from the scene by the state news channel. And when the presenter had announced the first cables had been cut, the place had erupted into a carpet-beating frenzy of back-slapping and buying of vodka for toasts.

With his warning whistling up the chain of command back in the UK, Hewitt decided to go over and see the Americans to check on their plans personally. Dressed in his civilian clothes and accompanied by his Russian translator, Hewitt wandered up to the gargantuan C5 aircraft and tracked down the American Major who was in charge of loading and unloading.

'Are you guys leaving soon?' Hewitt asked.

'Like to, but I'm not allowed,' the Major replied, looking glum.

'I see. That's a relief, to be honest. We need to borrow your K-loader again or we'll be stuck here warming ourselves with cheap vodka for months. What's holding you up, anyway?'

'I just had a call from top brass telling me I'm not allowed to leave until some Brit says that I can,' said the Major.

'That's what I like to hear. I'm Squadron Leader Keith Hewitt, by the way.'

'Hewitt?' the Major replied. 'You're that Brit!'

Tuesday, 9 August
Morning
Kamchatka

As the crews returned from the ships, the MIGs that had previously loomed as ominous but silent Cold War silhouettes were now swarming with activity. A pilot sat in the open cockpit of one, apparently running pre-start checks. It took one of the RAF crew to point out the missing turbine blades and the grass growing up around the wheels.

Such theatrics were confusing – and a little amusing – to Squadron Leader Hewitt. During the long hours of waiting for news from the rescue team, he'd astonished one of the Russian Air Force officers on the base by inviting him on board the C17 to have a look around. The man had been wide-eyed at seeing such cutting-edge foreign military technology – some of the latest that NATO aircraft had to offer – and at being given the chance to inspect it up close. Hewitt smiled and told him to take pictures if he liked, that there was nothing to hide. It wasn't quite true; Hewitt had carefully placed a couple of newspaper supplements over the more sensitive bits of gear.

But the gesture of trust had evidently not diffused very far. Squadron Leader Hewitt and the other RAF pilots were having all sorts of hassle planning the return trip across Russia. While their outward trip had been blessed with humanitarian status by the Russians, Hewitt and the other pilots were now being forced to go through a tortuous series of hoops and to clear hurdles to gain the necessary diplomatic and flight clearances for the flight home.

The Russian Admiral who was in charge of the Elizovo airbase appeared at the aircraft as the pre-flight checks were finally being conducted. He was invited on board, where he made a presentation to the RAF crew of some vodka and salmon caviar.

Hewitt smiled. It was extraordinary to have been welcomed into a major military centre of a nation that had for so long been considered such a threat to British security and Western civilisation. There was a quiet satisfaction to knowing that he and his boys had played an integral part in freeing those Russian sailors from a frozen, suffocating underwater hell. The rescue would have been impossible without the RAF. It would have taken a long time to arrive on a boat, that's for sure. His particular glow of fulfilment was known to all air transport crews, familiar as they are with supporting the glory boys in bombers or fighters. As the tanker pilots say, 'Nobody kicks ass without tanker gas.'

Once the Admiral was off the plane and the pre-flight checks were finished, Hewitt called for clearance and the C17 started rolling towards the runway holding point. At 11.00 local time, Ascot 6564 lifted off, routing for Scotland, back across the frozen Russian north.

The sensations inside Stuart Gold could not have been more different from when they'd left Prestwick. The gnawing nervousness that had kept him shifting in his seat had been replaced by warm, comfortable satisfaction. It felt as though everything he'd ever done had been preparation for the events of those last 72 hours. His time on submersibles, his period as an electrical engineer, all of it felt as though it had played a part. When the incident had finally happened, it wasn't anything like any of the scenarios they'd practised, but still they'd pulled it off. Fifteen years ago, he'd been a lowly computer repair man, underneath some teenager's desk outside Edinburgh, when he'd decided that there must be more to life. Now he was, he realised, the person he'd always wanted to be. He found himself singing to himself with Midge Ure's twang, his voice swelling as he hit the title line:

'a good man in a storm'

Looking down the aircraft cargo bay, Riches observed that the team were all much better prepared for the return journey than they had been on the way out. They might not have the sleeping bags and DVD players that the RAF boys had, but at least this time they had found warm clothes and makeshift blindfolds to keep out the light and made earplugs to shut out the roar of those huge Rolls-Royce engines.

As the aircraft climbed to its cruising altitude, he could feel himself gaining perspective on everything that had happened. The incessant interviews he'd already done since the rescue had worn a deep groove in his brain about how things had gone: the brotherhood of the sea, the integrity and selflessness of international rescue, the bad luck that had led to the situation and so on. The truth was more complicated, but looking back on it he also felt a glow of fulfilment. Some of his worst fears had come true and problems he'd not even dreamed of had been thrown at the team, but they'd pulled it off. It wasn't commanding a nuclear submarine, but he'd led an extraordinary mission on the far side of the world. His thwarted dreams of submarine command suddenly didn't seem so bitter. Lots of submarine commanders had spent their careers training for battle with the Russian Navy, whereas he'd been involved in a much rarer thing: a genuine encounter between the two sides that had saved lives, not destroyed them.

August/September 2005
Moscow and Petropavlovsk

When Captain Jonathan Holloway boarded his Aeroflot flight 24 hours later, he too felt a changed man. Twelve years earlier he'd jumped at the chance to serve on the Royal Yacht, but it had set him off down a path of Naval diplomacy that sometimes felt rather insubstantial. The last few days had proved otherwise.

All of the trust-building relationships, the exchange visits and the invitations to participate in exercises had paid off. The value of all that talk was minimal until it came to an actual incident, and the acid test of sincerity had now been passed. The value of international cooperation was now clear. If their efforts had failed, there was a risk the suspicious internal prejudices in Russia against working with foreigners would have been reinforced, and the UK's relationship with Russia would doubtless have suffered as a result. But as things turned out, they could expect new levels of cooperation. The Defence Minister, Sergei Ivanov, was evidently personally grateful, and had given the team private gifts.

With the crew of *AS-28* walking in warm, fresh air once more, hopes of a new era of peaceful mutual collaboration soared.

'These are moments worth living for,' said the head of the Pacific Fleet, Admiral Fyodorov. 'Today was a very happy event.'

The celebrations over the safe return of the submariners played out across the television channels in Russia and across the world. But the festivities cloaked an unwillingness to discuss the circumstances of the accident. When Ivanov decided to visit the hospital and meet the submersible's crew, he invited along the sailors' wives, Yelena Milachevskaya among them. Sitting in the hospital's lounge, the minister had exchanged some pleasantries before asking the men to recount what had happened that day, 200 metres beneath the surface of Berezovya Bay. But when one of the men began to answer, Yelena was astonished to hear the group's commander cut the sailor off abruptly and make it very clear that openness was not required.

The men promptly fell silent, and the Group Commander steered the subject towards less delicate, everyday matters. Gennady Vasiliyevich Bolonin, the engineer who as the only civilian on board could have disregarded the Group Commander's order, had been transferred to a different hospital shortly before Ivanov's visit. Afraid of getting her husband into trouble, Yelena bit her tongue, but was outraged by what she saw as a blatant direct cover-up by the military.

When the media were allowed to meet the sailors in their hospital ward, however, their stories had become strangely uniform. Contrary to what he'd said to his wife when he'd first seen her, Slava Milachevsky now told reporters that he'd never been worried or written a note, that he'd always known he was going to be rescued. The rest all repeated the same story – that they knew rescue was imminent, and that none of them had been concerned enough to write a farewell note to their loved ones.

Estimates of how much breathable air had remained on *AS-28* also changed dramatically soon after the men had reached hospital. Initially, they had said they'd thought death was four hours away, perhaps six. But when Captain Lepetyukha officially announced that there was at least 36 hours of oxygen remaining on *AS-28*, the rest of the crew said the same.

By silencing the crew of *AS-28*, the quest to quell the raging media interest in the story had started in earnest. It wasn't just the sailors who were muzzled. Local journalists were prevented from meeting foreign reporters to stop them from passing on inconvenient details.

Yelena Milachevskaya's emotional outbursts stood in stark contrast to the continued silence of the wives of the other submariners. Tatiana Lepetuykha and two of the other wives even went to visit Yelena after the rescue to try to talk her into quietening down. Veiled threats still hung in the air. 'You'll wreck your husband's career if you don't quieten down,' the wives whispered to her, as though in confidence.

But Yelena was having none of it. To her, it was all part of a bigger plot to incriminate her husband. 'You'll see, they will hold my husband to blame, say it's because he is young and inexperienced,' she told Guzel Latypova and other journalists. 'But Slava is a virtuoso at the controls of that craft. He knows the Priz like the back of his hand and couldn't have made a mistake.'

Yelena insisted on refuting Russian attempts to claim a role in the rescue. 'Our husbands were saved by us, the wives, and by you, the press, including the foreign press. I am grateful to the British and the journalists – they saved my husband.'

She was right. Whoever it was that called Guzel Latypova's radio show on the evening of 4 August had accelerated the Russian Navy's response to the accident. If it had remained a Naval secret, even if only until the following morning, rescue would have come too late. In celebration of Latypova's role, Yelena and Slava Milachevsky asked her to be the godmother of their two girls, to which the journalist agreed.

Yelena's forthrightness appeared to be punished. After her husband's long stay in hospital, Slava was sent to a sanatorium to continue his 'convalescence'. Once recovered, he was immediately sent to Vladivostok to watch over the submersible. After several months, *AS-28* was sent to Nizhny Novgorod by train. Slava was given a month at home, but was then sent 6,500 miles away to Nizhny to remain with the craft for the two years that it would take to repair and refurbish. While Yelena and the kids had to remain in Zavoyko, they would see Slava only once a year when he came home for leave.

Still, the wife of Vyacheslav Milachevsky had no regrets about speaking out. 'I may have destroyed my husband's career,' she announced. 'But I've saved the father of my children.'

EPILOGUE

The members of the UK team settled back into their normal lives, swathed in a warm glow of achievement and relief at having proved themselves and saved seven lives. Riches stepped back into the everyday routines suddenly free from the nagging sense of frustration with the hand that fate had dealt him, the ghosts laid to rest.

In Russia, the ripples from *AS-28* were not as benign. On 4 September, less than a month after the rescue mission, the Commander-in-Chief of the Navy, Vladimir Kuroyedov, was fired by Putin. He'd survived the *Kursk*, the sinking of *K-159* and the Navy Day damage to the Baltic flagship, but the *AS-28* debacle finally brought him down.

His former Chief of Staff was appointed in his place, but Admiral Vladimir Masorin was under no illusions about the task he was being given. 'I am not experiencing euphoria at being appointed Head of the Navy,' he admitted with disarming honesty.

'The Russian Federation Navy has the biggest submarine fleet in the world after the United States,' he said, adding that thanks to a lack of resources Russia was 'lagging behind perhaps not just a little but rather a lot'.

'One thing is clear. To continue in the condition which we are in and do nothing is simply not possible,' he concluded.

Captain 2nd Rank Novikov, commander of *AS-28*'s mothership, the *Georgy Kozmin,* was relieved of command as the US Assistant Naval attaché had foreseen, having been found guilty of negligence by the Pacific Fleet prosecutor's office. Although later found innocent after a loyal campaign by colleagues, he has not returned to active command.

In October 2005, Vladimir Putin travelled to 10 Downing Street to visit the Prime Minister, Tony Blair for the first UK/

Russian summit in some time. All of the team were invited along to meet the leaders. Stuart Gold, Pete Nuttall and Riches along with Captain Holloway and Squadron Leader Hewitt were ushered into the Pillared Drawing Room with their families and the rest of the team behind them, where Blair welcomed the Russian president, who then emerged and took position behind his own microphone stand. The body language of the two leaders made it clear they were men in the exploratory stage of striking up a friendship after a period of acrimony.

'We in Russia remember vividly remarkable examples of outstanding heroism, demonstrated by the British seamen in the operation of the so-called Northern Convoys,' he said, referring to the hardships endured by the Royal and Merchant Navies in taking essential war supplies to Northern Russia during the Second World War. 'And I was pleased to note that even today you have made your contribution in substantially increasing, up-lifting, and deepening, and broadening our cooperation. In reality you have continued the traditions . . . in the relationship between our two countries . . .'

It was flattery to compare the 72-hour rescue mission to the heroism of the Arctic convoys that had kept Russia in the war against Hitler despite savage predation by the German submarine wolf-packs, but the sentiment touched everyone.

Putin then presented Gold, Nuttall and Riches the Order 'For Naval Merits', awarded for outstanding service in the Russian Navy. Squadron Leader Hewitt and Captain Holloway were both given the Order of Friendship. Originally the medal ceremony was slated to have been held at the Imperial War Museum, but the venue was changed to Downing Street. This, and the briefing that followed the medal ceremony to update the press on the achievements of two days of discussions held between the two leaders, left Riches feeling that Blair and Putin would not have been standing there together had it not been for their successful rescue.

For Holloway, Hewitt and Riches, the Russian medals presented a slight problem. To wear the foreign decorations alongside other medals on their uniforms they needed special permission from the Queen. Luckily Her Majesty was understanding, and gave her consent.

The next year Riches was to meet the Queen in person when she appointed him an Officer of the Order of the British Empire (OBE) and honoured Roger Chapman as a Commander of the Order of the British Empire (CBE). It was a big moment. Riches hadn't realised how much he'd craved formal recognition for serving his country and the international community of submariners. He now felt as though he'd earned the right to be one of them again, and it swfelt good.

The spirit of harmony surrounding Putin's visit to Downing Street soon deteriorated; 2005 turned out to be the zenith of the cooperative relationship between the two nations.

The first big crack appeared when a political enemy of the Russian government was apparently assassinated on British soil. On 1 November 2006, KGB officer-turned anti-Putin activist Alexander Litvinenko was poisoned while taking afternoon tea at a London hotel. He had been spiked with Polonium 210, a highly toxic and rare radioactive element that took three agonising weeks to kill him. British police named an ex-KGB man as the main suspect, but Russia refused to give him up to the UK authorities to face trial.

The insult to British sovereignty was still fermenting when the ex-Soviet state of Georgia erupted into war in August 2008. The energy-rich nation was leaning ever closer towards the west, wooed by Britain and America with military hardware, training, and the possibility of NATO membership. Unwilling to challenge the US, Moscow directed its fury at Britain, accusing it of acting like a 19th-century colonial power.

More sinister yet, in Russia the free media has been forced deep underground. Oleg Kashin, one of the Kommersant journalists who covered the *AS-28* incident, was attacked and hospitalised in 2010 as a result of his reporting. Situations that are unflattering to the government are spun into propaganda, and the mauling that Putin suffered over the *Kursk* would be unthinkable today. But there are signs that the Russian Navy is now persuaded of the importance of international collaboration in submarine rescue. In 2011, a Kilo-class Russian submarine took part in NATO's rescue exercises off Spain. If there was another accident and Russia requested help, the new NATO rescue team would doubtless be deployed.

The lessons learned from the 21st-century submarine rescue have developed and strengthened the coalition of nations who work together to protect their submariners from the gruesome, prolonged agony of death beneath the waves. They train in the latest and most effective submarine escape and rescue techniques. Equipment and strategies may progress every year, but one thing stays the same: the ruthless ticking of the clock. Whoever is mounting the mission, the time to first rescue remains 72 hours.

GLOSSARY

A-Frame: An A-shaped structure that supports a lifting point high above the deck and over the water, allowing safe deployment of equipment overboard.

ADS: Atmospheric Diving Suit – a human-shaped pressure suit to allow divers to descend below 300 metres.

ATC: Air Traffic Control.

C17: Boeing's C17 Globemaster III is a four-engined cargo aircraft used by various militaries around the world. Wingspan of 51 metres, able to carry over 77 tonnes of cargo. Three crew.

C5: Lockheed's C-5 Galaxy is one of the world's largest strategic airliners. With a wingspan of 67.8 metres, it is able to carry over 120 tonnes of cargo. Crew of eight.

ILS: Instrument Landing System, used to guide aircraft in to airports.

ISMERLO: The International Submarine Escape and Rescue Liaison Office, based in Norfolk, Virginia.

K-Loader: A specialised truck with a large flat cargo bed that can be raised and lowered. Crucial to the loading of C17 aircraft.

KIL-27: The anchor-handling and buoy-laying Sura-class tug-boat used by the Royal Navy rescue team as their Vessel of Opportunity.

LR5: The UK Submarine Rescue Service's submersible, in service until 2009. Able to carry 16 rescued submariners.

MOD: The UK's Ministry of Defence.

NATO: The North Atlantic Treaty Organisation. A military alliance between 28 western nations.

NDB: Non-Directional Beacon. An outmoded navigation method still fitted as standard in aircraft, but rarely used.

Priz: The class name for the Russian Federation Navy's rescue submersibles. Used in all fleets and deployed during the Kursk.

ROV: Remotely Operated Vehicle. An underwater robot usually equipped with video, lights, and manipulators.

Scorpio: The type of Remotely Operated Vehicle used by the UK Submarine Rescue Service's. Rated for work at depths of up to 900m, it is a popular model with offshore oil companies.

SS: SubSunk. The code used by the Royal Navy to indicate the time at which a submarine is known to have sunk.

TTFR: Time To First Rescue. The all-important measure of how fast a rescue team can respond after first being alerted.

VOO: Vessel of Opportunity. A ship allocated to a foreign rescue team by the host country.

Zulu: The International time code for Universal Time, or Greenwich Mean Time. Used in all aviation communications.

ILLUSTRATIONS

DRAMATIS PERSONAE

AS-28 crew

Valery Lepetyukha (Валерий Лепетюха), Captain 1st Rank,
  Commander

Vyacheslav 'Slava' Milachevsky (Вячеслав Милашевский), Captain-
  Lieutenant, pilot

Antoly Popov (Анатолий Попов) – Warrant Officer

Sergey Belozerov (Сергей Белозеров) – Warrant Officer

Alexandr Uybin (Александр Уйбин) – crew member

Alexandr Ivanov (Александр Иванов) – crew member

Gennady Bolonin (Геннадий Полонин) – civilian engineer from the
  Lazurit Design Bureau, the designers of *AS-28*

Support Fleet

Sergey Ivanov – Defence Minister, Russian Federation

Igor Dygalo – Russian Federation Navy spokesman

Admiral Victor Fyoderov – Russian Federation Navy, Commander of
  Pacific Fleet

Alexander Kosolapov – Russian Federation Navy, Pacific Fleet
  spokesman

Captain Viktor Novikov – Captain of rescue vessel *Georgy Kozmin*
  (*AS-28* mothership)

Dmitriy Podkapayev– Russian Submarine Rescue Service pilot

Boris Doroganov – head of auxiliary ships fleet and Captain of *KIL-27*

Abul Avdoshin – head of operational department on Naval staff

Vladimir Masorin – Head of the Main Staff of the Navy, acting Navy
  commander on board command ship

Wives of AS-28 crew

Marina Belozerov – wife of Sergey Belozerov

Tatiana Lepetyukha – wife of Captain LepetyukhaYelena
  Milachevskaya – wife of Vyacheslav Milachevsky

Guzel Latypova – journalist